Women of Vision:

Sixteen Founders of the International Grail Movement

Marian Ronan and Mary O'Brien

APOCRYPHILE
PRESS

The Apocryphile Press
1700 Shattuck Ave. #81
Berkeley, CA 94709
www.apocryphile.org

Women of Vision
Copyright © 2017 Marian Ronan and Mary O'Brien
ISBN 978-1-944769-69-7

All rights reserved. No part of this publication may be reproduced, stored in a retrieval system, or transmitted in any form or by any means—electronic, mechanical, photocopy, recording, or any other—except for brief quotations in printed reviews, without the prior permission of the publisher.

Printed in the United States of America

Please join our mailing list at
www.apocryphilepress.com/free
and we'll keep you up-to-date on all our new releases
—and we'll also send you a FREE BOOK.
Visit us today!

Table of Contents

Acknowledgments iii

2016 Introduction vii

2003 Introduction: A Parable of the Grail: *The Old Woman Had Many Daughters* xxix

Part I: The Old Wise Woman (1921-1940)

1. Lydwine van Kersbergen (The Netherlands) 1

2. Rachel Donders (The Netherlands) 21

3. Frances van der Schott (The Netherlands) 41

4. Hilda Canters (The Netherlands) 61

Part II: Sent Forth Into the World (1940-1953)

5. Mary Louise Tully (The United States) 85

6. Elizabeth (Bep) Camanada (The Netherlands) 107

7. Eileen Schaeffler (The United States) 127

8. Antonia (Ton) Brouwer (The Netherlands) 151

9. Magdalene Oberhoffer (Germany) 171

Part III: The Vision Burned (1953-1970)

10. Maria Teresa Santa Clara Gomes (Portugal) 195

11. Marie Elizabeth (Mimi) Maréchal (Belgium) 215

12. Rebecca Nebrida (The Philippines) 235

13. Maria de Lourdes Pintasilgo (Portugal) 255

Part IV: Envisioning a Justice-Filled New World (1957-2001)

14. Elizabeth Estencia Namaganda (Uganda) 277

15. Imelda Alfred Gaurwa (Tanzania) 297

16. Honorata Lubero Francis Mvungi (Tanzania) 325

CONCLUSION: The Daughters Weave On 345

International Grail Vision Statement 2011 345

Bibliography 347

Index 353

Acknowledgments

As Mary O'Brien details in the 2003 introduction to this book, U.S. Grail members Eva Fleischner and Nancy Hennessy Cooney launched the process that culminated in *Women of Vision: Sixteen Founders of the International Grail Movement* when they suggested the writing of a biography of Lydwine van Kersbergen, the founder of the Grail in England, Australia, and the United States. When Lydwine, in classic Grail fashion, declined to be the sole focus of the volume, it evolved into the book before you, a collection of the stories of sixteen Grail women who started or directly facilitated starting the Grail Movement in multiple countries on six continents between 1921 and 2001.

In the twenty-two years since that initial suggestion, very many individuals contributed in large and small ways to the creation of this book.

First of all, considerable thanks to the Grail in the Netherlands, Lydwine van Kersbergen, and the Social Science and Humanities Research Council of Canada, for funding travel to and from the sites of the interviews that underpin the sixteen chapters of this book, and to the Dutch Grail for providing housing during the interview process.

Secondly, it's impossible to overestimate the scope and significance of Mary O'Brien's contributions to the research and writing of this book. From the outset, Mary spearheaded the process. She conducted the vast majority of the founders' interviews and then used them, as well as their introductions, to draft fifteen of the sixteen chapters that comprise *Women of Vision*. Without Mary's work, this book would simply not exist.

The second phase of the process began in 2015 when the International Grail Archives and History Committee, consisting of Carol Webb and Mary Gindhart of the U.S. and Loek Goemans of South Africa, asked U.S. Grail member Marian Ronan to undertake the completion of the book. The International Grail through the Archives and History Committee also provided the funding necessary to accomplish this. Marian revised, edited, fact-checked and up-dated the fifteen chapters and their introductions and wrote the remaining chapter, on Hilda Canters, and its introduction. She also wrote the 2016 Introduction to the entire volume, and this preface. Finally, she located a publisher, the Apocryphile Press of Berkeley, CA, U.S.A. Thanks to all of these women for their hard work and commitment.

Many others have also contributed to *Women of Vision*. Special thanks goes to Mary Omedo, administrative assistant to the Grail International Leadership Team at the Grail International Secretariat in the Netherlands, for answering very many questions in the past few years and for putting the authors in contact with Grail members around the world. Thanks, too, to Carol Webb, Mary Gindhart, and Loek Goemans for answering a great many other questions and responding as well to drafts of various chapters and papers related to the book. Thanks to Ton Brouwer in the Netherlands for the speedy and appreciative response to her own chapter. Thanks to Marita Estor of the Grail in Germany for comments on an earlier draft of the 2016 Introduction, and to Josette Kersters, Didine Petit, Mieneke Hage and other members of the Dutch Grail for providing photographs and answering questions.

Thanks as well to Aloysia Masoy of the Tanzanian Grail for responding to questions regarding the chapter on Imelda Gaurwa, and to Jeanette Loanzon and Monica Sophia de Leon of the Grail in the Philippines for information regarding the Rebecca Nebrida chapter and a picture of Rebecca. Thanks to U.S. Grail members Carol White, in Dublin, Ireland, for reviewing the chapter on Mimi Maréchal, and Marian April Goering and Mindy Burger for help with the chapter on Honorata Mvungi. Thanks to Jeanette Stokes, director of the Resource Center for Women and Ministry in the South, Greensboro, North Carolina, USA, for help securing a photograph of Maria de Lourdes Pintasilgo. Multiple thanks to Ieva Zadina of the U.S. Grail for copy-editing the entire *Women of Vision* manuscript. Finally, deep gratitude as well as our apologies to anyone whose contributions to *Women of Vision* we have forgotten to acknowledge here.

The authors and publisher also gratefully acknowledge permission to reprint previously published material from *U.S. Catholic Historian*. A revised version of "A Woman of Vision: An Interview with the Founder of the Grail Movement in the United States" by Mary O'Brien and Patricia Miller, *U.S. Catholic Historian*, 15.4 (Fall, 1997), 95-105 (not including the afterword) comprises chapter 1 of *Women of Vision*.

In conclusion, the authors express appreciation to the Schoff Fund at the University Seminars, Columbia University, for assistance in the publication of *Women of Vision*. Material in the book was presented to the University Seminar: Religion in America.

2016 Introduction

In the Netherlands, in November of 1921, a Jesuit priest and internationally recognized linguist, Jacques van Ginneken, founded three Catholic lay groups, the "Society of the Women of Bethany," the "Crusaders of St. John," and the "Society of the Women of Nazareth." The mission of all three groups was the conversion of the world.

Van Ginneken's focus on laypeople was part of the wider Catholic Church's turn to the lay apostolate, also sometimes called Catholic Action. Pope Leo XIII helped to launch this movement in his 1891 encyclical, *Rerum Novarum*, and reinforced it three years later in another encyclical calling on the laity in the fight against Freemasonry.[1]

Of the three groups founded by van Ginneken, only one, the Women of Nazareth, continued as a lay group; the Women of Bethany eventually became a congregation of Catholic sisters, and the Knights of St. John became a secular institute.[2] Each

---

1   Pope Leo XIII, *Rerum Novarum* (On Capital and Labor), The Vatican, accessed October 18, 2016, http://w2.vatican.va/content/leo-xiii/en/encyclicals/documents/hf_l-iii_enc_15051891_rerum-novarum.html; Pope Leo XIII, *Humanum Genus* (On Freemasonry), The Vatican, accessed October 18, 2016, http://w2.vatican.va/content/leo-xiii/en/encyclicals/documents/hf_l-xiii_enc_18840420_humanum-genus.html.

2   Rachel Donders, *History of the International Grail 1921-1979* (Loveland, OH: Grailville, 1983), 4; "The Congregation for Institutes of Consecrated Life and Societies of Apostolic Life," The Vatican, accessed October 21, 2016, http://www.vatican.va/roman_curia/congregations/ccscrlife/documents/rc_con_ccscrlife_profile_en.html.

group thus came under the control of the institutional church. Yet the particular kind of lay group van Ginneken founded the Women of Nazareth to be came with certain tensions, not to say contradictions.

There can be no doubt that van Ginneken founded the Women of Nazareth in 1921 with the expressed intention of using laywomen's extraordinary gifts in the battle to resolve the crisis in which Western society found itself. But he feared that the modern world with its many seductions would undercut the commitment required for the Women of Nazareth to achieve that goal. He therefore mandated a quasi-religious (that is to say, quasi-monastic) leadership for the lay group, a "fiery core"—later to be called "the Nucleus." The members of this core would be trained much as monks and nuns were, with a lengthy novitiate, severe ascetic practices, and the making of promises of "poverty, chastity and obedience," hopefully for life, but in any case, for as long as they belonged to the group.

The group was also hierarchically structured, with the superior called "Mother General" or "Mother Superior." Yet van Ginneken also mandated that the Women of Nazareth not take canonical vows, which would put them under the control of the Catholic hierarchy, or even have a male chaplain in residence.[3] As we shall see, this tension would mark the nearly hundred-year history of the group, eventually to evolve into the International Grail Movement.

Initially, some of the Women of Nazareth focused on working with Dutch factory girls. Others prepared to establish an institute of higher learning for women in Indonesia, one of van Ginneken's dreams for the group. They also assisted with retreats the founder

---

3 Janet Kalven, *Women Breaking Boundaries: A Grail Journey* (Binghamton, NY: State University of New York Press, 1999), 35-36, 111, 175-176.

conducted for non-Catholics. But in 1928, J.D.J. Aengenent, the new bishop of Haarlem, the diocese in which the Women of Nazareth were located, asked (well, ordered) the group to shift its focus to working exclusively with the Catholic girls of that diocese. This was part of his effort to push back against the growth of socialist youth groups.

In obedience, the Women of Nazareth launched the Grail youth movement. Despite their initial ambivalence about this shift, the founding of the youth movement in 1928 turned out to be a "true watershed in the history of the Women of Nazareth."[4] Among other activities, the group held a series of massive dramatic presentations in the Amsterdam Olympic Stadium; in Easter of 1931, thirty-two thousand people witnessed three thousand girl actors from all over Holland perform a drama called "The Royal Road of the Cross"; two years later, ten thousand girls enacted a Pentecost play in that same stadium. By 1931, three years after the start of the Grail youth movement, as Alden Brown details, the group had "twenty-three urban centers, seventeen outposts in rural areas, six hundred and forty leaders, and eight thousand members."[5]

The Expansion of the Grail Youth Movement

Because of the success of the Grail youth movement in the Netherlands, and especially because of the Grail's subsequent extensive public outreach efforts—silent processions to celebrate saints' days, speaking choruses in public squares, newspaper articles, and, in particular, the participation of two hundred members in the December 1932 International Eucharistic Congress in

---

4   Donders, *History of the International Grail*, 6.

5   Alden Brown, *The Grail Movement and American Catholicism 1940-1975* (Notre Dame, IN: The University of Notre Dame Press, 1989), 9.

Dublin—Catholic figures outside the Netherlands began inviting the leaders of the Grail to launch the movement in their countries. Almost immediately after the Eucharistic Congress, for example, Bishop Schreiber of Berlin invited the Grail to his diocese; six months later, twelve hundred girls were performing a salvation play in Berlin's enormous sports stadium. The Archbishop of Westminster, in England, Cardinal Bourne, didn't even wait that long; already during the Eucharistic Congress he invited the Grail to his archdiocese. Lydwine van Kersbergen, one of the founders profiled in this volume, along with five other Women of Nazareth, opened the first Grail center in London in 1933.[6]

It was there, in England, that the Women of Nazareth changed their name to the Ladies of the Grail in order to clarify their connection to the youth movement. Also in 1934, so as to confirm the group's loyalty and obedience to the church, the Grail youth movement, under the leadership of the Women of Nazareth, became part of the Vatican-approved "International Union of Women's Leagues," with the name "Feminine Youth Movement for Catholic Action, the Grail."[7]

The international expansion of the Grail continued throughout the 1930s and 1940s. In 1935, the bishop of Wagawaga, Australia, who had also encountered the Grail in Dublin in 1934, sent an Australian laywoman to be formed at the Tiltenberg, the Women of Nazareth's training center in the Netherlands. Then, in 1936, five Dutch Women of Nazareth, including Lydwine van Kersbergen and another founder profiled in this book, Frances van der Schott, set sail for Sydney.[8] In Australia, the group became known as the Ladies of the Grail, as they already were in England.

---

6 Donders, *History of the International Grail*, 16, 18.

7 *Ibid.*, 20.

8 *Ibid.*, 23.

The following year, the social-justice-oriented auxiliary bishop of Chicago, Bernard Shiel, visited the Grail in Europe; this led to a meeting in Chicago, in 1939, between Lydwine van Kersbergen, who by then had returned to Europe from Australia, and the archbishop of Chicago, George Cardinal Mundelein. A year later, van Kersbergen returned with another Dutch Woman of Nazareth, Joan Overboss, to plant the Grail in the United States.

After the Nazi invasion of the Netherlands in 1940, and then for the duration of the Second World War, the Women of Nazareth (the Ladies of the Grail) in England, Australia and the U.S. were cut off from the group's leadership. And the Nazis dissolved the Women of Nazareth and the youth movement in the Netherlands and in Germany. Soon after the end of the war, however, leaders of the group, including van Ginneken, van Kersbergen and van der Schott, reunited in England, and before long, the movement began to grow again.

It was also the case, however, that in these same years the Archbishop of Westminster, so as to have more direct control over the English Ladies of the Grail, forced them to separate from the Women of Nazareth. This was a devastating development. The Dutch women who had started the movement in England returned to the Netherlands, while two English women who had joined them there remained. The group in England eventually became a secular institute, as had the Knights of St. John previously. Fortunately, however, the Grail in Scotland remained part of the international movement and none of the other countries left.[9]

Grail Growth After the War

The Grail expanded steadily from the late 1940s through the 1960s. In 1946, a Dutch Woman of Nazareth and scholar, Elisabeth Allard, arrived in Indonesia, the mission territory of Father van

---

9   Ibid., 36-37.

Ginneken's dreams, while in 1947, another of the founders profiled in *Women of Vision*, Mary Louise Tully, travelled to Hong Kong in response to a request from the bishop there. In 1948, Ifis Seijbel led a Dutch team to Brazil, where, in the mid-1950s, Elizabeth (Bep) Camanada, another *Women of Vision* founder, joined them. In South Africa, groups of young Catholic women, influenced by contacts with the Ladies of the Grail in England, had been meeting in South Africa since 1936; the Grail was officially established there in 1950.[10]

Then in May of 1952, Lydwine van Kersbergen, "ever the pioneer," came from the U.S. to travel for four months with the former head of the Women of Nazareth, Margaret van Gilse, through Rhodesia, Nyasaland, Tanganyika, Kenya and Uganda. Another team visited Ethiopia, the Sudan, and Egypt, connecting in Cairo for the first time with Simone Tagher, the Egyptian woman who became the International President of the Grail in 1971.[11] Between 1949 and 1961, the Grail expanded to twelve different countries on the African continent.

Seven *Women of Vision* founders helped launch the Grail in these twelve African countries. The tireless labor of Rachel Donders, international leader of the Woman of Nazareth, and subsequently International President of the Grail from 1949 to 1961, drove the expansion.[12] By 1950, Frances van der Schott had moved, at Donders' request, from Australia to South Africa, so as to allow Australian Grail members to assume the leadership of the movement there. A few years later, in collaboration with an African woman, Elizabeth Muwonge, and over a period of six months, Frances started the Grail's secondary boarding school in

---

10 *Ibid.*, 36-38.

11 *Ibid.*, 49.

12 See Chapter 2, 21-40.

Uganda; she later returned to the school to teach for nine years. And a student in the school's very first class, Elizabeth Namaganda, eventually travelled to the U.S. for formation, joined the Nucleus, and became the leader of the Grail in Uganda.[13]

In 1953, Hilda Canters and another Dutch Grail member, Joke van Neerven, travelled to what was then called the Belgian Congo to work in a hospital. Some years later, Hilda moved to neighboring Burundi to begin a movement for women and girls.[14] Although the Grail eventually left Congo and Burundi, the work of Hilda and the other Grail members who served with her between 1953 and 1975 influenced the lives of many women and girls there. Among those members who served with Hilda was Ton Brouwer, who arrived in Burundi in 1958, and eventually moved to Tanzania, where she joined the staff of a maternity dispensary.[15] And in Tanzania, Ton met and gave considerable support to Imelda Gaurwa, who eventually became the first indigenous woman to start the Grail in an African country.[16] Another Tanzanian, Honorata Mvungi, who had previously received her formation with the Grail in Uganda, worked with Imelda to found the Tanzanian Grail. Magdalene Oberhoffer, a German and another future International President of the Grail, worked in Uganda for nearly twenty years, first as the medical director of a hospital in Kampala, and later, as part of the effort to "Africanize" the Grail there.

The founder of the Grail in the Philippines, Rebecca Nebrida "met" the movement when she and U.S. Grail member Audrey Sorrento were studying theology together at the University of Notre Dame (U.S.A.) in the summer of 1957. Rebecca went back

---

13 See Chapter 14, 277-296.

14 See Chapter 4, 61-84.

15 See Chapter 8, 151-170.

16 See Chapter 15, 297-324.

to Grailville with Audrey, and after three years of formation and Grail experience, returned home to an academic career and pioneering work with the Grail in the Philippines. From 1988 to 1993 Rebecca also served on the Grail's International Presidency Team, the three-woman structure that replaced the International Presidency in 1979.[17] Also in 1957, after encountering the Grail at a meeting of Pax Romana, the international Catholic students' association, and subsequently visiting Grailville, Maria de Lourdes Pintasilgo and Teresa Santa Clara Gomes launched the Grail in Portugal. Pintasilgo would go on to serve as the International Vice-President of the Grail and the prime minister of Portugal.[18]

It may seem, after this delineation of the history of the Grail from its founding in 1921 through its expansion in the decades after World War II, that we are ready to move directly to the profiles of sixteen of the founders that comprise the body of this book. But before we do so, it may be helpful to review briefly the historical context of the Grail's birth and development.

The Wider Context of the International Grail

As mentioned in the previous section, a development that contributed significantly to the birth and expansion of the Women of Nazareth, later known as the International Grail, was the Catholic "lay apostolate."[19] In the decades that followed Pope Leo's encyclicals in 1891 and 1894 that addressed the importance of the laity, and especially after World War I, the hierarchy and members of the laity themselves began acknowledging and promoting the laity's apostolic role, using the term "Catholic Action" to describe

---

17 Kalven, *Women Breaking Boundaries*, 308.

18 See Gomes, Chapter 10, 195-214 and Pintasilgo, Chapter 13, 255-276.

19 Pope Leo XIII, *Humanum Genus*, The Vatican, accessed August 11, 2016, http://w2.vatican.va/content/leo-xiii/en/encyclicals/documents/hf_l-xiii_enc_18840420_humanum-genus.html.

it.[20] For example, in his first encyclical, in 1922, Pope Pius XI strongly promoted the laity's role in Christianizing all aspects of the increasingly secularized modern world.[21]

Certain tensions existed, however, between the Vatican's recognition of the essential role of the laity in the battle against "modernity" and its desire to retain control over that same laity. Pope Pius XI expressed the tension in 1931 in his in many respects galvanizing social encyclical *Quadragesimo Anno*, when he described "Catholic Action" as "the participation of the laity in the action of the hierarchy."[22] And many lay associations that eventually came into existence did in fact remain under the control of the bishops, though this was not the case with all lay groups.[23]

At the heart of the lay apostolate was the theology of the Mystical Body of Christ, based in the Pauline teaching that all members are "one body" with a "single Spirit."[24] But in the promulgation of this theology, too, the Vatican struggled to discourage lay autonomy, as when Pope Pius XII, in his 1943 encyclical on the Mystical

---

20 Brown, *The Grail Movement*, 10.

21 Pope Pius XI, *Ubi Arcano Dei Consilio*, The Vatican, accessed August 19, 2016, http://w2.vatican.va/content/pius-xi/en/encyclicals/documents/hf_p-xi_enc_23121922_ubi-arcano-dei-consilio.html.

22 James M. O'Toole, *The Faithful: A History of Catholics in America* (Cambridge, MA: Harvard University Press, 2008), 146.

23 Jay Dolan, *The American Catholic Experience: A History from Colonial Times to the Present* (Garden City, NY: Doubleday and Company, 1985), 395-396; Debra Campbell, "The Struggle to Serve: From the Lay Apostolate to the Ministry Explosion," in *Transforming Parish Ministry: The Changing Roles of Catholic Clergy, Laity, and Women Religious*, ed. Jay Dolan *et al.* (New York: Crossroad Publishing, 1990), 212-213.

24 Ephesians 4:4.

Body, used distinctly hierarchical and juridical terms to describe the relationship between head and members in that "one Body."[25]

All this notwithstanding, because of the teaching's stress on the unifying role of the Spirit and on the mystical rather than purely organizational nature of the church, the theology of the "Mystical Body of Christ" introduced a strikingly more unified vision of humanity and a groundbreaking understanding of the church itself as a vital force for social and cultural change. The various papal calls for "Catholic Action," the dynamizing new theology of the Mystical Body, and the growth of an increasingly educated middle class, led to the emergence of a considerable number of lay Catholic movements and communities between the 1890s and the 1950s.

Dimensions of the Lay Apostolate

One noteworthy dimension of the lay apostolate was the Catholic Intellectual Revival. The revival was a cluster of intellectual, cultural and spiritual movements formed to counter the anti-religious rationalism of the Enlightenment and the evils of the modern world. Strongly influenced by the work of John Henry Cardinal Newman and the wider Oxford Movement, the revival was powered by the literary work of laymen such as G.K. Chesterton and Christopher Dawson in Britain and Charles Péguy, Léon Bloy and Jacques Maritain in France. By the 1920s, the Catholic Revival was underway in the United States as well, with the foundation in 1924 of the lay Catholic intellectual journal *The Commonweal*, and the opening in 1933 of the New York branch of the British lay publishing house Sheed and Ward, for the purpose of making the classics of the European Catholic Revival available to U.S. Catholics.[26]

---

25 John W. O'Malley, S.J., *What Happened at Vatican II* (Cambridge, MA: Harvard University Press, 2008), 85.

26 Campbell, "The Struggle to Serve," 226-227.

Another historical development that played a significant role in the growth of the International Grail was the Liturgical Movement. This movement to revive and transform the liturgy and the communal prayer life of the church emerged from the renewal of European Benedictine monasticism under the leadership of Dom Prosper Guéranger at the Abbey of Solesmes in France in the 1830s. Pope Pius X (1903-1914) had already energized certain aspects of the liturgical renewal, urging, for example, more frequent reception of communion, reducing to seven the age at which children received their First Holy Communion, and declaring participation in the Eucharist and the Divine Office to be the source of the true Christian spirit.

Though some aspects of these earlier phases of the liturgical renewal may seem romantic, a nostalgic attempt to return to the Middle Ages, the effects of the movement's emphasis on the communal nature of prayer and worship was quite the opposite. Already by the late 1930s, letters to the editor of the U.S. journal, *The Commonweal*, were demanding that the *Missa recitata*, or dialogue Mass, launched by the Benedictines at Maria Laach Abbey in Germany in 1924, be celebrated every Sunday in all parishes. Other readers, however, called for a crusade to help the starving instead, an understandable preference in the midst of the Great Depression.[27]

That reader's call for attention to the poor brings into view a third major development within Roman Catholicism during the years when the Grail Movement emerged, the turn to social action. Stimulated by various anti-Catholic *kulturkampfs* beginning in Switzerland in the 1840s and exploding in Bismarck's Germany in the 1860s, Catholic concern with social justice came further into focus with the publication in 1891 of *Rerum Novarum*,

---

27 *Ibid.*, 226.

the first Catholic social encyclical.[28] By the early decades of the twentieth century, clergy and laity alike were calling for Catholic social and political engagement in response to the problems of industrialization, urbanization, and poverty.

Lay groups played a significant role in the Catholic turn to social action. One of the most influential of these were the Jocists (Jeunesse Ouvrière Chrétienne), called the Young Christian Workers in English speaking countries, founded in Belgium after World War I by Father (later Cardinal) Joseph Cardijn.[29] Other such influential groups include the Catholic Worker, founded by Dorothy Day in 1933, the Canadian Madonna House apostolate, inaugurated in Toronto by Catherine de Hueck Doherty in 1957, and the Grail Movement.[30]

As noteworthy as the Intellectual Revival, the Liturgical Movement, and Catholic Action were in themselves, it would be difficult to overstate the extent to which they were interconnected.

---

28 It must be admitted, however, that ongoing Vatican hostility in response to the takeover of the Papal States by Italy sometimes outstripped Leo XIII's concern with social justice; eleven years after the publication of *Rerum Novarum*, the Vatican Sacred Congregation of Extraordinary Ecclesiastical Affairs under Leo XIII issued a document directing that the popular Italian Christian Democracy Movement, which called for a wide range of social reforms compatible with the 1891 encyclical, including reforming child labor laws, a minimum wage, and a shorter work-day, should focus its attention exclusively on the restoration of the temporal powers of the Vatican. "Pope Leo XIII," Notable Names Database, accessed August 20, 2016, http://www.nndb.com/people/387/000088123/.

29 The Editors, "Catholic Action," The Encyclopedia Britannica, accessed October 25, 2016, https://www.britannica.com/topic/Catholic-Action.

30 Susan Kim, "*La Croix*," *French Media Studies*, accessed October 20, 2016, http://frenchmediastudies.blogspot.com/2010/10/la-croix-susan-kim.html; Campbell, "The Struggle to Serve," 240-241.

In the United States, Dorothy Day, the charismatic leader of the Catholic Worker, is known primarily for her total commitment to social justice, yet for her, the liturgy was the core of that work.[31] Similarly, a leader of the European Catholic Intellectual Revival, Sheed and Ward co-publisher Maisie Ward, became actively engaged in the liturgical renewal in the United States, and considered the dialogue Mass an essential building-block of the lay apostolate.[32]

These dimensions of the lay apostolate, the Catholic Intellectual Revival, the Liturgical Movement, and Catholic social action converged remarkably in the Grail. The Grail's earliest incarnation, the Women of Nazareth, had been explicitly founded as part of the lay apostolate, and their ministry focused from the outset on serving the poor and disenfranchised, working with Dutch factory girls and planning to start a university for women in the Dutch East Indies (now Indonesia) based in Javanese rather than European culture and languages.[33]

The founder, Jacques van Ginneken, an internationally known psycholinguist and ethnologist and the only Jesuit ever elected to The Dutch Royal Academy of Sciences, might himself be characterized as a force in the European Catholic Intellectual Revival. As historian Marjet Derks suggests, van Ginneken's

---

31 Katharine E. Harmon, *There Were Also Many Women There: Lay Women in the Liturgical Movement in the United States 1926-59* (Collegeville, MN: The Liturgical Press, 2012), 51, note 62; Mark and Louise Zwick,"Virgil Michel, Benedictine Co-Worker of Dorothy Day and Peter Maurin: Justice Embodied in Christ-life and Liturgy," Casa Juan Diego, accessed October 25, 2016, http://cjd.org/2000/02/01/virgil-michel-benedictine-co-worker-of-dorothy-day-and-peter-maurin-justice-embodied-in-christ-life-and-liturgy/.

32 Harmon, *There Were Also Many Women There*, 136-137.

33 Brown, *The Grail Movement*, 21.

vision of a mystical, profound and vigorous Catholicism aligned with those of radical Catholic thinkers such as Léon Bloy, Jacques Maritain, G.K. Chesterton, and the Dutch Catholic author, Gerard Brom.[34] In addition, Lydwine van Kersbergen, one of the first members of the Women of Nazareth and founder of the Grail in Great Britain and Australia as well as the United States, had studied the Oxford Movement in Britain after completing her Ph.D. at the University of Nijmegen in 1936.[35]

During the 1920s and 1930s the Women of Nazareth and the Grail Youth Movement were not explicitly involved in the European Liturgical Movement. Yet as Katharine Harmon argues, the Grail's massive dramatic performances in the Amsterdam Stadium beginning in 1929, with many thousands of girls dressed in bright colors enacting the Christian message and dancing to Gregorian chant, launched the Grail as "one of the most courageous and public realizations of Catholic Action in the years between the world wars."[36]

As the Grail spread throughout the world, its overlapping commitments to the Liturgical Movement, the Catholic Revival,

---

34 Marjet Derks, "Female Soldiers and the Battle for God: Gender Ambiguities and a Dutch Catholic Conversion Movement," in *Gender and Christianity in Modern Europe: Beyond the Feminization Thesis*, ed. Patrick Pasture *et al.* (Leuven, Belgium: Leuven University Press, 2012), 180.

35 The Oxford Movement was a response from a number of High Church Anglicans in the early part of the 19th century to what was perceived as the secularization of British culture. One of the leaders, John Henry Newman, eventually converted to Roman Catholicism and became a Roman Catholic Cardinal. *The Oxford Movement: Europe and the Wider World 1830–1930*, edited by Stewart J. Brown and Peter B. Nockles (Cambridge, UK: Cambridge University Press, 2012); Kalven, *Women Breaking Boundaries*, 39; Brown, *The Grail Movement*, 25.

36 Harmon, *There Were Also Many Women There*, 35.

and Catholic Action became increasingly apparent. A founder of the Grail in the U.S. (as well as in England and Australia), Lydwine van Kersbergen, attended the convention of the (U.S.) National Catholic Rural Life Conference, a group committed to improving the lives of rural Catholics, a bit more than a year after the Grail's arrival in North America. And the other U.S. founder, Joan Overboss, spoke out at the National Liturgical Week meeting at St. Meinrad's Abbey in Indiana in 1942.[37] Indeed, the first direct contact by the Women of Nazareth with the American church was a 1936 letter from van Kersbergen to Dorothy Day. And a number of the founders profiled in *Women of Vision* speak of the profound impact on them of the dialogue Masses and liturgical music, especially the Gregorian chant that they experienced during their training at Grailville and took back with them to their home countries. Liturgical spirituality was a driver of their subsequent work to educate, provide medical care for, and liberate women and girls in Asia, Africa, and North America.

This mention of the Grail's particular focus on women and girls calls attention to another aspect of the group's identity, one that distinguishes it considerably from other lay groups: their stress on the essential function of women in the lay apostolate. For while women like Dorothy Day and Catherine de Hueck Doherty played pivotal roles in Catholic social justice activism, and a significant number of women made invaluable, if too-often unacknowledged, contributions to the liturgical renewal around the world, the Grail Movement has highlighted the role of women in the transformation of church and society from its founding in 1921. A story about the Grail's work in Uganda that Magdalene Oberhoffer relates in her interview in chapter 9 suggests the impact of this focus on women in the work of the Grail around the world:

---

37 Brown, *The Grail Movement*, 28-29; Harmon, *There Were Also Many Women There*, 51, note 134.

We then started the secondary school for girls, not the way the British had been running them; we wanted to give it an agricultural base. So Josephine Drabek and Jessica Stuber arrived from Grailville with a tractor. The people of the village couldn't believe it—a woman driving a tractor. They marched behind the tractor—it made a lovely story.[38]

The Continuing Tension

A certain ambiguity has marked the Grail Movement from its inception. Founded as a lay movement, but with a "fiery core" that made promises (not vows) of poverty, chastity and obedience and underwent rigorous spiritual training, the Grail has elicited curiosity, and sometimes skepticism, from the church as well as the wider public. In her interview in *Women of Vision*, Hilda Canters recalls becoming interested in the group because she wanted to check out the unsavory rumors going around about the Women of Nazareth living in the same residence as the Crusaders of St. John, the Dutch laymen's group also started by Jacques van Ginneken. Who knew what was going on in there, people suggested. Hilda wanted to find out.[39]

Nor did the Grail's expansion beyond Europe resolve this ambiguity: a year and a half after van Kersbergen and Overboss arrived in the U.S., an article in *Time* magazine described the women as "Nuns in Mufti" and a "new religious order."[40] And lest that article seem to have appeared too long ago to signify very much, in January of 2016, the *Global Sisters Report*, a channel of the liberal *National Catholic Reporter* newspaper, published an

---

38 See Chapter 2, 21-40.

39 See Chapter 4, 61-84.

40 "Nuns in Mufti," *Time* (July 21, 1941), accessed August 22, 2016, http://content.time.com/time/magazine/article/0,9171,765827,0.html.

interview with "Sister Imelda Gaurwa, the First Tanzanian Grail Sister," in which the Grail is described as "an international order."[41] Gaurwa is one of the Grail founders profiled in *Women of Vision*, and in her interview she mentions specifically joining the Grail because it was *not* a religious order.[42]

In some respects, the size and success of the Grail in the United States after World War II contributed to the ambiguity that has shadowed the movement since its foundation. In part because of the severed communications between the founders of the Grail in the U.S. and Australia and their superiors in Europe during the war, and perhaps also because of American egalitarian tendencies, the Grail in the U.S. under the leadership of Overboss and van Kersbergen emphasized the lay rather than the quasi-convent dimension of the group's identity. In her interview in *Women of Vision* Frances van der Schott speaks of how impressed she was when she visited Grailville during the war by the emphasis there on the lay reality rather than on hierarchical structures. When she returned to Australia she worked to shape the formation program there to be more open and less cut off from the world, as she perceived the U.S. formation program to have been.[43]

Yet in 1951, the International President of the Grail, Rachel Donders, in order to strengthen the structure of the whole international movement after the departure of the English Grail, mandated the dedication of the first twelve members of the "fiery core" or Nucleus of the Women of Nazareth in the United States. The commitment took place in a semi-secret ceremony in the main

---

41 Melanie Lidman, "Q & A with Sr. Imelda Gaurwa, the First Tanzanian Grail Sister," *The National Catholic Reporter Global Sisters Report*, accessed August 12, 2016, http://globalsistersreport.org/blog/q/q-sr-imelda-gaurwa-first-tanzanian-grail-sister-36661.

42 See Chapter 15, 297-324.

43 See Chapter 3, 41-60.

hall at the national center of the U.S. Grail, Grailville. The newer students were sent off on a picnic, while the twelve women swore "absolute obedience to the International President of the Grail" and promised to live in apostolic poverty and virginal chastity for life.[44] Thus, the historic tension between the "inner circle and the outer circle," the "nuns in mufti" and the laity, continued, at least in the short term. And the continuation of that tension in the U.S. would have a significant influence on the International Grail for years to come. Because of the size and scope of the resources at Grailville, many of the future leaders of the Grail, including seven of the founders profiled in this book, received their training there, thus taking the tension in the Grail's identity back to their home countries with them.[45]

It might seem that repeated questions about whether the Grail is a lay organization or a congregation of Catholic sisters would at least mean that the Grail's denominational identity is unambiguous, but neither is that entirely the case. In the Afterword to his 1989 study, *The Grail Movement and American Catholicism 1940-1975*, Alden Brown argues that by 1975, the Grail in the U.S. had effectively moved beyond the bounds of "Catholic affiliation." Brown attributes that disconnection to the absence of any principle of reform in the Catholic Revival, the movement that had played a major role in the International Grail's pre-Vatican II identity, as well as to the wider rejection of hierarchy in the post-Vatican II U.S. church.[46]

And while the move in the U.S. Grail from a Catholic to an ecumenical or even "spiritual" identity beginning in the late 1960s

---

44 Kalven, *Women Breaking Boundaries*, 110-111.

45 The last U.S. Grail member to join the Nucleus did so in 1975, but half of the approximately one hundred members of the Grail in Tanzania were Nucleus members in 2016. Mary E. Gindhart, telephone conversation with author, August 26, 2016.

46 Brown, *The Grail Movement*, 174-175.

is evident in some other countries—the Lutheran group in Sweden was recognized as a national Grail entity by the International Grail in 1998—in other countries, for example, Tanzania, Germany, the Philippines and Portugal, the Grail membership is still almost entirely Roman Catholic.[47] Efforts to have a Eucharist celebrated jointly by an ordained Lutheran Grail member and a Catholic priest at an International Grail spirituality forum in Portugal in 2007 provoked controversy; separate Catholic and Lutheran liturgies were celebrated instead, though the female Lutheran minister did stand at the altar as the priest celebrated the Catholic Eucharist.[48] According to figures collected at the 2011 International General Assembly in South Africa, nearly a third of the countries in the International Grail have an ecumenical and/or interfaith membership, while between 85 and 100 percent of members in the eleven other countries are Roman Catholic.[49] The International Grail Vision Statement passed by that 2011 International General Assembly recognizes these differences, even as it acknowledges the Grail's Catholic roots and the radical call of the Gospel.[50]

Toward the Centenary of the International Grail Movement

In some respects, it might be difficult, in 2017, to argue that the International Grail, with its approximately 850 members in seventeen countries around the world, is having as massive an

---

47 "Where We Are: Countries: Sweden," The International Grail, accessed August 23, 2016, http://www.thegrail.org/index.php?option =com_content&view=article&id=82&Itemid=108; "Where We Are: Countries: Tanzania," The International Grail, accessed August 23, 2016, http://www.thegrail.org/index.php?option=com_content&view= article&id=83&Itemid=109.

48 Mary E. Gindhart, telephone conversation with author, August 26, 2016.

49 Carol Webb, telephone conversation with author, November 10, 2016.

50 See Conclusion, pp. 345-346.

impact as the Grail youth movement had in the Netherlands in the 1930s with its "six hundred and forty leaders and eight thousand members."[51] On the other hand, the Grail today has definitely moved beyond its European origins, playing a not insignificant role in Christian ecumenism, interfaith dialogue, environmentalism and the liberation of women and girls around the world in the years since the Second Vatican Council.

It is also the case that the lives of many of the 850 or so current members of the International Grail and their communities were deeply affected by the Grail founders profiled in this book and the other Grail women who worked with them. These women opened and staffed schools and hospitals, taught the Christian faith, farming, and women's empowerment, organized bicycle workers, served in Parliament and even, in one case, became the first (and thus far only) woman prime minister of Portugal.

And today, as we approach the centenary of the founding of the Women of Nazareth, Grail members around the world continue to engage in significant work: conducting two secondary schools and a residence for Masai girls who have refused female genital mutilation in East Africa,[52] bringing together young women from around the world each year at the UN Commission on the Status of Women in New York City,[53] working with women in Brazil on economic solidarity, environmental sustainability, and women's

---

51 Brown, *The Grail Movement,* 9

52 What We Do: About the Sofia Fund of Tanzania," The Grail in the U.S.A., accessed August 24, 2016, http://www.grail-U.S..org/aboutthesofiafund?.

53 "Where We Are: The Bronx Grail Center," The Grail in the U.S.A., accessed August 24, 2016, http://www.grail-U.S..org/where-we-are/the-bronx-grail-center/; "What We Do: the Grail Link to the United Nations," The Grail in the U.S., accessed August 24, 2016, http://www.grail-U.S..org/what-we-are/grail-link-to-the-united-nations/.

health issues,[54] offering much needed preschool education in poor communities in the Philippines,[55] working for thirty years with an income-producing program for women in Johannesburg, South Africa,[56] supporting programs for aboriginal women and children in Australia,[57] and much, much more. Indeed, when we consider that the Women of Nazareth began in the 1920s with only four members, and that the Grail survived the Nazi occupation of the Netherlands to spread to seventeen countries around the world by 2016, who knows what Grail women will achieve in the years to come?

Marian Ronan
October 2016

---

54 "Where We Are: The Grail in Brazil," The Grail, An International Women's Movement, accessed October 25, 2016, http://www.thegrail.org/index.php?option=com_content&view=article&id=101&Itemid=96.

55 "Where We Are: The Grail in the Philippines," The Grail, An International Women's Movement, accessed October 25, 2016, http://www.thegrail.org/index.php?option=com_content&view=article&id=78&Itemid=104.

56 "Where We Are: The Grail in South Africa," The Grail, an International Women's Movement, accessed October 25, 2016, http://www.thegrail.org/index.php?option=com_content&view=article&id=81&Itemid=107.

57 "Where We Are: The Grail in Australia," The Grail, An International Women's Movement, accessed October 25, 2016, http://www.thegrail.org/index.php?option=com_content&view=article&id=69&Itemid=95.

2003 Introduction

These are the stories of sixteen remarkable Grail women, told for the most part in their own voices. They represent eight countries and four continents. Many of them are now in their eighties and nineties. All but three of them have died since they were interviewed.

It all began in November, 1994 with a phone call from Eva Fleischner and Nancy Hennessey Cooney to me, Mary O'Brien. Eva's and Nancy's original idea was to honor Lydwine van Kersbergen by having a biography of her life written. At that time Lydwine was eighty-eight years old and living in Amsterdam. Her response to having only her story recorded was characteristic of a woman who has spent most of her life working in community for the liberation of women. She was emphatic in stating that she was only one of many women who had stories to tell about their Grail experiences. So the initial proposal expanded into a much larger project, that of recording the stories of several Grail members, and thus portraying the diversity of women who had taken a critical role in the international development of the Grail.

From the beginning, we established two major criteria for selection of women to be included: those who had participated in an original team of women who sought to root the Grail in their own country, or in a country other than their own, and women who had served as an International President or as a member of the International Presidency Team (IPT). One of our major concerns was that women who were chosen to be involved in this project did not begin to include all of those who satisfied these criteria. There are many more Grail members both living and dead who have had significant roles as members of an original team and there are more who have served on the IPT. However, a shortage of available financial resources made it impossible to interview everyone who might have been included. Intrinsic to the stories presented in this publication, and the stories of all Grail women, is each one's commitment to the international dimensions of the Grail.

From the stories in this book we get glimpses of each one's involvement in four generations of Grail women in the worldwide vision and expansion of the Grail. We discover in these women's stories the significance of the contributions of women who defined themselves as laywomen in the twentieth century. Although their lives were not always grounded in the tenets of the modern women's movement, their stories, like those of all Grail women, do reveal innumerable ways of addressing and confronting women's issues in the church in different times and cultures around the world. In referring to the significance and urgency of this undertaking, Eva had this to say:

> This project, I believe, will be an important addition to the history of the Christian church in this century....The Grail was conceived as a movement of and for Christian laywomen. In its theological breadth, liturgical practice, social involvement and, above all, view of women's role in the church and the world, the Grail was far ahead of its time, and helped prepare the soil which eventually gave birth to the Second Vatican Council.
>
> I sometimes speak of women's liberation in the church forty years before anyone had heard of "women's liberation." All this was the work [in the beginning] of a handful of young women—all deeply committed to their Christian faith and belief in its power to transform the world, inspired by a vision of making the Kingdom of God more of a reality here and now. Strange as it may seem (and is!), the lives of these women,

the role that their faith played in their spiritual journeys, have never been studied. Time is running out if we are to obtain their first-hand testimonies. To fail to do so would, I believe, mean a significant loss to our understanding of the church.[58]

Early in the project we decided to use narrative, or story telling, an oral account of lived experience, as the primary source of recording and writing about these women's lives. Narrative acknowledges the interpretation of historical events as equally important as the recording and accuracy of the events themselves. During the interviews, each woman was encouraged to form her own interpretations of influences on her life choices and her history within the Grail as it unfolded in the context of culture, race and ethnicity, class and religion. Thus, open-ended questions were used in one-to-one interviews to allow her to weave together two levels of her story, the factual occurrences of her life along with personal memories, feelings, and reflections. Accordingly, each narrator could reconstruct significant life events, often emotionally laden, while sharing her particular experiences and expectations. She could reveal her perceptions of what it was like to be a woman who embraced non-traditional leadership roles in the context of church, society, and culture in the early, mid- and late-twentieth century. All of these factors would allow the uniqueness of each woman and her experiences to emerge.

The specific questions asked each woman explored these experiences within the "community of memories," that is, within the various frameworks of her life. We began with childhood reflections of home, parents, siblings, church, and school, and how the integration of these associations and relationships had influenced and helped form early thinking, behavior, and what one respondent termed "great religious feeling." An essential part

---

58 Personal correspondence from Eva Fleischner to Mary O'Brien, November 1994.

of each interview was given to each individual's experience of the Grail as community from her first encounter to the present, with particular emphasis on international participation. Why did this woman become a Grail member and how did her early experiences within the Grail influence her life choices and preparation for the Grail work she was to undertake? What was her specific role, what did she do, how did she actually think and feel about what she was doing? What did she perceive as her greatest contribution to the international growth of the Grail? How did each woman experience and face change—cultural, religious, and social? How did each woman feel about retirement and what has it meant to her? How was she managing the aging process and how did she feel about old age? What did she see as her task in the present? What were her reflections on death? What could each woman offer as advice to younger women about spiritual growth? Finally, what were the threads of meaning from childhood, which continued to provide a sense of purpose and continuity over the entire life cycle for each woman?

All interviews were taped, recorded, and transcribed. Transcripts were then sent to each woman and she was asked to make changes, such as deletions or additions, if she so wished. Some sections of each story were deleted at the request of the narrator, but more often because of the writer's decision as to what was most important or appropriate to the purpose of the project. To facilitate brevity and continuity, the sequence of the original material was often rearranged. Continuity was furthered by occasionally inserting connecting phrases along with making some word changes. Incomplete sentences were sometimes made complete. Language usage was occasionally changed for those whose first language was not English. The women we interviewed also had difficulty using the first person, "I," in talking about their lives and expressing their feelings. The stress in the early Grail was on a particular kind of community participation whereby group priorities held sway over individual preferences, influencing how women referred to themselves and their work. So that each story recorded here is in the voice of the speaker, and reflects her experience, the communal "we" has been changed to "I" when considered appropriate. Again, in order to create a consistency for each individual woman's story, the editors blended their questions with each narrative and thus wove one story.

We have made every attempt to be true to the original meaning of each woman's story by reading each transcript many times before beginning to write, so that we became familiar with story and ambience. We critiqued one another's choices and selections. Eventually we realized that just as a person's life story is a work in progress, so is the way we have chosen to write. Without arriving at conclusive answers to our concerns, we have realized that the recording, analysis, and reporting of any narrative is a blending of the narrator's voice and that of the writer. If this allows for bias, it also provides opportunity for exploring and suggesting the universal aspects of each woman's life while preserving her uniqueness.

Having acknowledged this, and knowing we most likely have not met the expectations of all of our narrators, we hope readers will discover each woman's vision of transformation and the connection of that vision to the larger web of life. The Grail women whose lives are included in this volume took strong leadership roles that constantly evolved to meet the needs of their times and the differences in cultures. As their stories reveal, openness to new currents of thought in church and society, and consistent efforts to integrate fresh and innovative ideas into a living reality, enabled them to remain on the cutting edge of dialogue, caring, and responsibility with a global scope.

The narratives are divided into four sections, each section connoting a significant time period in the twentieth century. The themes for each section and an appropriate selection for each woman's chapter, have been taken from "A Parable of the Grail"[59] which follows. We felt this would further weave these stories into the larger vision of each time period and the accomplishments of individual women.

For instance, the section, "The Old Wise Women (1920 - 1940)," chronicles four women who were some of the earliest Grail pioneers, and were among the first to answer the invitation to begin a worldwide movement of women. In the second section, "Sent Forth Into the World (1940 - 1953)," are examples of great courage in the face of war, exploring new ways of spreading the work of the Grail, and handling tremendous changes in the Grail itself. The third, "The Vision Burned (1953 - 1970)," illustrates heroic commitment to balancing the determination to end oppression and the fostering of the contemplative life. And lastly, "A Vision of a Justice-Filled New World (1957-2000)," presents us with new cultural ways as African women implement the Grail in Africa.

A Parable of The Grail

The old woman, strong for her years
And wise beyond her years,
Had many daughters.

Daughters of the sunburned prairie,
Red canyon, dusty mesa, swamp and bayou,
Mountain and valley, ocean sands,
City...Village...Farm.

Loving them dearly,
The old woman sent them forth into the world,
Setting for them
The task
Of weaving

---

59 From Ruth Gallant, "A Parable of the United States Grail," U.S. Grail General Assembly, 1988.

*The web
Of justice.*

*And to each daughter
The old woman gave precious gifts.*

*To the eldest,
...Compassion for the timid, the fearful,
The desperate, the outcast.*

*To the second,
...The heart of the clown for laughter
That unifies.*

*And to the others,
...Persistence in the face of adversity,
...Passion of anger against oppression,
...A calming touch in the midst of chaos,
...Tears for the sufferings of others,
...Dreams of brighter tomorrows,
...Courage to speak the truth in love,
...A meditative self open to the breath of the spirit,
...Grace for sharing hearth and home,
With friend and stranger.*

*And to the youngest,
... Reverence of all that has gone before.*

*And most precious gift of all,
The old woman gave to each a piece of
The vision of the web of justice, a vision of
"The radical call of the gospel
For the transformation of the world."
And in the soul of each daughter,
The vision burned, lighting the way
For herself and for others.*

*Now the daughters setting forth to weave
The web of justice were guided by many signs.*

Many followed Christ.
One lived the sacraments.
Another dwelt in fervent prayer.
A fourth discovered the way of Zen.
One, collecting faith-evolving symbols,
Hung them from the cross.
Others sought wisdom of the goddess
Or opened themselves to the energies of the cosmos.

And the many signs led to many paths.
There were those who took on the hungry,
Heart-sore journey with the poor.
Others marched against racial strife.
Some raised their families,
Some raised other people's families.
Some joined the struggle for women's rights.
Some wrote poetry, danced, painted and stitched.
Some learned the language of scholars.
A few traveled far building schools
And hospitals and hope.
Some planted in the fields, others harvested.

The daughters took many paths,
Yet each path connected to the whole.
And they discovered in the connections
Strength in each other,
Rest for the weary,
Solace for the lonely,
And the vision made whole.

So the daughters wove on
Steadily, fitfully,
Boldly, painfully,
Striding, stumbling,
Falling, rising.
And so the web of justice grew—
Fragile, mended, broken, tough.

Deep within its crisscrossed threads, on-lookers
Caught glimpses even in the darkness of
Singing, dancing, story-telling,
Feasting, fasting, meditating,
Praying, birthing, dying.
And of the daughters finding each other
In the breaking of the bread
And the sharing of the cup.
In time, one by one, daughters dropped the
Threads, stopped weaving, slipped homeward.

And the old woman sent forth
Younger daughters who fastened new threads
To the old web lines and then wove on,
Pushing at the boundaries of the
Old weary world, true to their vision of a
Faith-centered, love-bound,
Justice-filled new world.
A world in which all share joyfully
In the fruits of the earth,
The energies of the sun,
The tides of the moon,
The light of the stars,

And the old woman.

Mary O'Brien
February 2003

PART - I

The Old Wise Woman (1921-1940)

Lydwine van Kersbergen, The Netherlands, 1990s

1

Lydwine van Kersbergen[1]

The Grail's vision, from the beginning, has been that it is a spiritual movement rooted in God, a women's movement for and by women, a cultural movement, a worldwide movement with a world-embracing vision.[2]

Lydwine van Kersbergen was a great Catholic woman of the twentieth century, advisor to Dorothy Day, friend of Catherine de Hueck, admirer of Maria von Trapp, and a major liberating force for American Catholic laywomen. Until the end of her life, she empowered women with her global vision of spiritual women transforming the world.

---

1 This chapter, except for the postscript, is a revised version of "A Woman of Vision: An Interview with the Founder of the Grail Movement in the United States" by Patricia Miller and Mary O'Brien. *U.S. Catholic Historian*, Vol. 15, No. 4 (Fall, 1997), 95-105. Used with permission.

2 Lydwine van Kersbergen, interview by Mary O'Brien, Amsterdam, The Netherlands, May 1994 (see transcript, Grailville Archives, Loveland, Ohio). Unless otherwise noted, all quotes and material are taken from this interview.

4   Lydwine van Kersbergen

Lydwine was one of the major leaders of the International Grail Movement of women founded in the Netherlands in 1921 and the president of the United States Grail from 1940 to 1962.[3] After returning to the Netherlands in 1965, she urged the present generation to keep the vision of the Grail, believing and trusting that the world can be transformed to a newness that they helped to create, to a new way of living, to a new womanhood, to a new society, a new church, a new culture, a new cosmic view, a new relationship among all men and women. This has been, and is, the vision of the worldwide Grail, felt at work and expressed in its ups and downs, through periods of lightness and darkness over its nearly hundred year history.

The Grail women's movement has always recognized the inner strength that comes from spiritual search and the support of women from all walks of life who help one another reach their full potential. Lydwine's awareness from childhood of her own unique talents developed into the power to recognize other women's greatness and encourage them to make a special contribution to the church and the world.

Born in 1905 in The Hague, The Netherlands, the second youngest sibling among five boys and two girls, Lydwine identified early in life the significant influences on her sense of self. She attributed the foundation for her spiritual life to her mother, Johanna, a woman she admired and who had the greatest influence on her. "The Grail gave me a vision for life, but my religiosity I have from my mother."[4] "I breathed religion. The whole atmosphere

---

[3]   The movement began in the Netherlands as "The Society of the Women of Nazareth." Although the original group of women maintained this name for several decades, especially in reference to its core members, the name Grail has been the official name for the movement for many years.

[4]   Lydwine van Kersbergen, *Age Wise,* publication of the U.S. Grail, December 1993.

was Catholic, was spiritual. My mother was really—and I don't exaggerate—a holy woman."

Lydwine's journey began with her mother setting the stage for her daughter's spiritual quest for an integrated Christian life. Lydwine's early years included pilgrimages with her mother to holy places all over Europe, fasting and doing penance with other pilgrims. Her spiritual life was an integration of daily Mass, religious shrines set up in the home, artistic expressions from artwork, and plants her father grew in greenhouses. In addition, "My mother had visitors—priests, learned men. Everybody came to my mother for advice." Of lasting influence on the young Lydwine was her mother's sense of social justice, which she admits was at times difficult when she would have to accompany her on Sunday visits to the poor and houses for old women. Her mother "was a spiritual woman, a business-like woman," who also gave "everything she had to the poor."

From a very early age, Lydwine knew with certainty that her vocation was to be single. Indeed, she was only seven when she realized that she wanted to dedicate her life totally to God and had no interest in marrying or having children. She thought that the way to live out this vocation was to become a nun, which was the only option for women of her time. Later, however, another option presented itself to her, which changed the course of her life.

Influenced by her mother whom she perceived as a "risk taker," Lydwine, as a young adult, set her sights on a university education rather than pursuing the traditional women's career paths. Later, at the insistence of her mother, she completed her Ph.D. in Dutch literature. However, in 1924, at the age of nineteen, while at the University of Nijmegen, she met Professor Jacques van Ginneken, S.J. Although the Catholic Church in the Netherlands had emerged in the nineteenth century from two hundred years of suppression since the Reformation, a ghetto mentality prevailed.

Van Ginneken observed that the time was ripe for countering this mentality by bringing women together within a strong Catholic Action movement. At that time, women had had the vote for seven years; they were eligible for parliament and higher education, and careers were opening up for them. Furthermore, Catholic women were coming together in a women's league and, more and more, they were also employed in factories and offices.[5] Of van Ginneken, Lydwine said:

> He was the man who had a great influence on me. First, he said that what we needed in our time were laypeople. We had priests, we had nuns, but in the time in which we were going to be, we needed laity responsible for church and society. And secondly, he said that patriarchal culture in Europe was over and the influence of women was coming. That was for me a terribly important point—this vision he had that women should lead women. The third point was that we needed a world vision because, in Holland, the emphasis was on smallness and beauty, and that was not enough.

After two years of study, Lydwine, with three other women, left university to begin training to join the Women of Nazareth, a group van Ginneken founded to enable laywomen to use their talents to convert the world to God.[6] According to Lydwine, they focused their work on preparing to start a women's university in Indonesia. Aware of the great woman emancipator, Raden Adjeng Kartini, who worked with Javanese women "in the spirit of [cultural] adaptation," they sought to do the same. "That vision

---

5 Rachel Donders, *History of the International Grail 1921–1979: A Short Description* (Loveland, OH: Grailville, 1983).

6 The other three women were Mia van der Kallen, Elisabeth Allard, and Louise Veldhuis. Yvonne Bosch van Drakestein, Gré Hackenitz, Clara Trel, and Debora Judith Bouwman soon joined them. Donders, 6.

was given at Nijmegen—to start as laypeople in Indonesia. That is what I was interested in."

The year 1929 was critical. Plans for Java collapsed when the new Bishop of Haarlem insisted that the Women of Nazareth stay at home to work among young factory girls, "in the chocolate factory, in the cigar factory and with seamstresses, etc. That was a tremendous shock for us," Lydwine recalled. Dismayed at first, the women accepted this decision and thus the Grail movement began. With this change in focus, "we went," according to Lydwine, "from a clerical approach" to an approach where women "worked out their own ideas. I was twenty-three at the time and I felt very old."

In her opinion, organizing the Grail as a women's "movement" brought about a significant change. Parish-led events for women were "paternalizing little clubs of sewing, gymnastics and singing. We wanted to change entirely that pattern from [paternalistic] caring to a movement. We were from the beginning a movement within which the members take an active part." The growth of the movement away from the parishes caused some conflict with the local churches, "but we were educating ourselves for the conversion of the world." This included the poor people, the working girls, the middle class and the students.

The birth of the Grail movement was formed in the context of a cultural climate that fostered many youth movements.[7] However, the Grail movement attracted thousands of young women to participate in all kinds of courses, "some of which were religious and spiritual, singing, music, sports—whatever they wanted to

---

7 Other youth movements considered idealistic at that time were such groups as the Russian Komsomol, the Boy Scouts and the Girl Guides in England, movements of university students, and, in the Netherlands, the Young Socialists and the Young Workers. Donders, *History of the International Grail: 1921 – 1979*, 7. Another group that shared some of the practices of these groups was the Hitler Youth.

have." But, according to Lydwine, "what was terribly important were the mass plays we had in the big stadium," organized and directed by the first Grail team.

> We had the Royal Road of the Cross, the Pentecost play with 10,000 young women, the Saint Lydwina play with about 6,000. Saint Lydwina was the patron saint of Holland. We put on Everyman in England in Albert Hall as well as the Hound of Heaven. The idea was to appeal to the masses, a current thing at that time which now would not be possible .... It worked. It had mass appeal and those who had joined in have never forgotten it.

On the other hand, "many of the clerics were very much against us because they had lost all their prestige, all their influence on the young women."

Summarizing the foundation of the Grail movement in the Netherlands, Lydwine said, "We organized the whole Grail movement," while Van Ginneken viewed the Grail project as "just a side line." His minimal guidance of the Grail from its beginnings, however, was intentional, taking seriously his own advice to remain a "pious union" and not seek canonical status as a religious congregation.[8]

Never did the Grail stray from being a movement directed by women. To attend the Eucharistic Congress in 1932, Lydwine took a ship from Amsterdam to Dublin with three hundred women.

---

8   A pious union is an association of the lay faithful recognized in Roman Catholic canon law but not as a religious order or institute. "Associations of the faithful," Wikipedia: The Free Encyclopedia, accessed July 11, 2016, http://en.wikipedia.org/wiki/Associations_of_the_faithful. The category was eventually dropped from canon law.

There was another organization of women on the boat and they were there with their bishop, and I think, fifty priests, and there I was with 300 women and no priests. It was a hard time for me. I gave a big lecture every day, with the priests looking on.

Her insistence on autonomy for women is again reflected in her personal stance: "I have also refused to have a [male] spiritual director. We wanted to go our own way." Lydwine has fond memories of countries where she helped to establish the Grail: Australia, England, Scotland, and Germany. Thinking back on the expansion of the Grail, she noted:

> The name Grail was quite a good thing because it was an international name, chosen on purpose ... because we were searching for love, for peace, for social justice, how to save the world .... So, you see, it was a worldwide search for good.

Key to this search, according to Lydwine, was community: "If you are women together and if you are united and have an appreciation for each other, then great things can be done." And on her own spiritual quest over her lifetime, she said, "I have grown with the Grail, yes, but in America I have grown the most." This statement embodies her great love of the United States and her admiration for its people, which grew from her own experiences over twenty years in her work in the education of women, helping them recognize and develop their talents.

Lydwine was a major force in establishing a unique education experiment, the "Year's School" of the lay apostolate, at Grailville in Loveland, Ohio, in 1944. The Grail had moved from its original U.S. location near Chicago to Grailville, an 183 acre farm near Cincinnati, with the support and encouragement of the Archbishop of Cincinnati, John T. McNicholas. The "Year's School" was a program designed for formation of Catholic laywomen and was based on the integration of liturgy, the land, culture and women.[9]

> I have always searched for an integrated life,... for the training, the liturgy, the land .... So I was interested in the liturgy, I was interested in agriculture ... and I believe, personally, that reading books and listening to lectures is not enough, especially for women. That is why I wanted women to have contact with nature, with animals.

This tall, handsome, self-possessed woman with a powerful presence recalled that, "I had been quite good looking and that helped of course. I could manage, especially bishops and people in authority. They trusted me." This, combined with her strong sense of the importance of culture, enabled her to discern what was alive in America at that time: the liturgical revival and the rural life movement. "I tried to join with the best of these people."[10] At the same time, she always used her commitment to the question of women's role in church and society to critique the best of these new ideas. For example, "Although back to the land had never been part of the Grail, I joined the rural life movement" in the United States. While attending a meeting of the National Catholic Rural Life Conference in the early 1940s, Lydwine listened to its leader, Monsignor Luigi Ligutti, talk for two weeks.

---

9   Alden V. Brown, *The Grail Movement and American Catholicism, 1940-1975* (Notre Dame, IN: University of Notre Dame Press, 1989), 43-66. For a more extensive understanding of the centrality of the liturgy for the Grail, influenced by Lydwine, see Janet Kalven, "Living the Liturgy: Keystone of the Grail Vision," *U.S. Catholic Historian*, 11:4 (1993), 29-35.

10 Some mentioned in the interview were Dorothy Day, Martin Hellriegel, Reynold Hillenbrand, Ermin Vitry, Damasus Winzen, Christopher Dawson, Jean Daniélou, Evelyn Waugh, Godfrey Diekmann, and Gerald Ellard.

Then she got up and said, "It is a beautiful convention but I have not heard a word about farmers' wives. Could they not have something to say, too?" So Ligutti made her vice-president of the Conference.[11]

Lydwine's knowledge of culture and literature was always part of her search for an integrated life; this enabled her, at the time of the interview on which this chapter is based, to say, "I have the vision for what I want." She synthesized her ability to take religious ideas, dramatize them and turn them into cultural events, with the new learning opportunities she found in the United States: the liturgical reform from the Benedictines, intellectual thought emerging from the Catholic Revival, and the importance of the back to the land movement, while keeping in mind the same question, "What is the role of women in the modern world?"[12] Lydwine had a remarkable ability to integrate these great movements into a living, learning, experiential program to train lay women leaders. Her understanding of the importance of the relationship between land, liturgy, culture and women was deep. Implementing Lydwine's vision required, first, that the women be intentionally exposed to the variety of programs at the "Year's School," so that:

> Women at least get a touch of everything, and perhaps for several months. Then they stick to one particular department—some to agriculture, some to culture, some to writing, some to the study and discussion of womanhood .... With great difficulty I had to adhere to that integration, and not to be drawn by important leaders into one department.

---

11 See also Janet Kalven, *Women Breaking Boundaries: A Grail Journey, 1940-1995* (Albany, NY: State University of New York Press, 1999), 65.

12 See Lydwine's three articles combined in her book, *Woman: Some Aspects of Her Role in the Modern World* (Loveland, OH: Grailville, 1956).

Thus, farming, gardening, baking, cooking, spinning and weaving, along with community liturgical celebrations expressed through daily Mass, participation in drama, dance, literature, readings, art, music and the chant, permeated the very atmosphere of Grailville.[13] Lydwine believed that her greatest contribution to the Grail in the United States was building Grailville and helping women discover their gifts and talents for the lay apostolate.

One of Lydwine's most significant talents was her extraordinary capacity to realize and foster the greatness in individual women. This ability stemmed from her faith, which underpinned her unshakeable trust in God and in people.

> I believe that we are created as unique persons, that we all have a mission, and I am very much inspired by John Henry Cardinal Newman. God created everybody to render a special service. We have our talents, gifts from God, and I am convinced that we are all unique … . As Newman says, young or old, man or woman, rich or poor, each has a mission in life… . I have always believed that, and I still believe it … .
>
> I had the gift of delegation … .We are very clear about the faults we have … . But very often we do not see the greatness of others. And I have learned that, from people you least expect, you can have the greatest performance … if you give them the chance, they can accomplish great things … . From the beginning Joan (Overboss) and I had tried to help women to become conscious of their talents and their possibilities and

---

13 Lydwine mentioned as examples readings of plays by Paul Claudel such as *The Satin Slipper* and *The Tidings Brought to Mary,* T.S. Eliot's *Murder in the Cathedral* and *The Cocktail Party,* readings from great writers such as Charles Péguy, Josef Pieper, Romano Guardini, John Henry Newman, G.K Chesterton and Eric Gill; and religious dance led by Dom Ermin Vitry.

to help them create ways they could work out these talents wherever they go.[14]

Lydwine felt she succeeded in her goal of "trying to develop every woman in line with her talents."

Lydwine's own experiences in the United States and at Grailville left a lasting impression on her.

> The most beautiful years of my life have been the years at Grailville—living in community, fasting and feasting together .... I had my most beautiful time in America. I love the American people .... I must say also that I was touched and impressed by the youthful energy, élan, generosity, spontaneity of the young women who were with me [because] I always wanted to help in educating young women in service for others, for God, for society. I've always been a spiritual person.

Lydwine's vision of building a worldwide lay women's movement had a lasting influence on the international development of the Grail. Early on at Grailville she encouraged women from other countries to come for training at Grailville, with the hope that these women would take the idea of the movement back to their own countries. Although she later talked about the value of women remaining in their own countries for education and training, she nevertheless believed the international presence at Grailville brought a rich, reciprocal dimension to the learning experiences of American women. She also helped establish the Institute of Overseas Service in Brooklyn for the training of laywomen for overseas work

> ... which was new ... to work in the medical, social and educational fields.... Up until that time—until the Grail came—you

---

14 Joan Overboss, a German national, was the co-founder of the Grail in the U.S.A. See Kalven, *Women Breaking Boundaries*, 1, 3, 22, 84, 221 and throughout.

had only priests and nuns going to countries in Africa and South America.

The Grail's commitment "was to start and help, but work so that the indigenous women could eventually take over." Talking about some of the eighteen countries where the Grail movement existed at the time, she said, "I think it worked."

The Grail in Africa, in particular, had special meaning for Lydwine. Lydwine talked with great animation about her "two big trips through the whole of Africa" in the 1950s, the first being with the Grail's International President, Margaret van Gilse, to explore possible placements for women training for overseas work.

> So I went from Capetown by car, all over Africa, through the Sahara ... to preach the lay apostolate, to talk to bishops, to say you should have lay women ... and saw all the bishops and the governments and we chose Uganda ... with great care because of the opportunities there.

The bishop was black and, according to Lydwine, none of the other bishops, all white, were interested in the training of laywomen and their contributions to church and society. "So we got there and then did what we wanted."

She spoke enthusiastically about the Grail in Africa, which was run by indigenous women:

> I think the most beautiful spirit lives at the moment among the Grail women in Africa. They stick to the first idea of simplicity of life, of living as poor as can be, of giving themselves totally without reservation. They are in the first era of beginning, the joy of the beginning. And I feel that, at the moment, we have to learn from them.

Her travels for the apostolate during the 1950s also took her through all of South America and Mexico. And before she returned to Holland, Lydwine and several other Grail members attended sessions of the United Nations under the auspices of the International Movement for Fraternal Union Among Races and Peoples (U.F.E.R.), a non-governmental organization. U.F.E.R. represented hundreds of young women from many professional backgrounds who, according to Rachel Donders, a past International President of the Grail, "put their skill and energy at the disposal of their sisters and brothers" in their home countries. [15]

Reflecting on her time in Mexico, Lydwine said, "I loved Mexico. I have a great love of the Spanish language, and I would have loved to have stayed there." However, she returned to Holland in 1965 at the age of sixty and began to study Spanish at a university there. She found returning to Holland difficult, "but I did it and ... it was good that I was not that old, to start a new life here." And indeed, she did start a new life using her Spanish in work with migrant workers—"guest workers" as they were referred to—helping them to find housing and learn the Dutch language and culture.

> I went with them to the doctors because they could not understand. All these things I have done and done with great pleasure and with great love. I know how they felt, and how they felt lonely here. It was a very beautiful time working among these people. I still have contacts with many of them in Spain.[16]

At the age of eighty-nine, when she gave the interview on which this chapter is based, Lydwine's thinking remained alive and vital, and

---

15 Donders, *History of the International Grail: 1921 – 1979*, 50.

16 Lydwine's interest in the Spanish language extended to literature, much of it South American. As she said, "I have a whole Spanish library that's world literature," including works by Cardenal, Neruda, Borges, Marquez and others.

reflected her awareness of what had changed and what had continued in her thought. "We are at a turning point of history, so the old, to a certain extent, is over and the new is coming, but what that new is going to be we don't know yet." And of the Catholic Church:

> I think we even have to go down a little bit further so that, out of the ashes, something new still comes ... if I may say, a new vision of religion, of spirituality. And the essence of our religion, which is so simple—love God and love your neighbor—these will always remain.

Her vitality of thought and openness to new ideas were again revealed in her statements on women and religion:

> Take the point of women and the priesthood. In my time, when we started the Grail, we were very emancipated. However, that subject (priesthood for women) was not discussed .... Nowadays it is at the center of women's concerns. And they are right. I am convinced it is going to happen. Only we need more time. We are growing and growing through development of women.... I say that history has hardly started because women have not had a real chance to come forward .... For me the hope of Christianity is the women's liberation movement and liberation theology, the church of the poor .... Why is not the whole church behind the women's movement? Why does it not back liberation theology?

Having been one of the leaders of the United States liturgical revival, Lydwine suggested new directions for women and liturgy today. "We have to get new symbols, we have to get new liturgical prayers, we have to get new women's services in the church ... we also need womanly symbols."

Lydwine also pointed out that, from its beginning, the Grail, because of its autonomy, has had the ability to be flexible and changeable to incorporate the practical realities of women's lives.

I never believed in holding fast to what has been, but searching together in new fields, to new approaches, to new ways of life ... . I firmly believe that the essence of the Grail must stay ... everything around it, the projects, the ideas, the growing development in feminine thought, in theological thinking, has to be accepted and worked at ... the essence of the Grail stays, women for women, the spiritual mission, a world vision, and it has to be related to the world now. And that is the task of the younger generation.

Finally, Lydwine acknowledged: "I am not particularly fascinated by what I have done and what my ideals are, but I gave the vision and now that is everything for me in my life. I see how much we are developing, the growing evolution and the greater consciousness of women. I am part of it. But I am old. I wish I were twenty-five. I would start again."

Postscript

Lydwine lived another thirty-three years after her return to the Netherlands in 1965. During most of those years, she lived in Amsterdam and gave Spanish, Dutch and English lessons to young and elderly people, gave talks to various professional groups and was an active member of a discussion group in her parish. She also cared for her younger sister, Leentje. During her time in the United States, Lydwine had little contact with her family, something she regretted. She cared for her sister for many years, until Leentje's death in a nursing home in Rotterdam.

In these later years, Lydwine loved the saying "In omnibus rebus respice finem," that is, "Keep your eyes always fixed to the end." After falling down in the street, Lydwine was no longer able to care for herself, so in 1995, at the age of ninety, she moved to a senior care center for religious people in Mariengaerde, in Warmond. Four other Grail members were already living there, each with her own single room.

Lydwine died on Christmas Eve, December 24, 1998. Two other Grail members were with her. She had expressed the desire that U.S. Grail member Catherine Leahy attend her funeral, and indeed, Catherine and two other U.S. Grail members, Teresa Wilson and Audrey Sorrento, arrived in time for the evening memorial vigil in Mariengaerde, Warmond, on December 30. Lydwine was buried the next day at the Tiltenberg, with many people in attendance..

Toward the end of her life Lydwine said, "I keep living in faith. A new church is growing, a new world also through our devotion now. I pray for the help of our faithful friend John Henry Cardinal Newman 'that I may persevere till the end.' And as Father van Ginneken often prayed, 'that I may die nicely, like the golden leaves from the trees in autumn.'"[17]

We conclude with Lydwine's advice for our time, a text of St. Teresa of Avila, translated from the Spanish:

Let nothing disturb you.
Let nothing frighten you.
Everything will pass.
God doesn't change.
Patience conquers everything.
Who trusts in God
Will miss nothing.
God alone will do.[18]

---

17 Translated from the booklet, *Lydwine van Kersbergen 1905 – 1998 Een vrouw van de twintigste eeuw: Lydwine aan het word* (Lydwine van Kersbergen 1905-1998 A Woman for the Twentieth Century: The Words of Lydwine). Texts collected and introduced by Rachel Donders with the help of Helen van Cleef (The Grail in the Netherlands, 2000).

18 *Ibid.*

Rachel Donders, The Netherlands, 1990s

2

Rachel Donders

> *This is the Grail saga:*
> *there is a plan and it comes*
> *from within each of us.*

Under Rachel Donders's leadership as International President of the Grail, the movement reached a turning point in its identity. Rachel assumed this position at a very difficult period in the history of the world and the Grail, a few years after World War II. Just as there was enormous national and global fragmentation in the late 1940s, so too, the Grail in Holland and around the world needed a renewed sense of purpose and unity.

Rachel grew up in a country marked by centuries of religious division and she herself experienced religious discrimination as a child. Born in 1911 into a Roman Catholic family, she grew up in the town of Alkmaar, in the predominately Protestant north of the Netherlands. Although proud of her Catholicism, she was aware of differences, particularly when Protestant children were not allowed to play with her because she was a "Roman."

Discussions at home, though, went well beyond the borders of the Netherlands and she remembers talk about the Russian revolution of 1917 that she knew even then "had something to do with religion." So very early in life she became fascinated by the world and by history. According to her, these experiences from childhood were the primary influences on her eventual realization of how interest in the world and love of travel could blend with perceptions of religion and God.

Rachel recalls her parents telling her how delighted they were to have her since she was the "youngest by far" of seven children, born when her mother was forty-five. Both her parents came from the south of the Netherlands. She describes her mother as "very religious—a conscientious Catholic and very old-fashioned in a sense," while her father was "religious in his own way, but he did not go to church and he was quite liberal."

Although Rachel's father, a tailor who made uniforms for a military academy, worked at home, he was seldom present. Nevertheless, both parents had a lasting influence on their daughter. While she remembers her father as "more fun—more my friend," her mother endowed her children with their religious appreciation and taught them how to behave. Rachel remembers her mother taking her children to church, leading them in the family rosary and in prayers before meals. She also set an example of helping the poor and Rachel remembers that "I always had to bring things to the poor, and there were so many."

While Rachel's mother was her "religious educator," her father, in contrast, gave her a "cultural education." He had more formal education than her mother; for example, he was fluent in French, a language Rachel spoke with him, and he loved to travel. She later reflected back on how each of their approaches to life helped integrate her own worldview that would eventually form her future:

> As a child, I always thought that I would travel. My father took me on journeys. I liked the world, I liked nature, I liked culture and I liked people. I had an interest in life and then

suddenly all of these fell into place with my religiosity, which I got from my mother. Although at the time I could not express it this way, that's how it worked for me later.

In the face of the division between Protestants and Catholics, the Catholic schools in the northern part of the Netherlands, imbued with "the old time religion," helped to solidify and create community for the Catholic minority. Rachel at first found school boring but eventually became interested in languages, an interest stimulated by her father and his friends. Over time she studied French, German and English. The Dutch language particularly fascinated her and at a very young age she decided she wanted to become a writer, an ambition she dropped when she went into teacher training. However, she wrote many essays throughout her student years and describes herself as having been a good student and found high school "wonderful—I loved it."

Rachel decided early on in her life that she would most likely enter a convent. She had gone to a school conducted by Catholic sisters, and even though she wasn't "so keen on becoming a nun," she was "religious by nature." Meeting the Grail in 1930 at the age of nineteen while in teacher training challenged her with another possibility.

Although Rachel was immediately attracted to the Grail and fascinated by its vision, she thought that joining a religious congregation, and particularly the contemplative order of Carmelites, would be more difficult, and therefore, heroic. She recalled that this was the first time in her life she could consciously remember consulting a priest for help. He was a Dominican and when she told him of her dilemma, he cautioned that her reason for thinking she should be a nun rather than joining the Grail was groundless. "I was so relieved," she recalls, "and I never thought about it again; I dropped the whole thing at that moment and I knew then it was the Grail."

After making a lifetime commitment to the Grail, Rachel made known to Father van Ginneken three desires: to leave the Netherlands, to go to Russia, and if she couldn't do either of these, to become a prayer member of the Grail. First, though, as president of the Grail youth movement, she guided the Dutch Grail through very difficult and often dangerous times during the Second World War, when some members went underground. Eventually, however, Rachel did leave the Netherlands for many years, first as International President of the Grail and then when she accompanied two other Grail members to Japan for twelve years.

As International President (1949 to 1961), Rachel nurtured the Grail during the postwar period with her breadth of thinking and innovative ideas for rebuilding, renewal and new directions. During these twelve years the Grail experienced a remarkable expansion to twelve African countries, several new places in Europe, and Singapore.

Rachel's inspiration and encouragement, combined with her discretion and balanced perspective, sparked the beginnings of the evolution from the Society of the Ladies of Nazareth and their works beyond the Netherlands to the formation of the International Grail Movement. Rachel's particular gift was to move the Grail in directions in keeping with the times while preserving the original vision.

Rachel's aspiration to be a praying member of the Grail was realized when she and other Grail members formed a house of prayer in Israel in 1974. Throughout her life Rachel had consciously sought to combine the contemplative and the active life. Her experience in Israel gave her the unique opportunity to bring this particular passion to the Grail since, as she noted, this is what had attracted her to the Grail in the first place.

Subsequently, after spending a few years in Portugal, Rachel returned to The Hague in 1993 where she lived alone in a beautiful apartment that dated back to the seventeenth century. She found that her special task at this time in her life was "to help, as much as possible, those who are my age." She was also an avid reader and she felt that her own creativity had always come more from reading than anywhere else. In this way she continued to keep abreast of current theological, religious and spiritual thinking that was reflected in the many articles, essays and poems she sent to various Grail publications and newsletters.

One newsletter Rachel edited, *Let Us Celebrate*, grew from her "love for celebration and ritual." It consisted of contributions from Grail members around the world describing ways in which they celebrate feasts and special occasions. She also participated in functions at the Tiltenberg and often welcomed visitors into her gracious home. And she continued to travel in Europe to visit friends and Grail centers.

Rachel died in a car accident in March 2001 at the age of 89. Until the end of her life and amidst all of her outward endeavors, she still reserved time each day for prayer and meditation. The myriad aspects of her resolute nature and breadth of commitments came together and were symbolized by an exquisite crystal chalice displayed in her apartment. This receptacle was a visible reminder of her deep reverence for the Grail myth. It also signified how Rachel lived out the ever-emerging realities and mysteries that continued to the end to shape her quest.

Interview

The Grail Quest

I have always known that I was made for the Grail. It's where I belong; I would never have been happy anywhere else. I have been all over the world and seen so much but the Grail has something that I have not met in any other movement.

What has carried me these past seventy years of my Grail membership is the spiritual purpose, the idea of a striving, a search, a quest. We come through many different doors with a variety of symbols and approaches but our togetherness is in the Grail quest, the Grail saga.

I have always seen a difference between religion and belief. Since I was a young child I have had a sense of religiosity, the feeling, the knowing there is a mystery around all of us and I am made for something beyond. And when we search for something beyond ourselves, when we ask the question about our spiritual purpose, we already have the answer within us, so we search for something we have already found in a way. This belief, and the symbol of the cup, the beautiful chalice of receiving and giving and sharing, have been my inspiration since 1931.

I knew early on in my life that I did not want to marry; although I knew several young men, I had never been in love. But the evening I met the Grail, I was absolutely lost; I was in love with it right away and I have never lost my love for the Grail. There was something so fascinating about this movement and immediately I wanted to be a part of it.

The Grail was a new movement starting with women and girls for the conversion of the world, which was the expression of that time. I was so taken by this; what was beginning was not just an ordinary youth group, but something great, something with more breadth than I had ever known.

Two things particularly appealed to me. One was the idea of changing the world, the opening up of the world to that great mystery. I had always been a religious person and what I found right away in the Grail was a combination of prayer and contemplation. And the Grail appealed to my sense of the heroic with the importance of sacrifice, of giving up and doing difficult things. That doing of the difficult still appeals to me.

At first I stayed in Alkmaar where there was a Grail house because I was still in teacher training and I lived at home. Thus, I was what was called an external leader in the youth movement and was a leader of the Grail house. I organized groups, and I took part in the great plays. There were about 600 women and girls connected with that house. At that time, in the early 1930s, the purpose of parish youth groups was to keep girls and boys off the streets. When the Grail took over the girls' groups and the girls became Grail members, there was a great difference; instead of being kept from the streets, they were sent into the streets. This movement was not for them, but for them to have influence in the world.

By the end of 1932 I had finished my teacher training and was still in the youth movement as a leader. I knew then I had to take the next step and move on. This meant leaving my parents and going to the Tiltenberg because I was convinced that I wanted to make a lifetime commitment in the Grail. I wasn't hesitant about this, although I knew it meant not marrying; it meant giving myself and going wherever I was sent. My father and mother and I went on our first big journey together to the Tiltenberg and when my father left he proudly said to Margaret van Gilse, "You have a good one."

The Tiltenberg, at that time, was the center for spiritual formation for lifetime members of the Grail. We had lectures by Father van Ginneken, we had a lot of time for prayer, and we did a lot of singing. At table, we always had readings on the spiritual life, usually about the virtues. It was the old spirituality, but we took it seriously.

We also worked very hard cutting trees and washing dishes, and there was lots of silence. Since we were all young, we found it wonderful and easy. Even the sacrifices we had to make, not seeing our fathers or mothers for a long time, or not going for a holiday was just the order of the day. Everything and anything was possible. It was a simple life. We were a group of women with our own leadership and our own spirituality.

My formation program was combined with being in Amsterdam where the Grail eventually had seven houses. And very soon I was placed in The Hague and went out to the villages from there. Eventually I went to Rotterdam where I worked with all kinds of youth. Three times a week, though, all of the Nucleus members had a meal together and that is when we had discussions and made decisions. So I wasn't in formation for very long.

In 1936, I became president of the youth movement. We didn't have the big mass productions then; we were more geared toward the parishes. In Scheveningen we had courses for young girls to give them more awareness of society. For instance, we had lectures on women and the role of woman.

As I look back on those years I realize that we were misunderstood and that was painful. We were often accused of not being serious enough because we wore uniforms and bright colors. We also did not accept the leadership of the priests; in fact we took away their leadership of the young women and they didn't like that. Of course, these things were not easy to cope with but they strengthened us. We were very optimistic, always moving toward the future together in great friendship. We were absolutely united with each other and we still have that very strongly now with the older members. A number of the younger ones have that too, but there is something between those from before the war, from the early youth movement, which is irreplaceable; the bonding among us is still something very special.

World War II and After

In 1940 the Germans came into the Netherlands and it was rather quiet in the beginning. Then came the changes; everything became Nazi. Everyone, the leaders, the university professors, the medical doctors, had to go underground if they didn't want to be in the organization. Many of them were sent to concentration camps. And, of course, the worst thing was the persecution of the Jews. They wore a star and I saw Jews being beaten in the streets.

Since I was president of the Grail, I got an order to come to the German headquarters. They knew the Grail in Berlin had been closed and they asked me about that. As a youth movement we were considered an enemy of the state. A short time later, the Nazis came and closed the house where I was living.

I just kept moving from one center to another because someone had to be there, and I did not want to just disappear. And of course, every time the Nazis came to close another Grail house, I was there. We destroyed all our files with membership lists and one day the Nazis came to our secretariat and asked what we had in a huge filing cabinet. We told them just stockings and sewing materials. They were disgusted when they found this to be true and one of them said, "What these women need here is a man."

Then the Nazis came to another center, put a pistol on the table and told us that we not only had to leave but we had to sign a document. I refused to sign anything and one of the men said, "You go." At that time, we were young and naive; I disliked the whole thing but I wasn't afraid. A few times they threatened me and finally the Grail was forbidden. All of the Netherlands was in the same boat.

The last place to go was the Tiltenberg. Convents were protected but since we were not a religious congregation even the Archbishop could do nothing for us. We hid most of what we could from the Tiltenberg with neighbors and finally the same Nazis came and they found me again. I was immediately taken and put in a German car and driven to the train station and let out. I hid for the next six months in a small town in the southern part of the country.

The Tiltenberg was taken and we had to decide what now, what are we going to do? We were told that if even two or three of us came together, we would be sent to a concentration camp. We all laughed, but of course we did take precautions. Grail members lived at home and some convents accepted us, but we still had meetings in Amsterdam and Haarlem. We met in small groups and we went on praying together and spreading pamphlets with meditations, some of which I wrote and were passed out in churches. We even had a retreat and a meeting with Father van Ginneken in 1944.

Several young Grail women were in formation and they hid in a convent in the south of the Netherlands so that their formation went on. Others became nurses and at a certain point we were asked to staff a Catholic hospital. So, one by one, about seven Grail members applied and they hid Jews in the contagious ward where the Germans wouldn't go. Also in The Hague we found milk for poor children. Each of us was doing what she could in her own way.

I kept in touch with members all over Holland and when Rotterdam was bombed I walked there from The Hague to see what had happened to one member who lived there. We were just trying to survive. The worst was the "hunger winter," the last winter of the war. We were eating tulip bulbs. The Germans were losing the war and sending all of our food to Germany. I don't know how many people died of hunger at that time. I spent much of my time then finding food for Grail members. All of this was horrible. It was a miserable, awful time because we didn't know what was going to happen. How would this ever end? We were always afraid. I was afraid at that time, not for my life, but for what was going to happen ... for the future.

When the war ended we went immediately to the Tiltenberg. The place was in terrible shape; it was empty and filthy. There were no windows and doors, the sinks and wood floors were gone. Almost everything made of wood had been burned as firewood. Some of the doors and cabinets were discovered later by one of our members who saw a man storing them in Amsterdam. After spending the first morning at the Tiltenberg, I went for an appointment with the bishop covered with fleas. I could hardly sit still. However, we did not get our Grail houses back.

It wasn't an easy time for any of us. We could not start a youth movement again after watching the Germans marching in the street wearing uniforms and waving banners. So the time of the youth movement was over. Many of us went back to our families. We had no houses, no Tiltenberg, no Grail, nothing. Some members trained for different kinds of professions and we kept the formation group together.

We did keep in contact with one another, but we didn't know what we were going to do as Grail. Even the bishop did not know what to do with us. Then a priest who was in charge of social work in the diocese of Haarlem asked us to take charge of five hotels in Noordwijk for Dutch women refugees who were returning from Indonesia and needed a period of recuperation. And then family service started and we began a training program for nurses to help out families in their homes. It was very institutional and we were all engaged in social work but we didn't have a movement. We had to grow and the question was: how do we influence other women in new ways? I wanted something different, another dimension.

An International Women's Movement

Until this time, nuns and priests went to the missions but they did not have lay people. I asked myself, why can't lay people—nurses, teachers, doctors—go? This was an idea that was new for the Netherlands. I thought that we could go out to the world, to women in the world.

I shared this with Margaret van Gilse, the International President of the Grail, who was very enthusiastic. We had to go to missionary congregations to find out how they trained their young men; we had to develop a curriculum; we had to find teachers. I helped to set up a mission training center at the Tiltenberg where we had our first course.

It caught on like fire. There were a lot of women who wanted to go. The first group went to Indonesia and then to Borneo. And because the whole thing clicked, we got a house in Ubbergen and that became the big missionary training center.

Then in 1949, we had our first official election and I was elected to succeed Margaret van Gilse who had been "Mother General." I had just spent some time in the Ark, a small new retreat house on the grounds of the Tiltenberg. This gave me time to pray and reflect on what I wanted to work for as International President.

Right after the war, we had had a meeting in England with members from various countries. Father van Ginneken was there and it was then that the English Grail decided they did not want to be part of an international movement. Even though we were not officially international at that point, we were moving in that direction, so the English Grail went their separate way. This was another painful time in the Grail. So I knew I had to work for unity, and that a way to accomplish this was through a movement which would be international in scope.

In the early days we divided the world; we went to other countries to serve in other capacities, to educate young women for their spiritual formation, to convert the world by women's influence, but not to start a movement. But now we were in a very complicated time when we had just come out of a terrible war and a big separation. Different countries were also developing in different ways. So I felt that unity for the Grail through an international movement could help us find our identity. What was the connection between Holland, the United States, and Australia? What did all of us have in common? Of course, this could only happen if there was contact between us, so I decided to go and visit each one. It was when I visited Grailville in 1951 and 1952 that we decided, Lydwine and I and others, to make some significant changes. Grailville was a center for the formation of young women, apostolic formation, spiritual formation, an opening to the modern world, but there was at that time no wider movement.

I remember the evening we came together. First we changed the terminology; I named the position I held "International President" and I had two assistants who were later called vice-presidents. More significant was the agreement that the core Nucleus group was no longer to be called the Women of Nazareth. We would begin a lay women's movement not only for Nucleus members but an international lay Grail movement consisting of Nucleus members, single women, married women.

Although this concept of a Grail women's movement grew out of the idea of the Grail youth movement, it was an evolution from an emphasis on youth to that of a movement made up of women from different walks of life who would take responsibility together, not just for education, but for the building of the movement. Keeping a Nucleus was consistent with what we had been doing since the beginning; these women had been the leaders of the movement, the ones who started it and who brought the Grail to the different countries. In a way, this was faithful to the original idea of Father van Ginneken.

I think this was a turning point for the Grail; the idea of the Grail as a women's movement was born. This vision had always been with us but no one had articulated or organized it, and I think clarification and the real identity came at this time. I am glad that I was instrumental in bringing that about; I don't mean that I invented it, it was already there. But I put my finger on it, and of course helped create and then develop it.

I brought this vision back to the whole community in the Netherlands and they were very open. I was fearful of what our bishop in Holland would say since he was not internationally-minded, but when I met with him he said, "I always thought this would happen." That, too, was wonderful.

My years as International President were largely devoted to the overseas expansion of the Grail. I continued to travel to each country. A big area of development was in Africa. The bishop of South Africa came to Holland for a visit in 1950, and then Margaret van Gilse went there to work with women. Shortly after that, I was invited to speak to the White Fathers, to talk about lay missionary work. They really wanted to collaborate with the Grail in women's work in the missions. This was just what we needed and it all helped. Lydwine and Margaret made a journey through Africa by car and as a result we sent women to help start a hospital in Uganda where previously all that the African people knew of the Catholic Church had been through priests and bishops and nuns. So we sent laywomen there, not just as doctors or nurses but to attract other women with the idea of starting a movement. Eventually some of the indigenous women attended nursing training at the hospital.

I was still concerned, though, about starting a movement and I travelled around preaching the movement, yes, preaching the movement. I knew that the doctors and nurses had their own work, so other Grail members came and eventually we started a secondary school there in Uganda. It was a very good place to send people from our training centers and at one time we had sixty people, all of them "foreigners," from the Netherlands and Germany and the United States.

We always supported these people but we knew that the Grail had to become indigenous. Therefore, certain Grail members began to work with the African women, to help them form their own women's movement and out of these efforts the Grail movement in Africa began and grew. Imelda Gaurwa who was subsequently on the international presidency team came to Uganda from Tanzania for training and then returned to her country to start the Grail.

The Grail also went to Nigeria and Ghana. We sent people according to what each country needed professionally. The Grail in Africa grew out of these early efforts. My period as International President was stamped, I think, by my efforts to help the movement develop with one name, with its own identity in many different parts of the world—in Africa, in South America, in Mexico and other countries.

After the Presidency

After my term of presidency was completed in 1961, I spent a quiet year in Holland. At that time there was a young woman from Japan, Akiko, who had come to the Tiltenberg and made her dedication in the Nucleus of the Grail. She wanted to take the Grail to Japan and she wanted Mimi Maréchal to go with her. They were both quite young so I said that I was willing to go with them to help. By then I was fifty years old and I knew that age at that time was appreciated in Japan. I went to Japan in 1962 and stayed for twelve years. We all lived together and Mimi and Akiko worked with students while I remained in the background.

I did have my work; I began with three bible groups for women in their fifties, Catholics, Protestants, Buddhists. The Catholics also wanted to learn more about their religion and especially about the liturgy after Vatican II. I did this for eight years and the Grail fascinated these women. They were so glad to meet a layperson because priests and nuns had always done all of this. And to put food on the table, I gave English language classes in a men's company for three hours each morning. It was really an exchange since we talked, too, about customs and the culture in different countries.

I also studied Oriental Art for a few years at Sophia University and although I never learned Japanese, Japan and its culture intrigued me. I learned a lot in Japan—that customs, values, even ways of talking can be different. The main value above all others in Japan was harmony. I loved a lot of Japanese people and I still have contact, thirty years later, with many of them.

One experience I had while in Japan had a lasting influence on my life. I was interested in Japanese religion and the Japanese are tremendously close to nature. It was Holy Week in 1970 and I was walking home from a church where we had just had a beautiful ceremony. I went through the park that was filled with cherry trees and blossoms.

I came to a pond and under these trees on a hillside were small groups of people, sitting silently, meditating, with the Japanese harp playing soft music. A little cloud was passing over the full moon. I can honestly say that for me this was a cosmic experience. This was cosmic religion. There was nothing theological about it; there was no celebration in the sense we know, just meditating in the moonlight. You could not ask a Japanese person, "What were you thinking while you were sitting there?" They can't answer; it's a total identification with nature. I thought to myself then, "East is east and west is west... never would the people sitting here be able to celebrate Holy Week as we celebrate it; it doesn't speak... it's an impossibility. It's another world." I will be eternally grateful for that experience. It was a conscious opening up and beginning for me of a completely different way of relating to religion. A few years later I would be into a new spirituality, a new way of thinking with a cosmic religious attitude.

When I left Japan, I was at a turning point in my life; I wanted to have time to pray. Although I'm not a contemplative and prayer for me has to be connected with life, all my Grail life, right from the beginning, I have felt that as Grail we needed places of quiet.

I had been thinking of helping to set up a place somewhere in the world, an international meeting place where we, as Grail, could meet for prayer, for quiet, for spiritual renewal. Another Grail member from Scotland, Anne Matthews, had been working in Israel on the staff of an ecumenical center. I joined her, and we found a lovely place on a hill between Jerusalem and Bethlehem with room enough for people to stay with us. We let it be known that people were welcome to come to visit the Holy Land but to do this quietly, not like the usual tourists and pilgrims.

The center was a great success; we had over seventy people of twelve different nationalities who stayed with us in the course of those fourteen years. There were women and men, lay and religious, married and priests who came for prayer, reflection, exchange and study.

We had a schedule which our visitors joined—Mass and prayer every morning and prayer again in the afternoon. We studied the Psalms and prayed them a great deal. We had a very beautiful room just for prayer that had windows on all sides and looked out on the desert and mountains. There was much time for quiet and reading and writing, whatever the person wanted to do.

A Cosmological Awareness

The spiritual has always been the most important thing in my life and in a way, my stay in Israel was the most spiritual time of my life. God has always been the foundation of my life and now my perception is more of presence, learning to live in the presence of God. I think I have always done that without sometimes knowing the expression.

My religious awareness has changed and expanded into a cosmological awareness. What I am coming to is the awareness of one tremendous mystery, inaccessible, untouchable, and from that great mystery emanates a power that is creation and is God.

However, this is also for me accessible, visible in nature, in the whole of creation, something that is not static but moving. My main interest, or rather I could say fascination, is with the contemporary currents and new approaches in religion in the widest sense, the changes these create in and around us, their meaning for life in this world and the hereafter. Of course science is the way to get to this, call it power, call it presence, call it energy. This power is in every atom. So, yes, I am living in God's presence.

This is a change from the old approach—naming—and has widened and deepened my understanding. I belong to those who in this time are searching for a new language through which old truths can be made relevant for us twentieth-century Christians. All-inclusive, yes, and interconnected as it is in mythology—not in a scientific way, but it's there. We are all interconnected, literally and materially, because we all come from that first moment of creation, from the development of the cosmos. This interconnectedness is for me divine, is the presence we call God. It is a consciousness that is for me a religious attitude, immanence far greater than we ever learned. I am happy that I am getting older in these times and am able to see the changes which are so great and wonderful: the new thinking, the new theology, the new currents, the new consciousness.

Now I am not a scientist or a theologian, but connected with this is the question of prayer. As I think back, that early influence of the Grail of an hour of meditation a day is still with me and even today I need that time of quiet, to sit and read and pray, to turn inward. Also, prayer for me is a way of connecting because of our oneness in creation. Rather than asking for trivial things in prayer, we can send another person what she needs, such as strength and courage.

This vision, this spirit and this connection are what give my life meaning at the moment. By living I contribute somehow to creation. That's my contribution. It's just life.

I also believe so much in the mystery of each one's calling. And it comes from within. It has to come from within; otherwise it does not work. I often say we are a feminist movement but I think what has been important in the Grail at its center goes beyond feminism to some extent, and that is our openness, our outgoingness to the reality of the world. I have always been an optimist, so I say we need to have a positive attitude toward the world and to look for opportunities to help and support and do the right thing, and to do this with hope.

At the same time, we have to have a consciousness of who we are as women, of our worth, and to stand up for that. I think we also have to have a deep interest in history and in the world—where we have come from and where we are going. This is what the Grail movement is all about.

Frances van der Schott, The Netherlands, 1991

3

Frances van der Schott

*To live is to change
and to live fully is to change often.*

On August 15, 1936, at the age of 24, Frances van der Schott sailed from the Netherlands with three other Grail members to start the Grail movement in Australia. They arrived in Perth on December 15 and a year later, when she was just 25, Frances would become the first president of the Australian Grail.

Frances had met the Grail in a rather unexpected way in 1931 when she was in her last year of teachers college. A young girl who was working for her family in their home was studying a little booklet during her lunch hour, "The Royal Road of the Cross," which was the first Grail play put on in the Amsterdam stadium. She was part of the speaking chorus and she sold tickets to the performance to Frances and her father.

A short time later, a Grail leader came to Frances's father's shop and invited her to a first gathering of young professional women organized by the Grail. The vision presented at that meeting, that of changing the world for the Kingdom of God, was one that Frances had never heard from the pulpit on Sunday. She immediately felt that this was where she belonged.

One of the first women to inspire Frances was Joan Overboss, who later helped establish the Grail in the United States. Frances became a part of the speaking chorus for the next Grail performance, which was put on at Pentecost in 1932. She attributes this experience to her making the decision to join the Grail. She made a lifetime commitment in the Women of Nazareth (later called the Nucleus of the Grail) at the Tiltenberg in 1935.

A strong link to community began early in Frances's life through the influence of her family and the church. She was the youngest of four children and grew up in a very harmonious home, surrounded by the love of her mother, father, and many relatives. Frances recalled that she had, in fact, two mothers since her mother's unmarried sister with whom she had a very close relationship lived with the family. Her father owned a religious goods shop which was in their home and she remembered her father and mother treating all people, as they came in and out of the shop, as friends rather than as customers.

Everyone in the neighborhood knew her father, so Frances developed a love for being with other people. She noted that her father's business suffered when the first communion age was moved from age twelve to seven by Rome. A greater emphasis was then to be placed on simplicity, which meant that the younger ones did not receive the same kind of elaborate gifts that the older ones had. Although this meant a loss of income for the family, there was always a peace and satisfaction with what each person had. In addition, needy relatives drained the family resources. And both of Frances's parents visited the poor and always left gifts.

On Sundays, when the shop was closed, the whole family went on long bike rides that her father organized. Her mother was a well-educated woman for her time, having been a teacher with a mastery of French. She refused to work in the shop since she thought it was not her work. However, she took care of many relatives, uncles, cousins and anyone who needed help, including a sister who had tuberculosis and who lived for a time with the van der Schott family.

Religion was the binding force in Frances's family. They were connected to the church and to each other. Her father, according to her, was more deeply religious than her mother, although he, like everyone else she knew, did not talk about religion in a personal way. He was a member of the St. Vincent de Paul Society and after forty years of service received an award "for his silent, quiet work for this organization." Frances, as a child, went to Mass each day; daily Mass was the most important thing in the lives of each family member. The family motto, although never spoken of aloud, but practiced, was "Love God, love your neighbor."

The pastor of their church, a priest very forward-looking in his approach to the celebration of the Mass, encouraged participation and responses in Latin so that parishioners could share more fully in this sacrifice. Frances credited his influence on her lifetime love for the tradition of the church, which, for her, focused on living the faith.

The summer Frances finished her teacher training, Lydwine van Kersbergen asked her and a few of the other young women who had been in the Pentecost performance if they would like to become Women of Nazareth,[19] that is, permanent members of what would eventually be known as the Grail. Although Frances

---

19 (The Society of the) "Women of Nazareth" was the name of the group founded in the Netherlands in 1921, which began the Grail Youth Movement. By the mid-1930s, however, new branches in English-speaking countries were called "The Ladies of the Grail," and by the 1950s, "The Grail" had become the name of the entire international movement, while members with permanent commitments were called the Nucleus of the Grail. Rachel Donders, *History of the International Grail 1921-1979*, 4, 18, 22 and throughout.

was taken aback, she responded whole-heartedly. By October she was at the Tiltenberg for training.

At that time, the Tiltenberg was completely closed off from the outside world. Silence, prayer, work, Mass, lectures, some singing and recreation were the order of each day. While she was at the Tiltenberg, Frances met Jacques van Ginneken, the Grail founder, who came for a few days to give her and the others in her cohort the vision of what women in the world could be.

Van Ginneken spoke to them about the great women of the Bible, of the Old and the New Testaments, and how Esther, Judith, Mary Magdalene and the other women had fulfilled their tasks—that only women were standing under the cross apart from John. He also talked about the three great movements of the world, communism, capitalism and Christianity, and told them that although they were not to do what communists did, Grail women were to have the same dedication and fire. Frances especially remembered that he never talked about priests or nuns. Her greatest inspiration at that time was not so much that the Grail was a women's movement but that she could be a part of bringing about the Kingdom of God as a layperson.

After a brief period of formation, Frances was sent to Rotterdam to be in charge of one of the fifteen Grail houses in Holland. This meant, at the age of twenty-one, she was the leader of a center which hosted 300 or 400 young girls at any one time. There were numerous clubs: some for choir; for acting; for mission work; for sewing; for folk dancing; for discussions; for meditation.

When the time came for Frances to go to Australia, she returned to the Tiltenberg for a few months of prayer and silence to prepare spiritually. She then spent the next fourteen years in Australia, mostly as president of the Australian Grail, where she helped to build a movement that spread to many parts of the country and attracted thousands of young women. When she left Australia in 1950 for South Africa, it was to allow for an Australian to take over the leadership.

In the early 1950's, Margaret van Gilse and Lydwine van Kersbergen made a trip by car from South Africa to several African countries with the plan of finding the appropriate place to establish the Grail. They decided on Uganda since the bishop wanted a secondary boarding school for girls; Frances went to get it started. She later returned to Kalisizo, a hundred miles south of Kampala, as teacher and principal of the secondary school there until 1970; at the age of fifty-eight she returned to Holland. She had been working for nearly thirty-five years in other countries.

When she returned to Amsterdam she worked in part-time teaching. She also immersed herself in work in the parish which included playing the church organ. And many Grail members will remember Frances's contributions to the international Grail newsletter, "AgeWise."

Eventually, Frances moved into an historic area, the Beguinhoff, which for centuries housed a group of semi-monastic laywomen, the Beguines, and was eventually turned into housing for older women. In this lovely place in the midst of Amsterdam, Frances was able to attend daily Mass and help other older Grail members who lived in the same area. She kept up a large correspondence with friends around the world. When asked in an interview what she did all day, she replied, "Well, I don't know what I do, but I'm busy all the time."

That interview, done in January, 1995, six months before Frances died, reveals her commitment and willingness to go wherever she could make a contribution; her openness and loving response to new cultures and her on-going openness to change; her quiet strength and great sensitivity; her warmth and love for people. It especially reveals her acceptance of life as it unfolded in old age.

Interview

Leaping Into the Unknown

Joining the Grail was an enormous step. You never knew where you were going to end up. I knew I wanted to serve God. From my childhood, what has always been with me is fidelity—fidelity to the church, to the Mass, to prayer, to seeking community—that love for being with other people and the love for the tradition of the church. I would never have expressed it in those words, but I had a great religious feeling.

I was a devout kind of girl and I loved going to church. When I was asked, "Wouldn't you like to become a Woman of Nazareth," I was overwhelmed with fear and joy. However, I knew it instantly. I immediately thought, "Yes, that is going to be my life, my vocation." We were so convinced that we could do something: women's conviction of being able to change things. That was the spirit of the youth movement.

The Grail caught me at a crucial moment. I never thought of marriage and I did not want to be a nun. I also did not really want to teach. When I told my parents that summer that I wanted to go to the Tiltenberg in the fall ... well, I hardly dared to tell them because I was the youngest. I really felt, "Oh, dear, can I do it?" I remember I had already gone to bed one night but I got up again and I thought, "Now I must tell them."

So I told my mother I wanted to go to the Tiltenberg, that I had been accepted. Well, it was a tremendous shock to her. My mother told me afterwards that she and my father couldn't sleep. They talked about it all night. The next morning I was sitting at breakfast ... I still know where I sat, with my back to the door and my father came in for breakfast and he said, "We've given you." I always get emotional when I think of this ... this tremendous step that he made and he loved me so much. I was nineteen at the time. He thought I was going to be a teacher and earn a little money, but

I never earned a cent for them. I only cost money. I never had a job that paid. That wasn't done in those days in the Grail. So, my parents accepted it and they came to the Tiltenberg to ask what I should bring and what I would need for the next few years. And I think they included some money, too.

Australia was the next big step and I know that was, of course, the second big blow for my parents. I later heard that my father hardly talked for the first few months after I left. I was not only leaving my family but my country and all my friends and all the ties that I had with everything. Nobody I knew had ever heard of Australia. This was 1936. Some Grail members had met Bishop Dwyer from Wagga, Australia, at a Eucharistic Congress in Dublin. When he saw all these young women wearing beautiful colors and speaking choruses and spreading joy, he thought, "Now this is something for Australia." And he was a very determined man. The story goes that as he sailed home around the Cape, he studied a Dutch dictionary and wrote funny little Dutch letters to the Grail people in Holland to say that he would like us to come ... to send some people to Australia to start the movement there.

That ship, the ship to Australia, I still feel it ... sailing into the unknown. From Holland, the boat stopped in England and my brother came to say goodbye. And then when we docked in southern France for a short time, Margaret van Gilse, the International President of the Grail, was there. She had come by car from Holland to the tip of France to say goodbye again. That night we all went out and drank a little too much wine. Margaret gave me a little movie camera that evening and I was told to take pictures to send back to Holland. And that is how I got the reputation as a filmmaker.

A Love Affair with Australia

Australia was a very welcoming country. When we arrived the bishop gave us a vision of what Australia was like. He helped us love the bush and the big, open stretches of land and the animals and the birds. He took us in his car to watch the birds and learn about the plant life. We laughed with him when we heard the kookaburra.

I loved the open spaces, the bush and the sea, the big waves; the largeness made me feel I had to be large myself. The Australians were big-minded. I had come from a little country where people were very critical and in discussions they often saw the dark side of things. The Australians felt friendly toward everyone. Eventually I felt very much an Australian; I had become one of them.

Although church dogma in Australia was conservative, I felt that in their behavior toward the people, priests were more democratic than in Europe. It was the whole spirit of the country, I suppose, that penetrated the church. Holland had political parties, which had religious affiliation. Australia had only the labor party and the conservative party, so no priest ever told you who to vote for. So we never felt held back because we were laywomen. Only twenty per cent of Australia was Catholic then and mixed marriages were much more common than in Holland.

Another thing we noticed right away was that married women in Australia did not have help in the home as they did in the Netherlands. They did everything themselves, and they also had smaller families. Actually, the women were quite organized. The Catholic Women's League, made up of women in their forties and fifties, raised money for the church and the Grail through garden parties and so forth. Although they often weren't Grail members, they took us under their wing as supporters of the "Ladies of the Grail," as we were called then.

We found that one of the greatest needs among young women was to help them deepen their faith. Often when they left even Catholic school, they would rather go to the beach than to church. In fact, at daily Mass there were just a few old ladies, whereas in the Netherlands, where the liturgical movement had started, there were many more young women during the week. I remember people in Australia saying the rosary out loud at Mass and only stopping for the consecration. In fact, one priest got annoyed with us because we didn't say the rosary at Mass.

We started off with what we knew from the Netherlands; we wanted to find a few girls who wanted to become part of the Nucleus and start groups in the big cities, but we also wanted to give marriage preparation courses. And, to start off, we wanted to give courses everywhere to make the Grail known. Bishop Dwyer had already done a lot of groundwork for us. So we accepted invitations from bishops to come and give courses to encourage girls to join the movement. We talked about women in the Bible, the task of women and motherhood, about the changing times and the communists against the Catholics, the simple life that should be led by women and the influence they could have in their places of work. I led folk dancing and singing and many celebrations with Grail and liturgical songs.

We did have uniforms but with no parades as we did in Holland. In the town hall we had a great choir with about a hundred girls and we did plays, for example, "The Royal Road of the Cross" in Sydney, as we had done in the Netherlands. When the war started, we did less of this but we always had a Christmas play in the big gardens in Melbourne and in Sydney. And we did experience some competition from the nuns, who thought we were taking young girls away from religious vocations.

We did get a few Nucleus members—Elizabeth Reid, Catherine Bagley and Beatrice (Kathleen) Sheehy. They came from the first courses in Brisbane. We were given a house for the formation of Nucleus members about fifty miles from Sydney, a house set in 30 acres of bushland in a place called Springwood. This place also welcomed visitors; it was a more open atmosphere than the Tiltenberg had been. We had courses for girls, and married couples came for Sundays and often for discussion.

Our training consisted of prayer, meditation, and Bible study. We had a visiting biblical scholar, a priest, who came and gave us talks. Eventually an Australian, Maria Malone, went to Holland for Grail training and then came back and worked with us. This was actually the bishop's idea since he thought that Australian women should be very involved right from the start. It was a great help to have Maria, somebody who had been through the training and knew what we were about. She stayed with the Grail all her life until she died of Parkinson's a few years ago at the age of seventy-nine.

Then in March of 1940, Judith Bowman, our president, was killed in a car accident on the way to the inauguration of a new bishop. I became president. I lived at the big center we had outside Sydney and I was organizing courses. I also travelled quite a bit to give courses in Brisbane and Newcastle.

Before Judith died, we had acquired a lovely old Tudor house in Melbourne we called Tay Creggan. She had plans to start a residential leadership-training center there for young women from Australia and New Zealand. They were to be trained to work in their own dioceses and were to be specially picked by their parishes and largely funded by the bishops. Helen van Cleef had come from Holland to help her with this.

And we began it and it worked very well for several years. Melbourne, an important center of the church, had many resources we could use: a big Catholic library, and scholars on church history, on social justice, on the Bible. Also, people from the Secretariat of Catholic Action came from the farmers' movement. We used to go out to exhibitions and plays. Some good marriages came of it. The program was called "The Quest."

The war changed a lot of what we were able to do: blackouts at night, women wanting to work to help the war effort and not having time for anything but an occasional meeting. After the war, we had just evening sessions and some weekend events.

An Experiment with Change

At the end of 1944, while the war was still on, it was decided that I would go to Grailville for a while just to make contact with what was going on with the Grail in other places. I went by a ship that was in blackout. When I arrived I spent the first few weeks at Super Flumina. My life was harder there than in Australia—getting up at five in the morning, saying lauds, walking a half hour in silence to Mass and singing the whole Mass.

We worked hard. No rest during the day. We had marvellous discussions and speakers. Catherine de Hueck, later the founder of Madonna House, spent time with us. I joined in everything—planting, harvesting—but I never milked a cow. This experience certainly affected me. I was there when the war ended and Lydwine and I sailed for England for a meeting with the English Grail. Two people, including Father van Ginneken, came from the Netherlands and we met with Yvonne Bosch van Drakestein, the head of the English Grail.

We gave reports on the development of the Grail and it was interesting to hear how differently it had developed between America, which had become very much a part of the lay world, and England, which had kept strictly to the Ladies of the Grail and the old customs. The Grail's development had been influenced in each country by national trends. And in Australia, we were somewhere in between. The bishop in England did not want the Grail to be taken to other countries, so there was a split; the English Grail separated from the international Grail. Now, of course, we are coming together again. The English Grail comes to European meetings and we go to their center for activities.

When I went back to Springwood, our formation center in Australia, at the end of 1945, we began to live more as they did at Grailville. We became more open and less separate from others, no more stress on the Ladies of the Grail. We did meditations the way they did at Grailville and began to till the earth. This was a smaller venture but we included our guests in the work. We read and discussed together.

We still used Springwood for Nucleus members to come for a year's formation and I would live with them the way I had when I was at Grailville. Then they went to the houses again and another group would come the next year. We also continued with the Quest but had it in the evenings rather than as a residential program. One evening would be social subjects, the other evening religious subjects, and so forth.

Adelaide Crookall started this version of the Quest in Melbourne. She became the leader when I left in 1950. Although the basic ideas remained the same, what we finally realized in Australia was that it was best to aim toward forming small, rather than large, groups of women who kept in touch with one another and were of support to each other. We no longer looked for great expansions and groups of people, but people who stood for something in their own lives. Not the coming and going of large numbers, but a steady continuity. In Sydney, for example, there is still a Grail choir. They have become ecumenical, they give performances in halls and churches, they sing at Grail weddings.

Saying "Yes" to Life

In 1950, Rachel asked me to go to South Africa because she felt it was time that Australians became the leaders in Australia. I was the last Dutch person to leave. Although it wasn't spoken then, it was the intention that we would start a real movement of indigenous people in Africa, too. Well, I know I left with great heartbreak because I loved Australia. I had become one of them. In a way I felt I belonged more to Australia than I did to the Netherlands.

But in those days, when someone said, "It's better that you go to South Africa," you went. I went with great sorrow in my heart.

Now we have the idea of personal responsibility, where everyone must decide with her own conscience. But all the same, life goes as it goes. I am very happy now that that move did happen because it gave me quite new openings in Africa. Otherwise, I might just have stayed in Australia—lived and died there—and now I've had so many new experiences.

This happened to Lydwine, too. It happened to many of us, I think. Sending out was not for a whole life. You stay in the Grail and you don't think you must stay in one place. The Grail is an international movement so we can exchange internationally. I think, especially as you get older, it's good to be back in your own place. I made the whole circle of the world and I came back to where I started because this is where I am most at home. This is where my roots are and I think I should also die here. Perhaps this is just my idea, but that's how I feel.

In 1978, when I turned sixty-five and retired, I went back to the Grail in Holland and found it wonderful to feel the spirit that had been kept. The older women were still as enthusiastic and as bright about the Grail as they were when they were young. The Grail had deepened. In a way it's no longer that fresh group, that fresh initiative, but it's more a steady group of people who want to influence the church and be a steady influence with non-Catholic women. I was there in the time of youth. However, I think that perhaps having more than one leader would have helped the expansion in Australia rather than one person who always kept the reins.

Bishop Whelan, an English bishop, had asked us to come to start the Grail in South Africa. There was already a small group of women there who called themselves Grail, who had been in touch with the English Grail through its publications. It wasn't a country I would have chosen, but at the end of 1950 I sailed to Cape Town and then went on to Johannesburg where there were about twenty young women.

Margaret van Gilse and I stayed at first in a convent. I had been wrenched from Australia and she had been wrenched from being international leader so we started out together in South Africa. We were there primarily to train women as leaders. Margaret had more of a feeling for building up a Nucleus than a movement. The bishop gave us a dilapidated place outside the city that we fixed up very simply and invited young women to come for weekends.

It was difficult at first trying to work with the existing Grail group but it eventually worked out. Of course, apartheid was growing and some of the women were not allowed to stay, so we started having the girls who were involved with us go out to the black townships. Some of these women, both black and white, went to Holland and the States for more training. It was difficult for the blacks since they experienced freedom at Grailville that they did not have in South Africa and some of them did not want to come back.

The white women were very similar to Australian women. There was also the openness and, of course, they lived in nice houses. But black women, in and of themselves, had a remarkable kind of strength. We felt they had a greater strength because they had lived under such difficult circumstances. At the time, we felt the need was for the white women to look beyond their little organizations and to feel more responsible for each and every one, black and white.

There was not much connection between them all. We tried to start that a bit, but of course, it was on such a small scale. Some of the white women were afraid of too much contact with the black women. There was always friction; it was very hard. Eventually, I worked in the Catholic Center, which was not Grail. Whites had set it up, but they had contacts with black Africans. It had a bookstore and a library. So we conducted weekends and joined existing organizations.

New Beginnings and New Challenges

I was in South Africa for seven years; I left in 1957. During the early 1950s Margaret van Gilse and Lydwine van Kersbergen took a trip through Africa to find places where the Grail might become rooted. In Uganda they made arrangements for us to take over a little hospital outside of Rubaga. And the bishop of Masaka wanted a secondary boarding school for girls. He was a very forward-looking man. The boys were far advanced but the girls were kept at home to help their mothers. Josephine Drabeck and Alice McCarthy were sent to start this new little secondary school in the Masaka diocese. However, they were delayed and since I had a teaching diploma, I went for six months to get things started.

There was a whole Catholic setup there—the cathedral, the school, the hospital, the priests' house. I started the school with an African woman, Elizabeth Muwonge, who later married. We had great fun, the two of us. When I saw the barracks and asked where the mattresses were for the girls, Elizabeth said the girls would make their own when they arrived, which they did from grass the men cut and sacks the girls brought with them. Elizabeth and I lived in the staff house without lights and water, a very rough building, but it was on a beautiful hill, among the high trees and the birds were always singing.

Well, it was there on this little "island" that the two of us started. Elizabeth knew just what to do with the girls. She was a tremendous teacher. Of course, I had no idea of African customs and she wanted the customs to be kept, so that the girls had to kneel when they came to ask something at our staff house. That was the custom of the Baganda tribe who were famous for their good manners. As a girl, one had to do this.

The girls were so eager to learn, especially English, which was very highly regarded. Among the first little group of twenty-eight on the hill came Elizabeth Namaganda[20] with her bare feet and her little bundle on her head. She eventually went to Grailville and joined the Grail. When I first saw her I said to Josephine and Alice, "Watch out for this girl." She was an all-around woman. She had a maturity about her and a kind of simple wisdom that you felt straight away. I felt she was someone who could become a leader of the real African Grail movement. She now is head of the Ugandan Grail and is very much respected in her country.

I went back to South Africa and then returned to Holland in 1957. In 1961, while I was doing some studies there, Dorothy Smith, the headmistress of the school in Uganda, asked me to come and teach. I went.

By now the school had moved to Kalisizo, about a hundred miles south of Kampala. I was there for nine years teaching English, singing, and Bible study. We made a Grail atmosphere with our singing and dancing and we put on plays. I was there in 1962 when Uganda got its independence.

Then came a really difficult period because Uganda got its own president and there was great dissension among the seven different tribes who each had their own king. Eventually the Baganda were suppressed and we always had to be careful about what we did, and we did not go out at night.[21] But we stayed on. At first we thought the new government would want the white people to go, but they still wanted those of us who had a definite work to remain.

---

20 See Chapter 14, 277-296.

21 The Ganda people, or Baganda, are a Bantu ethnic group native to Buganda, a subnational kingdom within Uganda. After Ugandan independence, the kingdom was abolished, but was restored in 1993. "Baganda," Wikipedia: The Free Encyclopedia, accessed November 15, 2016, https://en.wikipedia.org/wiki/Baganda.

At one point, however, a government inspector came to the school and said to the students in their own language, which we couldn't understand, "You learn well and you study hard because you must get rid of these foreign teachers." Afterwards the students began to become unruly and teaching was more difficult. I was fifty-nine by then. Helen van Cleef, who was back in Amsterdam, reminded me that if I was coming back to Holland it would be good that I came before I was too old to get a job. So, we gradually withdrew from the school and the Sacred Heart Sisters took it over and eventually they handed it over to African sisters. I know that since then they lost a lot of their customs because of European influence.

Africa particularly broadened my vision of adapting to cultures. You see that your own culture isn't the last word and that a culture can be totally different and still deeply affect people's lives. I think I became gentler through adapting to that, by addressing people in a gentle way, by walking peacefully rather than striding, by seeing the good, and through having a peaceful acceptance. I admired the women, who without thinking that they were doing anything special were living such holy lives, accepting what came their way. That's a very beautiful attitude, which is partly their faith and partly, I think, their natural character.

My greatest contribution abroad was in keeping the joy going, that Grail spirit of continuing to believe in what I stood for and always staying as the one who believed in people and believed in what I was doing—that kind of youthful spirit. The world did not convert. Changing the world really means trying to be in your own little spot, to be a person who can perhaps make a little change and become more modest as you get older, believing that what you do is very little and you accept that. The basic thing is to accept things as they come. Life itself is constantly changing. The changes don't worry me so much because I know they come out of the fullness of life. I always say I jump when the change comes; I go with it. Newman says, "To live is to change, and to live fully is to change often"—even if you yourself change a little.

Refocusing Life Again

As I get older I am letting go of certain things. It is better to let go. There is more withdrawing and letting younger people come forward, and you become the listening ear in the background. It's not passive; it's an active thinking of what is good for somebody else.

But I still feel needed here at the Beguinhoff, not just the physical help I offer but the moral help. And each of us has her own talents to contribute. It becomes more personal, helping others, and it is on a smaller scale. It is important to live in the now and to be turned to your surroundings and to see what comes to you, to understand that you must accept all the people who live around you and the people that need you and the people that you love and the ones that love you. That is the inner circle of your being that you have to pay great attention to.

And that means also to pay attention to the God who lives in you, that God and people, together, come to you through your eyes, through your ears and they are constantly calling on you and you are giving to them and they are enriching you and you are enriching them. I think that it is important to belong to this inner circle of people who are around you, at least it is for me; feeling that you belong to something bigger than yourself.

And first for me is the Grail, my little group here, and then the larger Grail, and then the church. Now I would say that God is the total reality of all that is and all that happened, the God that is living in me and helps me through His spirit to move out to others and to meet the day knowing I am loved and inhabited by Him.

It's a personal thing, and more universal, too. It is knowing that you are part of a whole and you are therefore intended to make everything more beautiful. Yes, I think of death everyday, but no one knows how we move from one life to another; everything we experience is limited. I have to let that go because I can't cope with it.

I don't know what we will be doing after death, but I know it is a full life. Zen has taught me quite a bit, that idea of turning inward to find God and to be one with all that is, of which you are a part—and the awareness of the now. And then I think of eternity. That is also the now, not just stretching out and out and out, but it is now. Eternity is the presence of the now which is being, with more intensity and joy.

And I hope that I will be surrendered enough to say "God, here I am, here I come," like that sudden decision that I made when I went to the Grail or when I went from one country to another, knowing that I had to do it. "Yes, now I do it;" I hope that the moment of death is also, "Here I am, here I go," that I may be conscious of it and that it may be a short moment, and then I will know where God is.

Hilda Canters, The Netherlands, 1994

4

Hilda Canters

*Lord let me grow to be
that for which you have destined me.*[22]

Hilda Canters was born into a prosperous middle-class family in the Netherlands on December 15, 1910. Her father was a notary. The family lived on a fairly large property and had servants; Hilda was educated at boarding schools.

Hilda's mother was the source of the family's stability and of Hilda's life-long trust in God. Hilda's father had been orphaned when he was eleven and was depressed a good deal. He could also be quite controlling.

During her last year in secondary school, when she was nineteen, Hilda met the Grail (called, in those days, the Women of Nazareth). At about that time, the group was undergoing a massive shift in

---

22 There are differences of opinion about the source of this saying. Hilda Canters, in her own interview below, attributes it to John Henry Cardinal Newman; others believe it originated with Jacques van Ginneken, the Grail's founder; still others attribute it to Caryll Houselander, the English Catholic mystic, poet and spiritual writer. Rachel Donders, *History of the International Grail 1921-197*, 97.

direction. The Women of Nazareth had worked previously with teen-aged girls, catechizing them and helping them to learn trades, and had taken part in Father van Ginneken's retreats for non-Catholics. But they were also greatly preoccupied with the idea of going to the foreign missions. Several Women of Nazareth, for example, were already working on the island of Java (now part of Indonesia).[22] Then the newly appointed Catholic bishop of Haarlem, J. Aengenant, asked the Women of Nazareth to turn their full attention to the Catholic girls of the diocese. That was the beginning of the Grail youth movement.[23]

After a two-week course in The Hague with Father van Ginneken, Hilda was sent to Amsterdam where she worked with other Women of Nazareth to establish the youth movement. The bishop was particularly concerned about a play for Dutch youth that the socialists had staged in the stadium in Amsterdam. In response, in Easter of 1931, three thousand Grail members performed "The Royal Road of the Cross" in the same stadium. The following year, Hilda and others staged an even larger performance there, this time at Pentecost.

Working with the factory girls in Amsterdam was Hilda's first encounter with "real people," people who were not very well educated. And the residence where she and the others lived was the first place she'd ever inhabited where you could hear the neighbors. Hilda, along with ten other women, made her dedication in the Nucleus of the Grail in 1932 at the Tiltenberg, the Women of Nazareth's new motherhouse, in Vogelenzang, between Haarlem and Leiden. Hilda returned there from time to time over the years for retreats and spiritual reflection.

After the Nazis invaded the Netherlands in May of 1940, life for the Women of Nazareth and the Grail youth movement changed

---

23 *Ibid.*

radically. If three of the women were seen together in the street, they might be arrested and sent to the camps. But they continued to have secret meetings and courses for girls, as well as retreats with Father van Ginneken. The Tiltenberg itself was destroyed during the war and then subsequently rebuilt.

After the war ended, the Grail in the Netherlands moved in new directions, and Hilda moved with it, working, for example, as a National Catholic Girl Guide leader. Eventually she spent four years in Edinburgh, Scotland, training as a nurse-midwife, and a fifth year studying tropical medicine in Antwerp.

Hilda had wanted to go to Africa since childhood, and in 1953 she and another Dutch Grail member, Joke van Heerven, travelled to what was then called the Belgian Congo to work in a hospital. Hilda served as director of nursing there. Then, in 1956, she moved to a neighboring country, Burundi, to begin a movement for women and girls. She and the rest of the Grail team led courses and workshops on health issues, agriculture, finances, and more. Hilda recalled that after seven years, she and her team members had organized ten thousand women and girls across the hills of Burundi.

But by the early 1960s, conflicts were already underway between the Hutu majority and the ruling Tutsi minority, a conflict that would lead to the massacres of large numbers of each group in 1972, and to the Rwandan genocide of the 1990s. In 1963, individuals related to one of the two groups, probably Hutus, killed Sis de Klerk, a young French Grail member who was working with Hilda and the rest of the team in the interior of Burundi. After Sis's death, all of the European members left Burundi; the Burundian men would no longer allow their wives and daughters to participate in the training.

From Burundi, Hilda went back to Europe, to study social organizing. In Paris she met a professor from the University of Wisconsin (USA) who invited her to come learn about cooperatives there. The work Hilda did in Wisconsin changed her fundamental view of the work of the Grail, making her understand that it was essential to have democracy, to work in teams, to engage people in discussion. When she returned to Congo, which was eventually renamed Zaire, she used this insight to begin, in collaboration with a local priest, a school of social work. In its first year, the school enrolled only six boys. For the first few years there was resistance from families (from fathers especially) against allowing girls to enroll. But after the first few girls did enroll and got good jobs after graduation, the resistance abated. By 1995 there were approximately two hundreds girls and boys in each of the four years of training at the institute.

As with a number of the other Grail founders profiled in this volume, Hilda's bravery and humility are quite striking. As if setting up secret meetings during the Nazi occupation of the Netherlands weren't enough, Hilda also chose to return to central Africa after her co-worker had been murdered. Someone less committed might well have gone back to his or her vastly safer home country and remained there. And have no illusions that Congo was safer than Burundi after the murder of Sis de Klerk in 1963. The period from 1960 to 1965 was a period of crisis and political chaos. During her nine years in Congo/Zaire, Hilda left the country a number of times out of fear for her life but then returned.

Hilda also made a number of significant contributions that she doesn't mention in the interview she gave in 1995. For example, during her early years at the maternity hospital in Congo, there was a serious problem: mothers, so as to be sure to have enough breast milk for their infants, would refuse to have intercourse with their husbands for as much as a year after the baby was born. This practice was contributing to the reduction in the number of Catholic families in Congo, since few men wanted a life marked by eighteen or so months of abstinence followed by a few months of normal married life and then another pregnancy.

So one year, Hilda spent her vacation driving around in a Volkswagen trying to identify an alternative food source for the infants. Finally, at a mission station, she learned that soybeans and sugar cane can be converted into a simple substitute for breast milk, something the infant could tolerate from its fourth month till it was able to eat solid food. Hilda and her teammates began immediately to educate the women about how to grow the sugar cane and soybeans and make the new food. She described herself at the end of her journey as "dead tired physically" but "happy beyond the telling."[24]

Because of the requirements of her pension, Hilda returned to the Netherlands from Zaire on December 31, 1975. She began living in an apartment in The Hague. A number of other Grail women lived in apartments along the same street and they formed a kind of community. At first, Hilda was worn out, and slept a lot. But eventually, she began to do ecumenical and interreligious work, even helping to get courses about world religions into local parishes.

Also, in 1981, she went back to Africa for six weeks, to Tanzania, to teach a course to the Grail members there. She especially enjoyed getting to know Imelda Gaurwa, one of the leaders of the Tanzanian Grail, with whom she found she had a great deal in common.

Hilda moved to a home for the aged in 1993, when she was 83, and died there thirteen years later, on March 23, 2006. During her last years she continued to be buoyed by the great trust in the Lord that she had learned from her mother, and that continued throughout her more than eight decades of Grail commitment. To paraphrase the saying that was popular in the early Grail, Hilda had grown to be that for which the Lord destined her.

---

[24] Elizabeth Reid, *I Belong Where I'm Needed* (Westminster, MD: The Newman Press, 1961), 189-197.

Interview

Childhood and Family

I had a happy childhood. My mother had a profound influence on my life. My mother gave me the idea that God is someone who loves you and that love is around you and in you—someone you can always talk with.

There were so many rules in the church in those days. When you went to communion, so many rules. All kinds of different difficulties. But when I came to my mother to talk about it all, she said, "The Lord is not troubled about those things." She taught me that God was not a man or a woman or a ghost that you cannot see but the love that is around you and in you and that you can speak with.

But we feared my father. Later on I understood that he was very depressed, for when he was eleven he had lost his father and mother in three days and then he was sent away to boarding schools. And he won a lot of prizes for he was always the best at everything, but there was nobody to rejoice in it. And he did not understand much about children because he was never a child.

My father was a notary. Laws and all that. And his office was at home. He heard everything. When one of us was playing the piano—we were very musical—and there was one note that was not right he came out of the office and said, "That's not right." But when there were difficulties with my father, my mother said, "Martin, go and look for a nice bottle of wine in the cellar..."

We had a very big garden so we always went far away to the part of the garden that our father could not see. The first part was the flowers and all that, and that my father could see, but then it went up a little bit higher and then we had a little garden house and then it went down. He didn't want us to run for he always thought that there would be an accident. He was always afraid of accidents.

Running was not allowed. So we walked to the garden house and then raced down the hill and did what we wanted.

At home, in the village, we had servants. Then I went to boarding school and everything was done for you, and you were closed off from the world. So when I went to Amsterdam with the Grail, it was a revelation. So much going on.

Early Years with the Women of Nazareth

I first heard about the Grail in my final year in secondary school. Secondary school is different here than in the United States. It's more like the first two years of university.

I was nineteen, and I was looking for something. I wanted to do medical studies. I didn't know what the Lord wanted but I did know that the Lord wanted me to be of Him, not a mother. It's not that I did not like children; I would have liked them very much, but I wanted to live for the Lord. And I didn't want to be a nun.

There was a lot of bad talk at that time about Father van Ginneken, that professor at Nijmegen who put the four women (the Women of Nazareth) into a house with the men, the Crusaders of St. John. You know where that's going to lead, people would say. They made them all out to be devils.

But I knew that people had made some of the saints out to be devils, too, so I thought I would see for myself. But I didn't know where the women were. Then I saw a newspaper article that they were in a parish near The Hague. I was on holiday, staying with my sister in Haarlem. So I took the train to Slivening and I thought I would look around, and then I don't know how I did it but I found them. So I asked if they were the Ladies of the Nazareth. They said yes. And I came in and they talked with me. They put me in a room, seated me on a piece of green and black furniture—simple but very nice. I thought, "Oh, that is nice."

Then Elizabeth Allard came—later on she was professor at the university in Indonesia and then at Nijmegen. She told me I had to return to meet Mother Margaret—Margaret van Gilse. So I came back in the afternoon and Mother Margaret asked me some questions and then she said, "Yes, you have to come straight up."

It was the middle of November and the training would start on the first of December. I had only two weeks to get everything arranged. My mother knew nothing of the group and my father had died in the same year. It was difficult. My mother had had a heart attack and was in bed—she was in bed for thirteen years before she died. But she said all right, the Lord wants you. She was very religious. She could not do anything to help me get ready, so in the end I had to make all the arrangements. I had to bring all kinds of things—so many pieces of underwear and so forth. Then I came on the first of December.

But we were not in the training center—we were in a house. When I was in my bed at night I could see all the stars—there wasn't a roof. And there were little cloth partitions between us when we slept. Next to me was Dr. Louise Feldhauser, a student of Father van Ginneken's, and she was a very bright girl, the best student he ever had, he said later on. I really saw the stars from my bed, which I did like very much. I was a bit spoiled materially and I thought this new life was marvelous; in the morning I had to take the brush and dust the floor. And I had to start where we were sleeping, for there were such holes in the floor and they went all the way down.

But after two weeks, Father van Ginneken came and gave a big course, a two-week course, about the whole world. We learned so many things, things that we take for granted now but that we did not know about then. It was 1930, so I had just seen a plane for the first time in my life. The technology was moving so quickly. Father van Ginneken said, "You think now it is difficult to travel, but you will see that in the end, the world will be one big village and it will be very difficult for all kinds of people—of different educations—of different habits to live together." So, he explained, he had founded the Women of Nazareth to practice living together with people from different nations. And that in our group we would have to learn how to live, all kinds of cultures together. And that that would be very difficult. But you are with the Lord, he told us, and with the Lord you will manage it. And then you can be the seed in different countries to help people to overcome those difficulties.

I thought it was marvelous, that view of the world. Because according to that view we have to live our whole life for Christ. Father van Ginneken told us that it would not be easy but you have to do it. They made us a little group and we went all over the world, and Father van Ginneken told us that the Lord would be with us and we just had to do it. So that's all. I thought it was marvelous. So I stayed.

I stayed, in part, because it was a woman's movement. At that time, especially in the Catholic Church, men always held the high spots. There was always a man who directed the women. But Father van Ginneken said, "That's finished. You are quite able to govern yourselves and I don't want to put a man in charge. I am a man, I can't help it, but you have to do it yourself."

I thought it was marvelous.

Before I came, there had been a long training for new women but at that time big changes were underway so Mother Margaret took me to Amsterdam. Up till then young Dutch women had always lived in families but now many of them were working in factories and the industrialization was demoralizing many of them. So then the socialists started a youth movement for them. And they held a play in the stadium in Amsterdam. So the bishop said to us, "Before all the girls in my diocese are going to join a socialist youth movement, you have to start a Christian youth movement for them." So we started to work in the factories with the girls.

At first there were all kinds of arguments against this, since we were founded to transform the whole world and some of us had already left for the missions. Yvonne Bosch van Drakestein and Clara Trel were already in Indonesia teaching the women there. Going out to the whole world as lay apostles was what we thought we were supposed to do. And then all at once everything changed. In those days we were fairly obedient to the church and at a certain moment our leaders said, "We have to do what we've been asked and when we do it, we will do it well." So they started the youth movement and that was the Grail.

For this new effort we needed some kind of a story, and Father van Ginneken said that a story from the Middle Ages, the story of the Grail, was very well known here in Europe and can be told in different ways. So we used that.

I didn't really get much training. We had to start the youth movement, so I went to the house in Amsterdam and there we started the youth movement. The only training I had was the two-week course with Father van Ginneken, and of course, the cleaning that we did. Working also trains you.

So there we were, with the real people of Amsterdam, you know, the people who are not very educated and all that. We had the ground floor of a house and on top of us there were all kinds of families living. I had never lived in a house where you could hear the neighbors. It was all new for me. And we had just one tap in the kitchen, so that was where we had to wash ourselves. And you had to sleep in the corner that they put in the wall and it was smelly. And then the people on top of you are dancing and everything like that so it was kind of different—the real world. The world which I never had imagined was like that.

I thought it was a revelation. And I thought: I have given myself to the Lord in this way. And there has never been a point in my life since then where it has been any different. The Lord goes with you. Everything in the world changes. When something does not change, it's dead. But the Lord is always the same. So the only thing on which you can count, that is the Lord. And when you can't stay with the Lord, you cannot support all the changes that you have to overcome. But with the Lord it works always.

In those days, I was not always in Amsterdam. At a certain moment I was in The Hague during Pentecost and I had to go with more than a thousand girls to Amsterdam for one of the big Grail stadium plays. What was always the thing for me was that we were a real women's movement—and we wanted to help women grow. You know, that saying from Cardinal Newman, "Lord, let me grow to be that for which you have destined me." Father van Ginneken said that we all have talents, so develop them. That's what we said to the girls, those poor working girls in the factories, so that they felt like they were persons.

I made my Grail Nucleus commitment in 1932, at the Tiltenberg. There were eleven of us, I think. Giving ourselves totally to the Lord—complete obedience. From time to time there were courses by Father van Ginneken at the Tiltenberg. We all had to come out of the work of the youth movement—for some days, or some weeks sometimes. Afterwards you felt filled up again.

Some of the greatest challenges were during the war. There were thirty-two Grail houses and we had a card system in those houses for the girls' addresses and we couldn't let the Germans see them. If the Germans saw three of us together we'd be sent to a concentration camp, so we were like thieves in the night, trying to get all those cards out of the houses.

And when the houses were closed by the Germans we still tried to have groups meeting in The Hague—little groups, after the larger ones were dispersed. For example, we had a course for girls who had earned their diplomas, an introduction to the bigger world. So we continued with them, secretly.

I was not very fearful, I think. You pass over. Twice we had to organize a retreat with Father van Ginneken in convents. One was in the boarding school where I had been a student; I organized it. But once someone talked to a policeman about us, so we had to shift to other places. To the Institute for the Blind in Gravaan, near the Tiltenberg, for example. But we survived.

New Directions

After the war, I went back to school. I had considered becoming a medical doctor—I wanted to study medicine when I was in secondary school. Mission priests came to visit my father when I was growing up, and we had a lot of mission magazines around the house, so I wanted to go to Africa. But medical school took seven years, and then you have to specialize. So I started nurse's training instead.

The Women of Nazareth already had contacts in Africa, mostly in English-speaking countries, where you had to have British certification to be a nurse. So I went to Edinburgh to study midwifery. But in the end, in 1953, I went to the Belgian Congo. Joke van Heerven and I went by boat to Angola, and then we travelled by train for nearly a week up to the Belgian Congo.[25] The conditions on the train were terrible. Ten times as many people as there were seats. And no toilets.

But then we came to the station near Kasongo. The bishop was waiting for us there, and another official, the director of the hospital. So they took us to the hospital.

The hospital was a real mess. The first morning I went to one ward—it was a big, big hut, with beds on both sides. Twenty

---

25 The Belgian Congo was a Belgian colony in Central Africa between 1908 and 1960 in what is now the Democratic Republic of the Congo (DRC). From the mid-1970s through 1997, it was called Zaire. "Belgian Congo," Wikipedia: The Free Encyclopedia, accessed July 17, 2016, https://en.wikipedia.org/wiki/Belgian_Congo.

men there, with their pants down, and they were using the same syringe on them all.

So I stayed on, and the medical director was happy that I stayed. And in my second year we started to build a new hospital. I was the director of nursing. And there were also twenty, or twenty-two dispensaries in the bush, so the medical doctor was often gone there to visit these dispensaries.

After two years we had the new hospital. People from the developed countries gave us all kinds of things, like incubators, air conditioners, and a marvelous electric kitchen with everything in it. But we did not have any oxygen or enough electricity for the kitchen, only electricity from a little generator. It was all political. Belgium had profited a great deal from the Congo—by putting very little in and taking a great deal out. Putting in what the people could not use. But eventually, we did mange to have a working hospital, and to run it from our own resources.

After three years in Congo I went to Burundi, to start a movement for women and girls there. Grail women who worked at the hospital in Congo gave half of their salaries to start the effort. That was in 1956. I didn't want to leave the hospital, but in those years there was still a very strong sense of obedience, and the leaders wanted me to go, so I went. As a consolation I was allowed to choose my companion, so Hanny Doesburg went with me. She worked with the girls and I worked with the women.

We started in the city of Bujumbura.[26] The Belgians would not allow white people to live in the same neighborhoods as black people, but we said that if we could live only with white people,

---

26 Bujumbura is the capital, the largest city, and the main port of Burundi, on the northeastern shore of Lake Tanganyika."Bujumbura," Wikipedia: The Free Encyclopedia, accessed July 17, 2016, https://en.wikipedia.org/wiki/Bujumbura.

we would leave. So the archbishop gave permission and we got a little house, but later, we moved to the interior where it was better. There we were able to build little houses, like the ones the people lived in.

We started programs for the women. They were intelligent, but they had not been to school. If the men came into where we were meeting, the women were not allowed to show their faces. The men would sit outside listening. We taught the women about cleanliness, about sterilizing things, to protect the children. We told them that just as a lion can kill your child, microorganisms can also kill them. We showed them with a magnifying glass. We taught them to use mercurochrome, or ashes from the fire, to sterilize the bottles. We had discussions about health issues, and about agriculture, how you could grow food for good health. And finances. And we taught sewing, so the children could have little chemises.

The priests were pretty accepting of us, but the nuns, not so much. They thought we were taking their girls. There was also trouble between the Tutsi and the Hutus. We had a Tutsi girl living with us in the house, Jean Marie, but usually the Tutsi men did not want the Hutus to learn anything. They threatened that if the Hutus went to school, they would burn the schools.

After seven years in Burundi, we had ten thousand women and girls organized over the hills. The greatest challenge was that we had such different norms. I remember when the Burundian bishop came to see our new house, and we didn't have curtains yet. In Burundi, in those days, a wife was not allowed to see how her husband eats and the children could not see their father; they all sat with their faces against the wall. And the bishop was eating with us, so he said, "I can't eat here for nobody may see when you eat." So we had to take the blankets off our beds and put them across the windows before he could eat. And many other things were different, too. So every evening we sat around a fire with the girls who were living in our house, and the first night they told us their practices, and the next night we told them ours.

The people there were much better Catholics than I was. Every Sunday they walked twenty kilometers (twelve miles) to Mass and then they stayed for Benediction in the afternoon to make the trip worthwhile, and then they walked home, ate and went to sleep. The whole day was dedicated to the church. And they sang all the way to church and back.

So our work grew, and we had reached ten thousand women and girls in Burundi. And then Sis de Klerk, the French Grail member who had joined Hanny and me, was killed. Her death came out of a struggle between the King and his son, who believed he was entitled to inherit the throne. So there was a revolt, and the Hutus murdered a white person, to get the other white people upset, and then they could blame the revolt on them. Some people believed that the Tutsis were also connected to the Chinese communists in Burundi somehow. Our team was working in the interior, and the other team members had gone to the capital to pick up a new team member who was arriving at the airport. That was when they killed Sis. It was in 1963. I had been in Burundi seven years.

After Sis's death we could not do anything more. The men forbade the women to come to us. And the Chinese communists and the Tutsis were working together. So we had to leave. But up until then, we had been pretty successful. We had organized the women there in a democratic way of governance, and they learned how to work together. And it is still going on, Aba Grail, the women of the Grail, though it has to be underground.

I was not happy at all about having to leave. But I would say we made a real contribution, teaching people to adapt to one another. That was a real technique. And I gained a great deal—my mind was broadened.

After Burundi, I went back to Europe. For a time I was at the Institute for Social Studies in Paris. A Grail member, Ifis Seybel, had worked in Brazil and studied co-ops in Wisconsin (USA), so I was interested in co-ops too. I didn't like Paris very much—it was all governing from on high, but I was lucky because I met a professor from Wisconsin. He told me the course was for five years, but he would allow me to just sit in on some of the courses. They gave me a little scholarship.

So I flew to Wisconsin and the professor got me a place to sleep, and I was there for one course, and I got a certificate for it. It was incredible. My father had been authoritarian, and the Grail was authoritarian, but I learned that there were different sorts of leadership. I got a lot of help from that.

Father Maes and I had decided that what was important was to start a school for social workers in Zaire, for workers who would really understand the people.[27] So I went back to the Netherlands to follow a course in social work and he went to study in one of the African institutes for social studies. And then we came back and started the Social Formation Center in Bukava. The first year we had six young men. They came nearly naked, only wearing little trousers, and we had to get clothes for them. On the road in they had to avoid robbers who would steal their stuff.

Then, for the second year, Father Maes wanted to include girls, but that was very difficult, because the officials did not like the idea of girls being emancipated, but we worked through the nuns'

---

27 Father Maes was a member of the Missionaries of Africa, commonly known as the White Fathers, a Roman Catholic society of apostolic life dedicated to evangelization and education. He had been in contact with the Grail in Africa for some time before he and Hilda started the Social Formation Center in Bukava. We have been unable to determine Father Maes's Christian name. Didine Petit, email to Marian Ronan, November 28, 2016.

secondary school and had one girl the second year. And the next year we had four, and then it took off. Once the graduates started to work, and they got paid well, then the parents realized that girls could earn a lot as social workers. When I left, there were something like two hundred students in the first year. We had four years training in all, like at university.

We had a lot of teachers, some from Belgium and from Canada. We put more stress on practice than theory. We trained the students to do community development in the cities and in the villages. All our emphasis was on that.

There was a lot of trouble in the country then, in Zaire. I left and came back several times. There were revolutions, and persecutions of the church. Sometimes I went to Uganda and then I went back to Zaire. I was there, at the Institute, for nine years altogether, and I had been there for three years before I left for Burundi. The second time, in Zaire, we didn't so much establish the Grail—it was too dangerous for that—but we built the the Social Formation Center. And then, after nine years, I went back to the Netherlands.

Return to the Netherlands

When I first came back, I mostly slept. I was worn out. I was sixty-five years old. The hardest thing was adjusting to the luxury—the children saying, "I don't like that kind of chocolate; I want a different piece," after working for so many years for children not to die from hunger. And there was much less Grail community, in a sense, than there had been before. At first it was all hard, but then I got used to it.

After my long, long sleep, I realized that I wanted to do ecumenical work. In Africa we had suffered for the Lord with all different kinds of missionaries and some were killed in the most awful way. So we came to understand that we were all one family in Christ. And gradually we helped people to see that ecumenical wasn't just

Christian, that you had to work with all kinds of people, Jewish, and from other religions too. Eventually we got a course into the schools here about all the world religions. And we organized to have a fair about the world religions. The ecumenical work and the multicultural work were the most important things I did after I came back here.

Also, in 1981, I went to Tanzania for six weeks, to help with the training there. Oh, that was a pleasure, to get to know Imelda Gaurwa[28]—she's now on the International Leadership Team. Her story is so much like mine—she too did not want to be a nun but didn't know how to find something else. And then she met Ton Brouwer, and eventually she started training catechists in an old house that the bishop had given. She started out sleeping on the floor, as I had done in my early days with the Grail. When I was in Tanzania that year, I taught the whole course that Father van Ginneken had given when I first met the Grail. And I talked with the young African bishop there and we agreed that things needed to be done in a whole new way, that the church had to become integrated with the culture.

This is what I had already come to understand when I went to the United States, to study co-ops at the University of Wisconsin. The church—and the Grail—had been very top-down, everything very Western. For a long time I thought this was just what the world needed. But then in Wisconsin, in those leadership courses that I took, I learned about democracy, and working in a team, and that you had to have discussions before you start doing things. That was completely different, and it changed me a lot. A lot of the older Grail women here in the Netherlands had trouble with all these changes, but I was happy with them. My commitment was to the Lord.

---

28 See Chapter 15, 297-324.

Changing, Getting Older.

In the early days, we were mostly concerned with the conversion of the world. This was what Father van Ginneken emphasized. By the time we went to Burundi, in 1959, we just wanted to help all women. We certainly weren't concerned with getting women to join the Nucleus of the Grail. By then, I believed that the work of the Grail was to help women develop their own talents. You shouldn't push people into something—that's not right. You have only to look for what the Lord is doing in them, seeing what's inside them.

You know, in the beginning, we learned we had to sacrifice ourselves, to look for suffering, but now I think, life itself gives us the cross, there's no need to look for it. Life gives a lot of things that we're afraid of. We were more attacking—we were young and we thought we would convert the whole world. And it was all going to be done by women. But it hasn't happened, I mean, it hasn't happened really in that way—the world is in some ways in bad shape. Your life makes you be more realistic—you are always thinking and speaking with the Lord—asking how is that possible? And then gradually you see that things are changing.

So I had to move from the original vision to what was actually happening. It was not so easy. I was in all kinds of difficulties in Africa, but I think that I now understand what Mimi Maréchal[29] and Carol White[30] and the others are saying, that they are looking for how the spirit is working in that person and then we build on that. I think it is a good thing.

---

29 See Chapter 11, 215-234.

30 Carol White is a member of the U.S. Grail who lived and worked at the Tiltenberg, the Grail center in the Netherlands, from 1982 to 1999. She now lives in Dublin, Ireland. Carol White, email to Marian Ronan, November 15, 2016.

So now I am eighty-five years old. When I was eighty, I stopped working. It was very difficult. People said, "Hilda, you can do it. Why are you not going on?" But I said, "Eighty, that is enough."

I wanted two or three years to myself. I always understood that when you are old you have to leave all the organizations. The age of eighty is a point of real turning. You are growing older, and you have to give it over to the Lord, and then He will say when it is enough. I am looking forward to meeting Him or Her.

I think death will be a very difficult moment. For I often saw births when the mother and child were in great difficulty. I think death is a second birth that will not be easy. I don't imagine that it will be easy—for a long time you have to ask for everything. But you have to pass by.

But on the other hand, I am happy here. At this point in my life, what gives my life its greatest meaning is the Lord. My task is to accept what He sends me and to open my eyes where I can do something. I think the good thing about old age is that you have a lot of experience and you don't always have to speak about it, but in the way you are with other people, you can more easily understand. You don't have to say, "I had this experience or I had that experience" but you know the way in which you have to ask a question—to let the others speak. In a way, this is doing the same thing I've always done. The day starts and you say, "Now what will it be Lord—here I am." And then I wait. And always a lot of things come.

What I hope for now is that the Lord forgives me for everything. Whether I live a long time or not, I don't care. The Lord accepts me so I have to accept myself. The revelation for me was when I thought you have to love everybody but you had to mortify yourself, with that strong cross. Now I think you have to love people, but you have to love also the creature that you are and that the Lord made also and that He loves. So you shouldn't spoil yourself, but the thing you have to do for another you also have to do for yourself. I learned this gradually, from my life experience.

What has sustained me through everything is the Lord—the contact with the Lord, that is always the most important. You are together. You do it together. You are not alone. They ask me, "Weren't you very lonely in Africa?" And I say, "I never was alone there, there was always somebody with me." And at times that sense was very strong—yes, when life is more difficult, then you feel it very strongly that there is somebody with you.

Of course, there are also moments when you feel alone and the Lord feels far away, as when you are playing with children, and they rush away and you have to find them. But there's always a certain strength within you. That is the Lord.

PART - II

Sent Forth Into the World
(1940-1953)

Mary Louise Tully, center, location and date unknown

5

Mary Louise Tully

I go where I am needed.

When Mary Louise Tully arrived in Hong Kong in 1947, she became the first American Catholic lay missionary in China. This was just one of her several groundbreaking experiences. She was also the first American to hear about the Grail and the first American to make a lifetime commitment in the Nucleus of the Grail.

Mary Louise had read about the European Grail in two Catholic journals published in the United States. She was in her third year at the College of St. Theresa in Winona, Minnesota, and was thinking seriously about what she would do with the rest of her life. That very summer, a professor of German was organizing a bike tour for students through Germany.

Mary Louise wanted to join the tour, but her father objected and, instead, took his whole family to Europe. He knew Frank Sheed, an author and a co-editor of Sheed and Ward publishers in London; Sheed put Mary Louise in touch with the English Grail. It can be truly said that she never looked back. When she finished college, she spent time with the Grail in London and later with the Grail at the Tiltenberg in Holland where she spoke no Dutch and found that English-speakers were also rare. But she was attracted immediately by the commitment and dedication she found among these women and knew she had found her calling.

Mary Louise was born on April 13, 1916. Her motivation to dedicate herself to something beyond the ordinary began when she was a child growing up in LaGrange, Illinois, an affluent suburb of Chicago. Her father, a Notre Dame graduate, manufactured radios, and her mother, also a college graduate, ran a smooth household for her husband and children. In many respects, Mary Louise's childhood was rather ordinary.

Mary Louise had loving parents who provided both emotional and financial security for their children. She attended a public grade school, a Catholic high school and a Catholic college and does not remember any traumatic experiences with the exception of the death of a brother when she was very young. However, when she talks about what inspired her as a child, she refers back to her susceptibility to bronchitis and pneumonia and her family looking for a better climate than Chicago where they could spend winters. So one year they drove across the United States to Los Angeles, California, where Mary Louise went to junior high school in nearby Pasadena; in late spring the family drove back to Chicago.

Mary Louise, being at a very idealistic stage in her life, remembers making a connection between the vast, open spaces of the country and wishing that everyone could know Christ. She was asking herself how she could announce her wish to the world. One way would be to go on radio, but she knew that people could just turn her off. She could write articles for the newspaper but she knew newspapers were used for garbage and she didn't want what she had to say go in the garbage. How about movies? She could star in one, but alas, she did not think she was photogenic enough. And, besides, she had met a girl in high school from Kentucky who had never been to a movie so she realized that movies don't reach everyone. When Mary Louise got to college, she decided she would just do whatever Jesus wanted. That was her answer up to the moment she read about the Grail in those two magazines.

The following years were anything but ordinary. They included several trips to Europe to train with the Grail; a thirty-six-day train and bus ride across southern Europe from Amsterdam via Berlin to Lisbon, fleeing the Nazi invasion of Holland; travelling around the United States laying the groundwork for the development of the Grail and the new lay apostolate; working with the Catholic Interracial Council in Philadelphia; earning a pilot's license, then becoming a ground instructor, navigator and civil air regulator.

Publicity followed the unfolding of the United States Grail. The *LaGrange Citizen* reported on a reunion Mary Louise had with friends when she returned to her hometown for a visit. Her friends, the newspaper accounts says, were eager to see just how the Ladies of the Grail looked and were quite surprised to find a "voguishly dressed young lady." The March 2, 1941 issue of the Catholic newspaper, *The Register,* reported from San Antonio Texas that Mary Louise Tully was "the first American novice of the Ladies of the Grail,"and that "in six days they (she and Joan Overboss) had fired the enthusiasm of both clergy and laity in the city ... at sixteen different meetings"... to lay "the groundwork for the development in America of a movement that has become one of the most potent forces of Catholic Action in Europe—the Grail."

In the mid-1940s, while Mary Louise was living at Grailville, the bishop of Hong Kong, Henry Valtorta, came for a visit and invited the Grail to send women to help build up the lay apostolate in China. So in December of 1946, Mary Louise set sail for Hong Kong where she became the only lay Catholic missionary among nine hundred Protestant missionaries. Hong Kong for her was intended to be the springboard for going to the mainland of China.

Mary Louise began supporting herself in Hong Kong by working at the Catholic Center started by Father Nicholas Maestrini after the Second World War. Maestrini, who developed a deep friendship with the Grail and had great admiration for its work, was a member of the Pontifical Society for the Foreign Missions and spent twenty years as a missionary in China. The Catholic Center was a crowded space containing the headquarters of the Catholic Truth Society, a free library where discussions on the social problems of China were discussed in light of papal encyclicals, and a chapel.

It was also a meeting place for people coming in and out of China, since Hong Kong was the gateway to China. The Catholic Truth Society printed and distributed pamphlets, books and periodicals. Mary Louise worked in the Center's publication office as editor, proof-reader, reporter and writer.

But Mary Louise's work extended well beyond the Center. Maestrini realized early on that lay people were essential for the work of the church since they were examples of Christian living right in the midst of society. He quotes a Chinese Catholic girl saying to him, "You tell us the theory, but these lay people show us the practice." [31] He further noted that Mary Louise "won the confidence and love of all the staff... within a few months (of her arrival) I sensed a real development of Christian life among our staff."

Mary Louise described her "real work" as that of living Christian principles, a God-centered life in everything she did, wherever she happened to be, whether at work, at recreation, at meals or in dealing with printers. Her unobtrusive manner and example of purpose and contentment inspired many to seek her out to talk about Christianity or sometimes just to ask how to live an integrated daily life.

---

31 Nicholas Maestrini, "Four Years with Lay Missionaries," *America* 86 (October 6, 1951): 12.

In order to be accepted and have an influence, she immersed herself in Chinese culture. She learned the language, learned the customs and even stayed for a while in a hostel for girls and later lived with Chinese families. In describing her overall work in the Grail that is also applicable to her role in Hong Kong, she noted that she was always more a catalyst than a founder. She made things happen or, as she says, "Things have happened because I happened to be there." One result of this role was her sending several young Chinese women to Grailville for training.

Ill health forced Mary Louise to leave Hong Kong and return to the states in 1950. She went back to LaGrange for a few years of rest before returning to the Netherlands where she lived at the Tiltenberg for ten years, assisting with Grail publications as writer and editor. In addition, she travelled to several countries with Rachel Donders who was International President during that time.

In 1962, Mary Louise moved to San Francisco, where she lived with three other Grail members until moving to Palo Alto in 1965 to share with her sisters the care of her ailing mother. At the same time, she earned a Masters in Social Welfare from the University of California, Berkeley, followed by several years of social work. One of the remarkable things about all the work that Mary Louise did, in the Netherlands, in China, and in the United States, is that because of her family's prosperity, she wouldn't really have needed to work at all. Indeed, during her years of membership in the Grail, she donated more than half a million dollars to the movement, a figure that does not include the financial support she gave to very many individuals.[32]

Mary Louise retired in 1981 and continued working with the Grail in various places in California. In 1983, she initiated an international

---

32 For example, in the 1980s, Mary Louise paid the tuition for the first semester of seminary for Grail member Marian Ronan, one of the co-authors of this volume.

newsletter for older Grail members called "AgeWise" and served as its editor for about ten years. Eventually she moved into a retirement home, Stevenson House, an independent-living housing complex for seniors in Palo Alto. There she continued her "apostolate" by assisting others who were in need of help. At Stevenson House, as in other settings, Mary Louise kept a low profile. A Catholic sister who lived there at the time was amazed to learn that Mary Louise was part of the Grail, since Mary Louise herself never mentioned it. She was remembered for thanking everyone for everything.

In her final days, Mary Louise lived at Lytton Gardens, an assisted living community affiliated with the Episcopal Church, also located in Palo Alto. She died on August 18, 2001. Carol Nosko, a U.S. Grail member who had supported Mary Louise at the end of her life, expressed gratitude that Mary Louise had not lived to know about the terrorist attacks on the World Trade Center and the Pentagon that occurred a few weeks after her death.

As Mary Louise reflected back on her life and her own work with the Grail, she pointed out that for her the Grail is not defined by projects or programs, but by something much deeper: a life orientation. What was most important to her was that "when someone begins to say 'we' instead of 'they,' she has grown into the Grail, a recognition of common values."

Interview

Breaking New Ground

I was probably the first American to hear about the Grail. I was in college. It was 1937 and I read about it in two magazines, *Ave Maria* which was published at Notre Dame University, and *Commonweal*, the liberal Catholic journal. Of course, at that time of my life I was asking myself what am I going to do next, what am I going to do with my life? When I finally had the opportunity to meet the Grail in England, I was impressed by a picture I saw hanging in the hallway as I walked in the front door. It was a painting of a young woman with her hands stretched out in front of her carrying a chalice that, of course, meant offering. It was very beautiful. And when I think of it now—yes, that inspired me very much.

Of course meeting the Grail was a turning point in my life. I had visited the Catholic Worker house in New York on the way to Europe that first summer and I certainly admired their values but I was not drawn to it. While I was in Europe that summer, we went to visit a cousin who lived in the Netherlands. Someone in the English Grail had given us the name and address for the Dutch Grail, but since there was a retreat going on at the Tiltenberg at the time, we couldn't go there.

However, since she spoke English, Liesbeth Allard, a Dutch Grail member, drove us around. We visited Grail centers in The Hague and Amsterdam. What I remember vividly are the bright colors the houses were painted with—orange and blue and red and green. Everything was completely colorful, and I always respond more to color than even to music.

I went back to college that fall and talked to a nun I trusted very much about the Grail. Although she had never heard of the Grail, she was in favor of my following my star, so to speak. And somewhere along the line, probably when I was attending a senior ball at Notre Dame, I talked with Father O'Hara, who later became the Archbishop of Philadelphia. He had been my father's roommate at Notre Dame. He advised me to think about it for a year.

It was good advice, but meanwhile, I did write to the Baroness, Yvonne Bosch van Drakenstein, who was the head of the English Grail and told her I would like to come to the Grail center in England when I graduated. She invited me to come as a paying guest for three months. It was a sensible response—come and get acquainted and see what is going on.

So in September of 1938, I went to the Grail in England and lived for a while at Sloane Street and at another center in the country outside of London that was their place for training. I worked while I was there, washing dishes, scrubbing floors and keeping silent. In December I went to Holland for a while. But since I had told my parents that I would return to Chicago, Margaret van Gilse, the International President, insisted that I keep my promise to them, so I did go back.[33]

By now I was convinced that this was what I wanted to do, join the Grail. After visiting both the Grail in England and in Holland, I was captivated by the completeness of the dedication to Christ. Of course there were lots of other people with this kind of dedication, but it was the lay part that was important, because that was something I'd been thinking about all my life. One thing I had been very clear about was that I did not want to become a nun, because I felt that this separated you from the people and the world. I realized that most of the nuns I knew were very connected to people, but that is what I thought at the time. I don't really know where I got the notion of dedication to the lay apostolate. It was certainly a novel idea at that time, that lay people would be so engaged in the apostolate. This seemed like a different theology, although I didn't use that word at the time.

An Extraordinary Venture

I returned to the Grail in England and stayed there for a time in training, doing housework and remaining in complete silence. In the fall of 1939, a group of us from England went to the Tiltenberg for a retreat. It was about then that the Nazis starting conquering

---

33 Mary Louise's reference to Margaret van Gilse as the "International President" here is an anachronism, since in those days, she was called "Mother Margaret." The title "International President" was introduced in the early 1950s. See Chapter 2, 21-40.

Europe. England was getting involved in the war, so the English women went back and I stayed at the Tiltenberg.

I did much the same things at the Tiltenberg that I had done in England. Of course the best place to learn utter cleanliness is the Netherlands. I do remember the prayer life. The liturgical movement had already come from the Benedictines in Germany. I had experienced some of this at the College of St. Theresa in Minnesota where we had Sunday vespers, something a lot of places would not have had at that time. And I had gone to daily Mass when I was in college.

Every evening at the Tiltenberg we went to the chapel and I would sit with the new people in the front, and someone would give me a book of prayers I couldn't read because everything was in Dutch. One woman from Sweden, Ingrid Brust, knew a little English and she helped me, but most of the Dutch people did not know any English. I was the first American to stay at the Tiltenberg. When I talked with Margaret van Gilse, she insisted we talk in English since, as she said, at least one of us would understand what was being said. I learned the Dutch ways of celebrating feasts. I especially remember celebrating the feast of St. Nicholas, which was a great family feast.

At that time, the fact that the Grail was a woman's movement did not particularly matter to me. I was a woman, but I did what I had to do; it wasn't a philosophical thing with me. I know that Jacques van Ginneken had instilled in a group of university students the conviction that women have a special contribution to make in the betterment, the transformation, the conversion of the world. For me the goal was life in Christ for men and for women, young and old, individuals and whole cultures. I did meet Father van Ginneken, but he couldn't speak English and since I couldn't speak Dutch, we never conversed.

One memory that is very distinct for me from my early time in Holland was the sound of planes flying over; if the motors were heavy, the planes were German. The lighter sounding motors were English. England was already being bombed, but the Nazis had not yet occupied Holland.

I was still getting letters from home and the American Consulate in Holland had notified Americans that it was getting more and more dangerous and advised them to leave. The Nazis had reached Poland and then Denmark. Holland was next. The Consulate didn't have my name and address. Lydwine and Joan left for the United States just one month before the Nazis came into Holland. Otherwise the Grail never would have started in the United States because I am not the kind to be the founder of something like that.

Well, when the Nazis did come into the Netherlands, it was decided that I had better leave. It would not be too convenient having an American at the Tiltenberg, so I moved to Amsterdam. Although I had an American passport, the Nazis had taken over all means of transportation. So every day I went to the American Consulate, took my lunch and waited. This went on for weeks. I remember walking along the streets in Amsterdam on my way to the Consulate and there would be men leaning against the walls of the building and saying under their breath in English to any one coming along, "Row you across the Channel for $50." There were no boats going across and they knew there were people who were trying to escape to England but didn't have any papers. And some people were taking them up on the offer.

By now the Nazis were in Belgium and northern France so I had to go to Germany—first, to Berlin. At that time, since the United States was not in the war, I wasn't in danger as an American going into Berlin. The Nazis still weren't in southern France, so the route for me was to leave through Berlin, go through Switzerland, then across southern France to Spain, across Spain to Portugal, and then hopefully sail home.

I boarded a train in Amsterdam. In the same compartment was a young married Jewish couple who had American passports and another Jewish couple with their children, ages fourteen and twenty. They had been working in Amsterdam as diamond cutters and also had American passports. And there was an American salesman who had come from Scandinavia. We stuck together in a compartment on the European train.

When we reached Berlin, we changed train stations. It was the day Paris was taken and all the flags were flying. When we got to Switzerland, the Jewish people looked up their friends and relatives in Basel and had a meal with them. The big question of the Jewish people we met was, "Have you seen my uncle? Did you see my cousin? Did you see my brother?" At this time, the Nazis had not started to take the Jews from Holland. They were still busy with Paris. But these people in Switzerland knew that the Jews were targets of the Nazis and that's why they wanted to know about their relatives. Jews in Poland were already being rounded up.

From Switzerland, we took a bus across southern France, down the east side of Spain and then across to Portugal. A truck carrying gas followed up since there were no gas stations along the way. When we got to Lisbon, I started studying Portuguese because I thought at some time the Grail would want to go to Brazil and I might just as well spend my time learning the language. This was my idea, of course. We would naturally go from the United States up and down North and South America; what else would you expect? If we had stayed in Spain, I would have studied Spanish. It was a difficult time for people because we had a long wait in Portugal and some had nothing to do but listen to rumors that were spreading about bombings and people being taken. Were the Nazis going to take Portugal and could we get out of the country in time?

Eventually a ship was found that could go across the ocean, they hoped. Actually, the captain had never been across the ocean before but we were all willing to get on anything that was going westward. Here was a crew, here was a ship, and here was a captain who apparently could steer a ship. There was nothing else to do but get on that ship—so we got on. We docked in Brooklyn and some people weren't allowed in because they didn't have passports.

When I got into New York City, I had just enough money for a bus ticket to Chicago and I called my parents and told them to meet me at the bus station when I came in. My parents had been very anxious since the American Consulate in Amsterdam had told them I had left but there was no further word concerning my whereabouts. When they finally met me, they weren't sure whether or not to be angry since they were so glad to see me. I say this in retrospect since that was not my perspective at the time. Anyhow, they welcomed me home and probably put me to bed. There was great notoriety in LaGrange when I returned since my parents were pretty well known. This included a write-up in the local newspaper.

Training for Leadership

Meanwhile, Lydwine and Joan were at Doddridge Farm, the Grail's first center in the U.S., outside Chicago, and had given some talks around the country and they were recruiting women. Among them were Janet Kalven, Barbara Wald, and Catherine Leahy (who had learned about the Grail through Monsignor James Coffey in Brooklyn). When Joan and Lydwine first arrived in the area, they stayed with my parents who showed them around and were very helpful to them. My father got Lydwine a car so she could travel around the United States.

My parents were always very supportive of the Grail even though I think they would have liked me to have chosen something closer to home. I had left home and hearth and country for total dedication, and my parents just kept supporting Lydwine and Joan and whoever turned up from the Grail. And then they sent me money and tickets when I needed to get back from wherever I'd gone with the Grail. I left them but they never left me.

As I look back on the support my parents gave, I am really impressed. It was their commitment to their daughter, undoubtedly, but as I have gained more life experience, I see this happening with other people, people who have been brought up in committed families. We take it for granted that people will do what they say they will do, like love their neighbor and help their siblings. One thing that was difficult for my parents to accept was the interest of the Grail in the rural land movement through Monsignor Luigi Ligutti and the National Catholic Rural Life Conference, the idea of integrated living on the land. My father really had spent his life getting off the farm in Illinois and into the city of Chicago and supporting his family so that they didn't have to get up at dawn and milk the cows and bring in the corn. So for him, my choice was a definite psychological setback. Why his daughter would be interested in the land—really, it seemed like going backwards.

While I was at Doddridge Farm, I helped with all kinds of office work and did a lot of travelling around the country talking about the Grail and the lay apostolate. I went to colleges, to high schools, to parishes, to seminaries, talking about participation in the lay apostolate and encouraging young women to come to Grailville. I spent time in New Orleans and in Philadelphia where I got to know Mary Kane's mother, Anna McGarry, who was active in interracial work. In New Orleans I used to ride the trolley in the black section. One day the conductor, who had been watching me with some suspicion, asked me if I was in the right section. I answered, "Yes." You see, I felt I was not lying.

As we travelled, we met a lot of people from other groups such as the Young Christian Workers, the Catholic Worker, and the Baroness de Hueck from Friendship House in New York. We were all on the speaking circuit. Each group had their own emphasis.

We, of course, were talking about women. So, there were about a half dozen of us speaking from one angle or another.

Of course one thing we talked about a great deal were new liturgical practices such as lay responses at the Mass. All of this was very original in the early 1940s. I talked to young women at several Catholic colleges at that time and I knew that sometimes the nuns were concerned that the Grail was taking vocations away from them. There was always the danger of this kind of competition. I recall that at one college, the reverend mother walked me to the door after I gave my talk and said that it was so nice that I had come but there was no room for me to stay overnight. At that time, even though the lay apostolate was being promoted, it still had to fit into the hierarchy of the church. It was really the participation of the laity in the apostolate of the hierarchy. Of course Lydwine may have looked up to the hierarchy but she really did what she wanted to do. What I was so enthusiastic about in the 1940s was the encyclical on the Mystical Body of Christ. It encompassed the whole and we were all a part of that whole.

Monsignor Hellriegel, the rector of the Catholic seminary that was close by, often said Mass for us. Eventually he became more involved with the Young Christian Workers than he was with the Grail, but in the beginning he was a great friend and a wonderful person who helped us. I remember going over to pick him up to bring him to Doddridge to say Mass and he would always ride in the back of the car. He wasn't going to sit next to a woman in the front. Things have certainly changed since then.

When I made my dedication in the Nucleus of the Grail in 1943, I was the only one to do so at that time. It wasn't called Nucleus at the time. We were the Ladies of the Grail, which didn't seem to go well with American psychology. Joan Overboss wanted to call us Grail workers. But then the question arose, would this include everyone who was working with the Grail. There were differences between Lydwine and Joan on this issue. I had been in England and in Holland so I made my dedication according to the formula that had been used before. The issue remained alive. Joan had a much more horizontal view of the world and of relationships and of the Grail. Lydwine's view was much more vertical. She was much more hierarchical, but things gradually worked out.

I didn't spend much time at Grailville since I was travelling a great deal. However, I do think that Grailville did have a great influence on young women. It awakened them to possibilities they hadn't even thought of before. Of course, it helped them define what they were going to do with their lives. They got the experience of taking responsibility that many of them didn't have and by taking responsibility they learned that they could do things they had not done before.

To Convert the World

Sometime shortly after the war, Father Nicholas Maestrini, an Italian missionary who had been in Hong Kong for many years, heard about the Grail. He was a real promoter and somehow he searched out the Grail and corresponded with Margaret van Gilse, the International President at the time. Bishop Valtorta, who was of the same group of missionaries, visited the United States and encouraged the Grail to send women to Hong Kong, a place he described as especially fertile ground for the apostolate. Eventually it was decided that I would go in response to these inquiries. Of course, we would convert China. At that time I had to look at a map to find out where Hong Kong was. I also had to find money to pay for my own passage on a boat, so I worked in a restaurant in San Francisco while I learned some Chinese.

Father Maestrini, whom I did not know, came to the boat in Hong Kong to meet me. He told me later that when he looked up to search out this new person who was coming to work at the Catholic Center, he saw a nun who was hanging over the railing calling, "C'est moi, c'est moi." He said his heart sank. He thought he was meeting a nun instead of a laywoman.

For the first few years in Hong Kong, I was employed at the Catholic Center; Father Maestrini directed the Center and became a good friend and supporter. Life in the missions, as we called them then, was a great adventure, but it was not always easy. We had to adapt to a new culture, an unknown language, a different climate, and unaccustomed food.

I did all kinds of work connected with the publication business—editing, proofreading, reporting and writing. The Center was much more than a publication house. It was the home of several English language publications, a library, a bookshop, a travel service bureau, the headquarters of the Catholic Central Bureau of China. It was here that I could really feel the pulse of the life of the whole church in China. Being in this position also allowed me to get to know the country, its people and its customs. Eventually, I could carry on a conversation in Cantonese. And there was a goodness, openness and generosity in the people that made them open and responsive to the Gospels.

A revolutionary idea was to forgive your enemies. It was almost disloyal to your ancestors to forgive your enemy. One time, I read the Gospel of the Last Judgment to a young girl, where Jesus says that whatever you do for the least of his brethren you do for him. And later, a whole new outlook was revealed to this same girl when I read to her the Gospel of the Good Samaritan. She later went to medical school so that she could be of practical help to the sick poor.

Another very vivid memory is of the young girl I helped prepare and sponsor for baptism, who said to me with great fervor, "I am free at last." I did sponsor others for baptism, including Rosaline Kew who later became a member of the Nucleus of the Grail.

We did not have Grail courses in Hong Kong. Our program at the Center was based largely on the church year. In this way, we tried to live in the spirit of the different liturgical seasons. During Advent, for instance, we would have talks and discussions with quiet time for reflection, ending in the evening with a family Advent wreath-lighting ceremony. We would make the wreath from bamboo rather than evergreens. On the Feast of the Three Kings, we had a picnic and three staff members acted the parts of the Kings who led the others to seek the star. During Lent, we had a study group during the noon hour on the Lenten Mass texts that culminated in a Holy Thursday Paschal Meal led by Bishop Valtorta.

And at Mass, the whole congregation joined in a well-understood dialogue Mass. Each Saturday afternoon, many of us gathered to prepare for the Sunday Mass. And four mornings each week, before the beginning of work, we had discussions of Scripture and Christian life. When I had been in Hong Kong for about two years, an elderly English woman I met on a ferry asked me, since I was a foreigner, if I had amassed a fortune. She assumed all foreigners did. I didn't have time to explain to her why I was there, but I felt that this was a place where the church could flourish like a seed planted in the ground. Eventually the flower would bloom.

However, the flower was not to bloom in China itself. I had seen Hong Kong as a base and I wanted to get Chinese young women for the lay apostolate to go and convert China. I learned early on that most people, including the young women we met and worked with who had left China for Hong Kong, did not want to return to China. They did not want to go back to the villages they had left; their plans for the future were elsewhere. Also, becoming a Catholic was a very dangerous thing to do because it endangered the possibility of marriage and people expected young women to get married. Then the Communists took over China. One woman whom I sent to Grailville, Yeung

Kwok Woon, later went to Canton as a member of the Legion of Mary and was arrested and imprisoned for many years. When her sister was finally able to get her released, she was very sick.

Hong Kong at that time was not a cohesive society with its own identity; it consisted of a collection of traders going in various directions and considering other places their home country. It certainly was not homogeneous and people were not so identified with it. One could almost call it a railroad station. It was actually a harbor with people coming and going. Very few people considered themselves Hong Kongites. Being there certainly expanded my view of the world and I admired a lot of things. All of this was a learning experience for me and just as I was getting acquainted, I got sick and had to come home because I needed care. I tried to hide this in the beginning, but I was exhausted and anemic. So I was in Hong Kong for three years.

Fresh Bends in the Road

I went back to the Tiltenberg in 1952. By then there were women from many other countries coming there for training and they needed English-speaking people. We developed a language that we called Tiltenbergese, a mix of Dutch, English and whatever other languages were being spoken there at the time.

Many of these women wanted to dedicate their lives in the Grail, so we had a lot of prayer based on the liturgy and meetings with them. The idea was to help people develop an integrated lifestyle with prayer as the basis. What I do remember well is that everyone, including the ones from rather wealthy families, did dishes together and shared the physical work. I am sure that this was a first for some of them. I became fluent in Dutch and helped with translations of publications and so forth. And I had the privilege of getting to know Rachel Donders and travelled with her to Ghana, Brazil and Rome.

In 1962, I returned to the United States and moved to San Francisco where I began my social work studies, which eventually led to working for the Santa Clara County Social Welfare Department. The 1960s were also taken up with looking after my mother so that she would not have to go into a nursing home. At that time, the Grail was also building up in San Francisco and in San Jose where I lived for a while after my mother died.

There was a lot going on. In San Jose there were courses for Papal Volunteers who were going overseas, ecumenical work was beginning as a result of Vatican II, and we were working with the United Farm Workers and Spanish-speaking people. And of course there was a lot of tension in the Grail in the 1960s—people disagreeing with one another but feeling safe in doing so. I felt sad when people left the Grail but knew that they did need to leave the organization of the Grail to be honest and find themselves.

Since my retirement from social work in 1981, I have travelled to Belize, to India and to Japan, where I taught English. Then in 1983, I started "AgeWise," as a kind of third-age international newsletter for older Grail members to keep in touch with one another. It was meant to help all of us share practical and spiritual matters, hopes and fears, suggestions and opinions we have as we grow older. Sometime later Victoria Jadez joined me. She did the formatting and I did the editing. It was both a labor of love and very interesting. And eventually Betty Rose and Margaret Shamansky in Wisconsin took it over.

Retirement for me has been just another chapter in my life. I have slowed down since I turned 75. I continue to work with the chaplaincy service at Stanford University Hospital and visit Ethel Souza, a friend of the Grail who had an aneurysm several years ago and is in a nursing home. And I am living in a retirement center here in Palo Alto that is HUD-funded where I visit people who need help in one way or another. And I go to Mass every day and often give rides to others.

One thing that hasn't changed for me is that Jesus is still the center of my life, which means to love my neighbor in all the different circumstances I am in. Just doing for people around me—whatever I am able to do for people at the present time. That might mean people living across the hall from me, or it might mean somebody on the other side of the world who would be glad to receive a letter. That's what it is—whatever needs I see.

Bep Camanada, location and date unknown

6

Elizabeth (Bep) Camanada

> *The big questions have to do with our attitudes toward life and death and solidarity with the poor.*

Bep Camanada's experiences as a young woman in the Netherlands during the Nazi occupation were instrumental in shaping the strong convictions that have guided many of her decisions and endeavors throughout her adult life. As she witnessed the deportation of Jews, the closing of her university, and worked with the student underground, she observed oppression and persecution first hand. Later she would choose to remain in solidarity with the poor in Brazil whose hardships resulted from living under a repressive government and the greed of multi-nationals.

When Bep was a student in a Catholic high school, she was already aware of her desire to do something unique with her life. Although at the time she did not know what this meant, she did know that she wanted to be a teacher, the profession which led her to Brazil and later to working in Holland with immigrants after she retired.

Elizabeth (Bep) Camanada

Bep was born in The Hague in 1921. She described her childhood as happy and she was especially close to her oldest brother, who became a Carthusian monk at about the same time she left to join the Grail. They were confidantes as they grew up together in a family of eight children, she the second oldest. The two of them shared their thoughts and concerns with each other, including their plans for the future. She recalls that ideas about missionary work came to her in early childhood through her brothers and the preachers and missionaries who came to the local church.

All the Camanada children went to Catholic schools and church, and religion was very much a part of family life. The whole family attended Sunday Mass and then had breakfast together. She especially liked accompanying her mother to an evening service in the church called Benediction.

Although her father was a religious man in his own way, her mother, who spent all of her time with the children, had the greatest influence on Bep. Her mother had wanted to learn German but was sent to a school to learn how to sew. Since she had not been able to attain the education she had wanted, she was the one who gave her children their aspirations for "something different." Her religiosity influenced two of her sons to become priests and Bep to join the Grail.

Bep's father was a very hard-working businessman who had left high school at the age of fifteen to take over the family business. He was what Bep described as "very interesting" and "self-educated." He read a great deal and introduced Bep to poets she still remembers and reads. He also encouraged the education of his children and insisted that Bep and some of her siblings go to a boarding school as teenagers so that they would receive a better education than that which was offered in The Hague. In this more disciplined atmosphere, Bep studied hard and was drawn to languages that she would later focus on in university and in her teaching career.

Bep went from the very protected atmosphere of her Catholic high school to the University of Leiden. At Leiden she was one of the few Catholics in a predominately Protestant surrounding where students were classified by the religious tradition they came from. She became active with other Catholic students, none of whom felt they were ready for any kind of dialogue with the Protestant students. She had her first "ecumenical experience" when both groups decided to put on a Pentecost play together in which, to her astonishment, a Protestant girl played the part of Mary, the mother of Jesus.

However, before Bep's first year as a student was over, in 1940, the Nazis had occupied the Netherlands, and after student revolts against the treatment of Jewish professors, the university was closed. She and several students continued to study together by organizing reading clubs. Exams were given for a while in Amsterdam, but when that became impossible students managed to go to classes in Utrecht until all university activities ended. She finished her studies several years later in a much different atmosphere; as a result of five years of war and living under the Nazi regime, Catholic and Protestant students became more unified around ecumenical issues.

When Bep met the Grail during World War II she was attracted by the courage of its members who continued to organize and meet even though the Nazis forbade them to do so. Although the international vision of the Grail had been obscured by the war and the Grail youth movement demolished, she found in the Grail at that time what she referred to as "those kind of first steps of the spiritual life" that she felt she needed. In 1948 she made a lifetime commitment in the Grail as a Nucleus member and a short time later, at the age of thirty-three, she responded to the invitation to go to Brazil to teach.

Bep spent the next thirty years of her life in Brazil and many of these were given to establishing the Grail movement. Beginning in Belo Horizonte and moving to São Paulo and eventually to the interior of Brazil required a remarkable ingenuity and faithfulness to her religious roots and her growing commitment to enculturation.

In the late 1950s and early 1960s, Bep served as the first president of the Brazilian Grail. In this role she travelled widely, listening to and consulting with others and following her own intuition about programs, training and how people could best use their energies and talents both in the cities and in the interior. Her linguistic and leadership abilities helped her to encourage a blend of the contributions of Dutch and American volunteers with those of Brazilian women.

In 1963, at the invitation of the new International President of the Grail, Magdalene Oberhoffer, Bep returned to serve as president of the Grail in Holland. When she returned to Brazil in 1968, a military dictatorship had taken charge, and their oppressive tactics, even imprisoning some members, had weakened the Grail there. Bep moved into the interior and spent the next years working with the poor in rural areas, using Paulo Freire's method of teaching literacy, helping to educate women on health issues and organizing cooperatives among farmers who worked at very low wages for big land owners.

A few years later Bep was exposed first hand to the exploitation she had observed earlier in Belo Horizonte and in other parts of Brazil. She assisted farmers who were forming a union; their land had been taken from them by multinational companies to raise eucalyptus as fuel for steel plants, a process that paid them very little and eventually destroyed the land. These experiences heightened Bep's own consciousness and deepened her sense of solidarity with the poor of Brazil as she realized more fully the sources of both their political and economic repression.

Bep describes her return to Holland in 1984 as "just changing places." The initial adjustment was difficult; she found little interest in Holland concerning an analysis of the socio-political situation in Brazil. However, she soon asked herself a question she had posed in each new situation over her lifetime: "what can I do?" and in a short time she was putting her international experience to use in service to immigrants and in a Dutch organization concerned with women in the Third World. She recalled participating in peace demonstrations and at one time speaking to twelve hundred women who were on a silent march in support of the mothers of the disappeared in Argentina.

Even in her eighties, Bep continued her commitment to "solidarity with others," becoming involved in providing care and support for more elderly Grail women who lived in a retirement home not far from her, women she referred to as "my dear sisters." She also took part in the difficult decision to close the Tiltenberg in 2003 and was pleased that a new Grail house for meetings and programs opened in Utrecht.

In 2011, Bep herself moved into Duinhage, an old-age home in The Hague, where she has her own rather small room. Until recently, she participated in the activities of the house and had good contact with some of her co-residents. Although she could no longer attend most Grail meetings, she remained interested in developments in the Grail nationally and internationally, and received visitors from abroad. In 2012, she celebrated her ninetieth birthday with members of the Grail, relatives and friends.

By 2015, however, Bep had become very tired and was avoiding visitors. Dutch Grail members report that she suffers from heart problems for which she has been hospitalized on several occasions. Even as our dear Grail sister slips from us, her extraordinary life inspires us to continue our work "in solidarity with others."

Interview

The War, the Grail, Ecumenism

I met the Grail during the Second World War when all the centers in Holland were being closed down by the Nazis. My father had insisted that I return home from university because the situation was becoming increasingly dangerous—students were being persecuted for resistance to the Nazis, especially their opposition to the repression of Jewish professors. I intended to continue my studies at home but without student support my motivation was low and the pressure of the bombings was always with us.

I was twenty-three years old and I felt lost. While in university I had been involved in ecumenical activities, Bible discussions and near the end in helping to organize reading clubs when classes were closed down. I had had great enthusiasm for these activities. I now wanted to find people to share social concerns with again and soon discovered a group of girls in the parish who were working with children from an underdeveloped area nearby.

I joined them. It was very simple and new to us; we went with the children to Mass on Sunday and got milk for them since they couldn't get it for themselves. Many of these children were from families having serious problems, so we also organized retreats for the parents by finding a priest who would give talks in the evenings. I discovered later that this project, called the "drinking milk club," was organized by the Grail, but was not a Grail project since the youth movement had ended.

While I was doing this, friends of mine from university who were very involved in the resistance against the Nazi occupation asked me to do some work for them. So I helped with communications by taking messages, books and letters from one person to the other. This meant distributing forbidden news releases, so I had to be extremely careful. I got a huge typewriter for them that I hid in my cupboard. I could not even tell my parents; my father was very afraid but my mother knew and she just kept quiet.

I was extremely busy, too busy, and I began to discuss this with my brother who was then deciding that he wanted to become a monk. I knew I had to make some decisions about my life and that is when

I decided to find out more about the Grail. I went to see Margaret van Gilse. Since this was during the war, there was nothing visible about the Grail but I knew at that particular moment that this was what I should do. The situation was that the younger women were all hidden together in a convent and, I must say, that attracted me. I was drawn by the enthusiasm of these young people who were in hiding. There was something spiritual behind this and it was something I could really engage myself in. It was not part of the Nazi philosophy; it was even forbidden.

So I spent the terrible last months of the war in an Ursuline convent near Haarlem. Rachel Donders and another woman were in charge of us and we studied Christian asceticism with Rachel. We were about fifteen in number. The sisters really cooperated and this was very dangerous for them. They told outsiders that the reason we wore ordinary clothing rather than nuns' habits was because of the war.

We helped the sisters with chores and biked to local farmers to ask for milk and vegetables. It was difficult at that time to get an international vision of the Grail since we were closed in a convent. We heard stories, but it all sounded quite strange to me then. What inspired me was the spiritual side. It was a time of discovering spirituality and trying to live with God. For me, personally, it was a time of stopping, of really thinking and starting to meditate and pray and quiet down. During that extremely cold and extremely dangerous winter I found silence. This was what I needed.

When the war ended, we were sent home; the Tiltenberg was completely broken down and there was no Grail youth movement. I realized later that the leaders of the Grail didn't know what to do with us. My home in The Hague had been destroyed. I didn't even have any books; everything was lost, but fortunately, no one was hurt.

Before too long I saw a poster in The Hague saying, "Students of Leiden, we will start again." I went and I expected to get right back into the rhythm of studying, but that did not happen. There had been an enormous breakthrough in student life during the war. We had learned to communicate, to cross the boundaries of religion, and now everything was going to be ecumenical. We took this very seriously. This was a whole new philosophy of academic life and we were determined to make it work.

I was on the board of a women's organization because I was convinced that there should be a Catholic presence. So, that's what I did, and I got almost no studying done for a long time. I went to the Tiltenberg occasionally for spiritual orientation and rest. It took a long time; I started university in 1939 and I finished in 1948 in Latin and Greek, language and literature.

In Brazil

Because of the immense dangers of the Second World War, there was a deep concern at this time to find places where the Grail could be planted and could blossom again. At the request of a Dutch bishop, two Grail members had gone to Brazil and then I was asked to join them in Belo Horizonte to work among university students. I didn't know anything about Latin America, since we had had no international contact during the war, but I thought that perhaps I could teach in a high school there as well as in Holland. The task was not all that clear; we were to somehow start the Women of Nazareth there.[34] I felt happy that my adult

---

34 (The Society of the) "Women of Nazareth" was the name of the group founded in the Netherlands in 1921 that began the Grail Youth Movement. By the mid-1930s, however, new branches in English-speaking countries were called "The Ladies of the Grail," and by the 1950s, "The Grail" had become the name of the entire international movement. Rachel Donders, *History of the International Grail 1921-1979*, 4, 18, 22, and throughout.

life was starting. I was about twenty-seven and I was ready. So I said, "Yes, why not?" But of course, I did not know that I still had to start all over learning everything. So away I went.

I got a scholarship from the bishop to study Portuguese and Brazilian literature because I needed to have my Dutch diploma revalidated in Brazil. I was the only foreign student in this new Catholic University and I started the whole project not knowing how much work it would take or whether it would be useful. I had to write seven papers a month in Portuguese though I could hardly read or write it. I was completely exhausted and feeling quite hopeless, but my teacher was very helpful.

However, I had known from the beginning that it was extremely difficult for students to do serious studying because they had no books. The library consisted of a bookcase full of books that students borrowed and often did not return. I don't know exactly how this happened but I became the librarian of the Catholic University and I stayed there for a few years. While I was both student and librarian I was living with the Grail.

The bishop asked us to start a *pensionato*, that is, a place for girls from the interior of Brazil to live and have their meals. Everyone thought we were sisters since nuns ran other *pensionatos*. It was difficult to change this way of thinking, but we kept quiet and started our *pensionato*.

In three or four months it was full of girls who often could not pay their rent. It was hard on us. There were no programs because the girls just came to eat and sleep and we could not communicate because of the language. It took me at least half a year before I had the courage to talk on the telephone. It took much longer to adjust to Brazil. For me the main problem in the beginning was that the women with whom I was living and working had such a different sense of the position of women. The greatest need for women at that time was to help them form their own opinions while depending a little less on their families. Gradually, though, I felt quite at home at the university.

But none of us felt comfortable with the situation at the *pensionato*. We eventually decided our staffing the *pensionato* had served its purpose. We knew the Brazilian way of life. Some Dutch people took it over from us and it went on.

Meanwhile, in 1954, Rachel Donders came to visit us and that was a turning point for us; she told us to start a Grail movement and to move out of existing institutions. Many of the girls already belonged to Catholic Action and we knew that the bishop would not want another lay movement in Belo Horizonte. For this reason Rachel urged us to begin in São Paulo so as to make a fresh start in a bigger city. We kept our contacts in Belo Horizonte and thought that eventually we would build a house there as a Grail training center.

Before going to São Paulo, I had a leave in Holland where I learned more about the Grail as a movement and then I went to Grailville in the United States for more international exposure. I visited city centers and came in contact with the idea of lay women in church and society. It was marvellous. We raised some money while we were there and bought a big house in São Paulo and some Grail women from the States came there to get experience working with foreign students. So we had people coming.

I didn't like São Paulo. It was a huge city but we did have a good start and in a few years we were working together, both São Paulo and Belo Horizonte. Our work in Brazil was influenced very much by the Netherlands and the United States and both Dutch and American women worked on teams.

In Belo Horizonte we developed the work around a very concrete issue in the squatter area. We had midwives and social workers.

In São Paulo we went on lecture tours and even went into the interior to attract young women. They came and we set up a training program for the lay apostolate. We had sessions on the rhythm of the Church year, on spirituality, the liturgy. We had art exhibits and courses for people who wanted to marry. We got everyone participating and during the holidays we met women from Belo Horizonte.

It was a twelve-hour train ride for us. The bishops of both places gave us their blessing. At that time we were very bishop-minded. We couldn't get around that.

Eventually a bishop invited us to train a group of people who could teach catechetics to rural people who lived in the mountains. We were to use "Popular Catechetics," written by a seminarian. So we took this on by recruiting people and getting them to São Paulo for a four-month course. Base communities didn't exist then, so our people worked with this catechism, organizing discussions around themes.

In the meantime, we bought a very lovely place about an hour and a half from São Paulo for rest and reflection, Chacara Manhangawa. We had the national secretariat there and when I was president, from 1956 to 1963, this is where I lived. I travelled all the time between Belo Horizonte and São Paulo. Little by little things worked out. We expanded Chacara as more Americans came and I helped train them in the language and culture before they began their work. Some women made their commitment to the Grail there in a beautiful ceremony. By the end of the 1950s the women from Holland had left and we were receiving Papal Volunteers. This was a difficult time since they didn't know the Grail and what we were about.

In 1963 the International President, Magdalene Oberhoffer, asked me to be the president of the Grail in Holland. Since the Grail movement in Brazil had been launched, I said, "Yes."

The Grail in Holland was faced with many internal problems during the 1960s. In fact, it was in crisis. For four years, I did my best. I helped to form a national team and this got people talking to one another. I wanted very much to get back to Brazil and I did not offer myself for a second term. In 1968 I went back.

Back to Brazil

Things had changed a great deal. When I left Brazil in 1963, liberation theology and the Vatican Council were just beginning, resulting in a new consciousness among the people. However, in April of 1964 there had been a military coup that brought in a dictatorship. When I arrived in Belo Horizonte I found everyone afraid and not doing anything.

Since I did not see a clear task for myself, I went back to teaching. I used Paulo Freire's methods. Latin had been eliminated from the curriculum, but I taught the students that they could still learn from Roman history about dictatorships and economic expansion so they could understand the role of the United States. This was in the mornings, and each afternoon I went to a poor area and worked in a project involving literacy classes.

Then we got into trouble with the police. Several of us lived close to one another in apartments and some of the people because of their own political convictions were offering hospitality to people who were working for the liberation of the country. The police arrested a young woman who had all of our addresses and for five days they ambushed everyone coming to our places. Finally, we were all arrested. There was no reason to arrest me but they had thirty of us in detention at a military training school and we knew they were torturing some of the detainees. It was a time of great anguish. Since I was the only foreigner, the Dutch consulate got involved and after five days I was released with a large group. Two Grail members remained behind and I worked for two months on their behalf until they were released.

This experience changed everything for me. The people working with us in São Paulo were angry; they thought this situation put them in danger and a split started. It was impossible to carry on after this and both centers closed. I was fired twice from the high schools where I was teaching because of the way I worked with Freire's conscientization. It was also too dangerous to be in the city because I would have the police at the door watching everything I was doing. So I moved to the interior and went to work on a project in the rural area that was not a Grail project.

I joined a team of two Dominican sisters and another layperson in São Domingos do Prata, about 150 kilometres (93 miles) from Belo Horizonte. The team had their own program but they didn't have anyone ready to teach literacy. At the time the government was promoting literacy but not raising the consciousness of the people. I changed that since I knew that if you only teach the mechanics of literacy to adults, they won't have the motivation to go on. People have to discover that reading and writing are cultural and political; it's liberation. So literacy classes have to be linked to a larger scope. We sat in a large circle and I was what was called a monitor since nobody is a teacher. They were all women and I just kept asking the questions. This is the method. I also helped organize training weekends for teachers and I taught them how to organize a library.

Working mostly with women raised questions about women's health. The women showed me prescriptions given to them by doctors, but they did not have the money to have them filled. So I started a health program. I began by using visual aids to show them the human skeleton and what was inside the body. Then I got x-rays from the hospital showing broken bones and explained that when this happens a person should not pull the arm or whatever but should get the injured person to the hospital.

We tried to help families where the child had psychological problems, but this was hard. We did a lot with home education by creating little theater plays to help parents understand how to allow children to grow more independent. We also talked about the numbers of children. All of this made people talk and they were very enthusiastic.

At the same time, these people were very oppressed but had very little consciousness of their oppression. After a meeting one woman came to me and said that she thought Brazil was moving forward. Actually there was so little movement. But when she compared the present situation with her youth, she thought things were really moving forward.

So what we were doing was giving hope by our encouraging people to take just one little step forward. In order to survive, many of the men rented themselves out to large landowners to work on the land at very low wages. We wanted to promote vegetable and fruit planting in that area as a pre-cooperative and got money from the government for technical assistance. I became secretary of this venture and did a lot of the organizing.

One evening I went to give a talk as part of a course about this to a group of people and they were very shy; they even kept their hands in front of their mouths when they spoke. I thought it was my Portuguese but I later found out that they were hiding the fact that they didn't have teeth. We took this course to many places and the people really learned and planted. At first the women did not want to eat the vegetables since they were used to rice and beans. So I made posters about salads and we made a salad look like a feast. This was a happy time; it was always fun and things were always moving along.

We grew to such an extent that a big government organization supported by the Inter-American Foundation came to offer money for this pre-cooperative. One of the persons who was key in this whole cooperative thing was the former pastor, a priest, who married his secretary and gave the whole organization to the politicians. Then he got jobs for all the brothers of his wife. The Dominican sisters also needed their rooms for getting a few girls to move in and so I moved to a very poor section of the town where I continued to work. After two years I became sick and I could not be treated there. I went to Buritizeiro for treatment and worked for a short time with farm workers who could not read or write.

The farm workers had sold their small pieces of land to large foreign companies who were planting eucalyptus to use as fuel in the steel plants owned by these sixty-four companies. The eucalyptus plantations provided work for the men. This process ruined the land and when the company finished they dismissed the workers and moved on. The men were starting a union and I was asked to be secretary. I again taught literacy, using Freire's method.

I finally returned to Holland for surgery and after a few months returned to Brazil knowing that I wanted to finish the work I had begun. All the years I had been in the rural areas I had maintained contact with Grail members. We were few and very scattered but for about ten years we met for discussions of what we were doing, mostly in base communities.

I also kept going to International Grail council meetings and once to a meeting in Mexico. We stayed with it. When I returned this time, the dictatorship had just about ended, so I went back to Belo Horizonte and helped the Grail get started again. We formed a small community and that took about two years.

Later Decades

I then decided to leave. I had very mixed feelings but I was sixty-three and I knew it was time to go back to the Netherlands. I felt I was not the right person to be with the Grail in Brazil and going back into the interior was too much for me. I could leave in a quiet way and still start over in the Netherlands.

When I look back on my whole experience of thirty years in Brazil, I realize that the people I worked with appreciated more than anything else that I was with them, that we worked together. What helped me and the Grail was the continuous insistence on discovering more about them and their country and having patience in trying to achieve. We had to realize that we were in a completely different situation and we had to wait and learn about how to start the Grail.

This meant that I had to drop a lot of my own baggage—cultural, spiritual and theological—and accept the simplicity of their ways. I saw their faithfulness and I came to the conclusion that it's not a question of who is "right." For instance, I did not always appreciate their religious ceremonies but I saw the people enjoy them, so there's a value there.

I have been back to visit and I still find the Brazilians so full of hope and joy about life. I hardly know where this comes from but it's contagious. Their community is not dependent on the celebrations; their community is always there. It is the hospitality, it is the whole of life, it is the way they welcome you. They ask about your family, they want to visit you and take you everywhere.

Today the Grail representatives from many countries, including Brazil, have really matured. The Brazilians know what they want and how to say it. They do not accept interference from the outside and they ask only for the help they want. I think the international Grail has to learn to work with a language other than just English and that language could be Spanish.

Coming back to the Netherlands has been a further opening for me; I have been able to use my international experience. After the initial adjustment I taught Portuguese to people who wanted to go to Brazil. And then I discovered an organization that taught Dutch to immigrants, mostly women who stayed at home with children and were forbidden by their husbands to go on the street.

A training course was started and I taught women from the Near East and India. I went mostly to their homes. Many of the women did not take even this step because of their husbands.

I also joined a Dutch women's organization concerned with women in the Third World and wanting solidarity with them. I was given responsibility for the Holland-Brazil connection. I had twenty groups in Holland and twenty groups in Brazil, which meant that I had to help the Brazilian groups write to the Dutch groups. That wasn't easy. I did a lot of travelling and speaking to groups and raising money for projects. People liked my enormous enthusiasm for this work.

I am now feeling my own physical limitations more and I do have some difficulty accepting that, but hopefully I am moving towards more wisdom and maturity. I hope that in the future I won't remain too attached to things. I don't want to fill my life, my house, so that I am not able to say "farewell" at the moment I should.

Acceptance is what I hope for. I've been busy all my life. Often I repeat to myself, "Just slow down." A spiritual turning point concerning this occurred for me after returning to the Netherlands. I knew that I needed a transition from all those active years to a new kind of life. There was a meeting of Grail Nucleus members in Italy that I went to and I observed people all around me doing yoga and meditating every morning.

Somehow I just couldn't stop moving so I took long walks around the grounds and each day I saw a sign for cars that read, "Please slow down." I finally said, "This sign is for me." Now when I have been very busy, I sit for a while, something I never did before. I pray, I have music in the evenings and I live more quietly. It's very simple.

What nurtures me now are two opposites: one is personal silence and quiet with a bit of reading and praying and some poetry and music. The other is friendship, meeting people, especially young people. That is definitely very important. That's why Brazil was so good. I was with young people in dynamic situations out in the world.

My experience in Brazil also changed my religious perceptions. As a child I thought of God in a very personal way and believed that Jesus was close by. In fact, my belief in Jesus as a person I could relate to brought me around when I was finishing high school to wanting to learn how to pray. I saw things in a more Christ-centered way.

The thing that broke through to me in Brazil was seeing God as more the God of history. This occurred to me at a time when I was getting more involved politically and in the liberation movement—seeing the role of the Spirit in human life and in history helped me be more open towards all the values around me in the world and to people from other beliefs.

I began to be more attentive to the signs of the time. I became aware of the effort that had to be made on the secular level to change things, and to see where political life comes in and to take a stand with political convictions. Little by little there was an opening up for me from Christ-centeredness toward seeing Jesus as an example of liberation as revealed in the teaching and living out of the gospels.

I feel very thankful for what I have received till now, and even though there has been a breakdown of many aspects of Catholic life, there is something that can blossom forth in new ways. There will be an opening to other people much more than before and the Gospel can be a guide for that. Even though I have criticisms of the church here and in Brazil, I want to remain faithful to my roots. At the same time, I want to be as open as I can to what is broader and deeper and what can be more universal.

Being in the Netherlands has opened me further since I have met so many people I feel very close to and who have completely different beliefs. Our country is full of immigrants who have all kinds of beliefs. If we want real meeting, we find that the deeper ground of everything is somehow the same for people from different religions. I think that if we want to find a real meeting with others, it's there. That's why it's so necessary to really deepen some knowledge of the mystics of the different religions to see if on that level there will be more of a meeting. Then we begin to see the different contributions that each religion makes to the whole picture. If we try to find ways to live on deeper levels, we will surely meet one another. The question to ask is how people from different religions live with ethical questions. Do they care for life? What are their attitudes toward the poor? These are the big questions.

*Eileen Schaeffler, right, Lydwine van Kersbergen, left,
Archbishop Karl Alter of Cininnati, center, The United States, 1950s*

7

Eileen Schaeffler

*My spirituality is to be open to the
energy that is available from the Spirit
—and acting from that center.*

When Eileen decided to spend six months at Grailville in 1950, she came with the intention of preparing for her upcoming marriage. Several months later while the man she was engaged to was visiting Grailville, Lydwine van Kersbergen presided over a high Sunday breakfast in honor of the couple and gave a homily on marriage.[35]

But by then Eileen was having doubts about marriage, and shortly afterwards she broke off her engagement in order to reflect seriously on a life in the Grail Nucleus. She had first heard about the Grail during her last year as a sociology major at St. John's University in New York when she attended a talk given by a Grail member, Mary Imelda Buckley, about the lay apostolate, the term used then for Catholic Action and social justice work done by Catholic laypeople in the secular world.

---

35 When Eileen went to Grailville for the first time, she was approximately 23 years old. She was born June 3, 1927.

Eileen was immediately inspired. She started spending time at Monica House, the storefront Grail center in Brooklyn. At Monica House Eileen resonated with the poverty of the area, since she herself had grown up during the Depression and came from what she described as a poor family. Besides helping to raise rent money for the Center and begging for food for their evening meal, Eileen was introduced to new forms of liturgy and Mass preparation that she taught to others with the man she still, in those days, intended to marry.

Eileen also felt an affinity for the Catholic Worker, the movement started by Dorothy Day to serve the poor. A very meaningful and influential time for her during her Monica House days was attending a retreat at Mary Farm, the Catholic Worker farm in eastern Pennsylvania. And her later six-month stay at Grailville, the national center of the U.S. Grail in southwestern Ohio, gave her a beginning insight into an integrated approach to life that continued to evolve throughout her life.

However, the years Eileen spent at the Gateway, the Detroit Grail Center, where she went from Grailville in the early 1950s, were what she recalls as the most formative ones. She discusses these three years of her life as "a charismatic time" and the most influential years of her own spiritual development. The Gateway had been started in 1949 by Joan Overboss, the co-founder of the Grail in the United States, who often worked in a factory as a way of identifying with and getting to know the needs of working class women in Detroit. Eileen had great admiration for Joan and her "socialist heart."

Like Monica House, the Gateway was a storefront in an urban area that was a changing interracial neighborhood. It had an interracial and international resident staff of fifteen, many of whom worked as teachers, nurses, social workers and secretaries, as well as over forty team members from throughout the Detroit area. Eileen joined in community neighborhood development projects there, as well as a family emergency service program, and work with international students. Prayer, study, work and recreation provided the framework for her daily life. Central to that reality was Eileen's participation in the liturgy at the local parish, St. Leo's, where staff from the Gateway worked with two priests—the pastor, Hubert Rhomberg, and his assistant, Walter (Joe) Schoenherr.[36] The creative arts, drama, dance and music were an integral part of the life of the Center and were shared with men and women, married and single, through lectures, discussions, concerts, dramatic readings, and feast day celebrations.

In order to have a better political and social analysis of the community development process and how she might apply it to her Detroit work, Eileen eventually attended classes at Wayne State University in Detroit. She was encouraged by one of her professors to apply for a Fulbright scholarship to do social research in Europe.

After receiving the scholarship, Eileen left for the Netherlands and eventually went to France where she came in touch with the "worker-priests" there[37] and John Vanier, founder of L'Arche. On November 1, 1956, while still in Europe, she made a lifetime dedication in the Nucleus of the Grail at the Tiltenberg.

In 1957 Eileen was appointed, along with Barbara Wald, to be on the U.S. Grail's first vice-presidency team. She and Barbara

---

36 In 1968, Rev. Walter Joseph Schoenherr became the auxiliary bishop of the Archdiocese of Detroit. (Email to Marian Ronan from Steve Wejroch, Assistant Archivist, Archdiocese of Detroit, U.S.A., March 13, 2015).

37 In the Worker-Priest movement, founded in France in 1941, priests worked in factories as a way of reaching out to workers. The movement was suppressed by Pope Pius XII in 1954. *The Chronicle of the Worker-Priests*, edited by Stanley Windass (New York City: Humanities Press, Inc., 1967).

searched out new places for city centers in the States and were responsible for helping to establish the San Jose center in California, with a mandate to work with Mexican-Americans. In 1962, Eileen was the first American appointed president of the U.S. Grail, succeeding Lydwine van Kersbergen. She served a five-year term. In 1964, she was appointed to the Grail international advisory board, and in 1965 became a member of the Grail International Council.

Then, in 1967, Eileen was elected to a four-year term as International President of the Grail, with Maria de Lourdes Pintasilgo as vice-president; they succeeded the presidency team of Magdelene Oberhoffer, Dolores Brien and Benedicte Milcent. She was the first U.S. national to hold the position. Her Fulbright experience and her ability to speak Dutch helped as she was called upon to continue efforts by the previous presidency team to bridge the differences between the Grail in the U.S. and in the Netherlands, the former with a growing movement of married and single women and the latter more Nucleus-focused.[38]

As International President she also relied on her political and social analysis skills gleaned from her Detroit days as she encouraged the founding of the Grail in Tanzania, assessed the potential for the Grail in Switzerland and Nigeria, and travelled to Grail centers in Uganda, South Africa and Brazil. Eileen's national and international leadership roles spanned the unsettling times of the 1960s when, after Vatican II, the Grail was trying to redefine its identity with the new emphasis on personal growth and decision-making in community, the burgeoning liberation movements, and the exodus of many women from the Nucleus of the Grail.

---

38 The International Secretariat had moved from the Netherlands to Paris, France, when the previous presidency team took office. (Note from Marie Marchall on an earlier version of this chapter, April 15, 2015).

Eileen returned to the United States in 1971 to face both critical personal difficulties and some new challenges. As she was trying to carve out a new niche for herself in New York City, she took care of two Grail members as they were dying of cancer. She also saw her younger brother through cancer and assisted his widow and two young children after his death. Eventually her new professional life began to focus as she acquired a master's degree, for which she wrote a thesis on women's work as a global issue. She then spent three years in Chicago working as director of the Women's Bureau of the Department of Labor, Midwest Region. In the following years she also travelled back to South Africa as a spokesperson for solidarity between trade unionists from South Africa and the United States.

Upon her return to New York City, Eileen worked as a Consultant to UN-related organizations from 1979-81, and from 1981-84 for the Pontifical Mission for Palestine, a Catholic fund-raising organization for Palestinian refugees that took her on a number of trips to the Middle East. Concurrent with all her other interests, she devoted many years to working in several different UN frameworks. Her familiarity with the UN came from an earlier experience in the late 1940s and 1950s in Paris when she and several other Grail members were part of U.F.E.R. (International Movement for Fraternal Union among Races and Peoples), representing the Grail at UNESCO. Eileen retired from her position at the United Nations in 1987, when she turned sixty, but remained in contact with different facets of that organization for many years.

Eileen's burning interest in the United Nations and her dissemination of UN literature inspired a number of Grail members to begin attending certain sessions and to find at the UN a forum for meeting women from around the world who share similar concerns. Located just twenty blocks from the United Nations' New York headquarters, Eileen's apartment in Manhattan's Stuyvesant Town hosted a steady flow of visitors from around the world. Her apartment also became the meeting place for a group of women who come together on a regular basis to discuss the relationship between spirituality and the political, now called the Grail "Politics and Spirituality" group. Eileen also contributed in an on-going way to process groups for prospective Grail members and provided invaluable historical context as an advisor to the Grail's international presidency teams.

Eilleen's most cherished activity in these later years, however, was participating in the New York City Labor Chorus, whose membership is mostly black. Singing in this chorus brought Eileen full circle. From growing up during the Depression, to working in the storefronts of Monica House and the Gateway, to witnessing apartheid in South Africa, singing with this group took her back to her early roots. For her it was her greatest spiritual expression in retirement, a "sacred activity."

By 2007, the mental decline that led to Eileen's death was becoming evident. During her final years, U.S. Grail members Dorothy Rasenberger and Joy Garland cared for Eileen with singular devotion, making it possible for her to remain in her Stuyvesant Town apartment with the help of both a day and a night aide. When Eileen slipped at home and fractured her pelvis, she was taken to Beth Israel Hospital, treated and then released to the Cabrini Nursing Home at East 5th Street and Avenue B in Manhattan, where she remained until it was announced on March 12, 2012 that the non-profit facility, run by the Missionary Sisters of the Sacred Heart of Jesus and serving 240 low-income elderly people, was going to close.

Dorothy and Joy were told that the previous owner, an unnamed family trust, sold the building for $25.5 million to a young East Side developer, Ben Shaoul. Cabrini was told that they had two months to exit the building even after the Archdiocese of

New York and local political leaders intervened to try to save it. Dorothy, Joy and others demonstrated outside the Cabrini Residence, but on May 4, 2012, Eileen was transferred to Mary Manning Walsh Nursing Home at East 79th Street in Manhattan. Dorothy went every day to visit, often staying till evening, with Joy visiting weekly and maintaining contact with the management. They celebrated Eileen's 85th birthday there on June 5th and sang "Happy Birthday" with her room-mate's husband playing the violin, to which Eileen responded by smiling and waving her hands in time.

Just three months later, on Saturday, August 4, 2012, the Mary Manning Walsh Home notified Dorothy and Joy that Eileen had passed away suddenly, possibly from a stroke. A funeral Mass was arranged in the chapel of Mary Manning Walsh and Eileen's many Grail friends and her brother Al's family came and then joined together afterward to share remembrances of Eileen.

Because Eileen wanted her ashes to be buried in the memorial garden at the Grail retreat house in Cornwall-on-Hudson, NY, a Mass with the local parish pastor there was arranged and Grail friends came from all over to attend it.

Eileen's poem "Glittering Words," written for Grail member Kaye Farmer in February 1997, expressed her undying love and hope for those left behind. It still echoes today.

Glittering Words

When I die
I would fly around the heavens
and sprinkle words
like glitter, sparkling glitter
that would catch the sunbeams
and leave the seers breathless.

The azure vault,
its pure blue,
and all the clouds
that hide our angels' nests,
would be alight as never before.

The glittering words
would come from those
who write and sing of love,
of pain, of joy,
of suffering,
of beauty, and of the
base lining of our souls.

These words would gently fall
into open hearts
and fill them with understanding.
Love would rise
and spread like a cirrus cloud,
each new word a diamond of ice
forming a rainbow of hope.

Interview

The Grassroots Struggle

I grew up during the Depression in a poor family, so when I received a scholarship to St. John's University, it was a fantastic chance. Two events of lasting significance occurred during this time—the Dean introducing me to a race relations course which was revolutionary at that time, and encouraging me to design a program for myself with an emphasis on racial justice. This program laid the foundation for the direction of most of my work in the Grail. And I met the Grail when Mary Buckley came to speak at St. John's about the lay apostolate. It was the first time I had ever met anyone who saw the consequences of her life and lived out that lifestyle. The time was ripe and Mary Buckley was meant to appear in my life—I was going to know something that I didn't know yet. I often call experiences like these "inside out" happenings; there was so much alive inside that I was pulled out by circumstances.

After graduation and working for a few years as a social worker at an adoption agency, I went to Grailville at the suggestion of Rachel Donders, who had made me more aware of the international dimensions of the Grail. By this time I was engaged, so I saw this as a preparation for marriage. The six months there turned me around quite a bit, with my having access to a different theology than we all had in our Catholic upbringing.

Grailville as a place, I think, was one of the biggest contributions because there's no place else in the world that the Grail would have been able to have that much property and that much ongoing programming. And the sense of community among the women, in the bonding of their energy. Most fundamental to all of this was the infusion of the practical with the spiritual. Engaging the Spirit and being sensitive to the Spirit, and nurturing the Spirit as an energy source for the work to be done.

The work was not as tiring as one would have thought because you were carried by this spirit. The holistic approach—everything was connected, the arts, music, poetry, drama. I worked on the farm and the lifestyle there on the land was very much in touch with the organic and with the principles of growth. I had never seen that possibility before, a revolutionary vision coupled with an earthly rooting at the same time. This kind of theological formation was mind-blowing for us Catholic college graduates.

At the same time, I was at Grailville as an engaged person, expecting to marry. The fact is, I never actualized Grailville and its way of doing because I was already committed to doing something else. So it was not the boundary of the universe for me. It was like a six-month retreat. However, at the end of that time, I knew the marriage was not going to work, so I went back to New York and broke the engagement. This left me free to follow Rachel's suggestion that I go to Detroit to help Joan Overboss with the beginnings of the Gateway Grail Center.

Joan had gone from Grailville to Detroit in the late 1940s and went to work in a factory as a worker on an assembly line so as to understand the youth. This was the kind of thing that impressed me tremendously. Every so often she would tell us that she needed to go back to the factory. "I'm losing my grip," she would say. And we would wave her off in the morning with her lunch pail. Have you ever thought of anyone else in the Grail in a leadership role who would have done this?

From the beginning, the grounding in the environment of the Gateway resonated with who I was. That was a big reason why I made the decision to go there. It was an authentic decision, not an easy one. The work at the Gateway was very grassroots and as with every turning point in my life, it was the integration of the spirit and matter that attracted me. It's not just that we were religious or that we believed, but that life had to be changed where we were from the strength of our beliefs.

Joan had found a storefront in a neighborhood that was changing from white to black. I eventually took a course at Wayne State University in an attempt to learn more about social analysis for this area of Detroit; we also got information from the Antigonish Movement in Nova Scotia about co-ops. I still get tired of political analysis when everything is just happening in the head. For instance you know what is wrong and you just keep dissecting it. That's not my cup of tea, because there's nothing about really being swept into these poor situations and being able to see some changes happening.

So once a month a group of us, including Joann Lamb and Anne Mercier, met in the home of one of the local women, Black or white, working with the Antigonish principles of cooperation and socialization. Our goal was that the women would understand that if we bonded around our common necessities which were food and shelter, we could transcend our differences. The multi-racial cooperative buying venture that we established was one way of fulfilling that goal. All of us had to take a turn at shopping in the market. Anne and I often went to the market to ask for left-over food. This may seem quite difficult but I was trained for it by Monica House where we had done a lot of begging for food. We had also been close to the Catholic Worker. Because we were more intellectual, more cultural as Grail, we needed that plurality that the Catholic Worker had. So I guess one of the reasons I felt all of these experiences as very authentic was because they were on the path I had started on before. They met who I was and what I wanted to become.

We were very connected to the local parish and we tried to help the Black parishioners use the idiom of their tradition for celebrations. The newly Catholic Black people had had their own culture put on hold and there was no bridge for really making that a part of their lives as Catholics.

So that was a big part of what we did—rediscovering the Black medium for the expression of the arts and expression in the church. We used to have a lot of choral singing. We had a jazz trombonist who became the director of music and we had paraliturgies in the church basement, knowing that we couldn't get away with them upstairs. I felt completely at home here because I knew that this was a part of my past and this was something I had been on fire about since my college days. And now, to be a part of this kind of parish. The Gateway was a real link with my past and something that kept recurring in my life. And as a city-bred person, I intended to live my life in the city and not on the farm.

Joan Overboss was determined, I think, to help me mature. At one point I was in charge of the whole household, doing things I didn't do well and that I had to prove I was willing to do. So that was quite difficult. However, our lives at the Gateway were not harsh. We had very modest lifestyles and we never felt deprived, because we had other kinds of riches.

A lot of professors from local universities came to do play readings. It was the first time I had seen the Grail in the United States incarnate all that we were dealing with intellectually and spiritually, in a milieu which was a desperate situation where there seemed to be no hope—integrating all aspects of life, and employing the kind of analysis that was required in order to do it in an effective way.

The cultural expressions had a great richness, so we didn't just get depressed by the situation. And the brilliance of Joan. I never met another woman like her in my life. She could be so playful. We used to sing it, we danced it, we would do dramatic things, we would conduct the buying co-op and credit union. The wholeness of it. Times of reflection and liturgies across the street or underground in the basement, and reaching out with play readings and singing. It was male and female. It was just wonderful.

While I was taking courses at Wayne State University in Detroit, a professor I studied with encouraged me to apply for a Fulbright scholarship to do research in Europe. I decided to apply. I wanted to do social research and understand things like the worker-priests in France. The scholarship was awarded, and at the advice of a professor at the University of Nijmegen in Holland who had known Joan Overboss, I went to Paris and invented my own program. Among other things, I explored the integration of mind and spirit among the worker-priests and spent time with John Vanier, the founder of L'Arche, a community for mentally-challenged adults outside of Paris. He was most helpful in supporting my interests.

Leadership Roles, National and International

In late 1956, while still in Europe, I made my dedication in the Nucleus of the Grail at the Tiltenberg. Immediately afterwards, I returned to the United States. Lydwine appointed Barbara Wald and me to be Vice Presidents—a first-time designation in the U.S. Grail. That was one of the great strengths of the Grail in the 1950s, its belief in women and grooming us for leadership. There was a trusting in women to take over all kinds of responsibilities.

Our main task was to travel around the United States to find new places for the Grail to begin. The most memorable trip for me was to California where Ethel Souza, a long time friend of the Grail, had this wonderful bookshop in San Francisco. She offered it to us, lock, stock and barrel, a wonderful situation in San Francisco. We said we would think about this and then we went on to San Jose. Barbara Wald had spent time in Brazil and she really had a Latin heart.

Well, we were driving down a street in San Jose and Barbara saw a big church and she said, "Let's go in and pray for some guidance." We did just that and almost immediately met the priest who gave us some property. It had been left to him by two women with the stipulation it should be for a Catholic women's group wanting to work with Mexicans. Just like that—he gave it to the Grail. We didn't really know what we were doing but it was given to us. And this has affected me very much. I think what I learned from this experience is that we need to become spiritual and receptive and expect "miracles." I really believe that much will be given, that things do reveal themselves.

In 1961, I was appointed by Rachel Donders to succeed Lydwine van Kersbergen as the national president of the Grail in the United States. I tried during my presidency to see that there was a collegial membership in the Grail. Things had been very hierarchically focused, with the absence of lateral communication. So we created a national board rather than having vice-presidents.

It was during my presidency and later, too, during my term as International President that the exodus from the Grail began among Nucleus members. They needed to have this in writing and I was the one they had to be in touch with. Answering people's requests for release from the Nucleus was very difficult for me. I was pen struck. I really am not a writer so my letters didn't convey my emotion.

We had a series of three retreats at Grailville and the theme was around what issues these departures of people from the Nucleus were raising for us. And it was an effort to make everybody feel free to reconsider their being in the Nucleus. I think out of loyalty to me many people stayed. I always respect the fact that people were kind enough to do it, but it delayed the process. Things that are designed to be more democratic and to give people more freedom are fragile in the end.

Also during my presidency, we had a meeting at Grailville with bishops, priests, nuns and married couples to look at the structures of the Grail and to explore what we really had to change. I always considered the church very reactionary and more so when I met the Grail because of the experimentation we had done and the kind of programs we had. We had that kind of bonding with people who were in the church in different ways, a mutual recognition. So we focused on issues that led to *aggiornamento* and everybody was so frank. Out of this came decisions to broaden and do more education within the Grail.

Then in 1967 I was elected International President of the Grail at the International General Assembly at the Tiltenberg. When we finally got to the point of voting, we were deadlocked. We were sent back to the chapel five times to keep praying for guidance. I don't think I was prepared for all this formality, nor, frankly did I want the job. I guess I always would say to myself, "If the community calls ... "

I had done part of my Fulbright in the Netherlands and I spoke pretty good Dutch, so I deliberately talked in Dutch, something that was not easy. The person who got the second greatest number of votes was Maria de Lourdes Pintasilgo. She served as my vice president. So what was really a blessing is that we grew to respect each other tremendously. We worked very hard together and we are loyal to each other to this day. We led the Grail together. I think having a collegial group to do it with instead of some of the lonely decisions I used to have to make as national president in the U.S. was very helpful. I made all the decisions in communication with others. We had a board and I wanted it to be an internationally representative board. For instance, Allison Healy came in from Australia, Alberta Lucker from Germany, Teresa Santa Clara Gomes from Portugal.

I think my greatest contribution as International President was my work in developing countries. I really tried to get with the grassroots situation in the various developing countries and to achieve communication with a lot of people who had been there for years and needed affirmation. I met Imelda Gaurwa, a Tanzanian, while she was in Uganda and she told me she wanted to start the Grail in Tanzania. I told her that I was there for a couple of months, why didn't we just go see.

So Imelda and I took a bus from Uganda to Tanzania in the middle of the night and the bus was loaded with people, with vegetables, and chickens. During the night she shared her dreams with me. And she brought me to meet the bishop. He wanted her to come and she wanted to be there. So we went ahead and we did it. I really felt good about that.

I was also excited about the prospects of starting the Grail in Nigeria. Evelyn Pugh was there. But I soon realized that the Grail wasn't going to take root there because there was such political turmoil. At the same time, Evelyn became ill with cancer and subsequently died that year.

However, before Evelyn left Africa she and I met a queen, Adebola, who was married to the king of their tribe, and he was a polygamist. She was a Christian and she presided over a house of many wives. They had met in Europe while they were at a university; they married and then went back into tribal life. It must have been awful for her.

I saw Adebola again when she came to an International General Assembly at Grailville and she said to me, "You know, my situation is unusual." We were in the kitchen doing dishes when she got called to meet some students from Nigeria who were studying near Grailville and had come to see her. So, she takes off her apron and goes out and the students prostrate themselves on the ground in front of her. She later said to me, "I am a little embarrassed by all of this." Of course, I did not expect this either. It was unbelievable.

And I felt good about the visit to South Africa. I think that's because I had done a lot of interracial work in the United States and could appreciate the risks that the South Africans were taking. Most of the Grail members in South Africa at that time were from European families. They were all needed professionally and they exerted influence through their professions and were making a sound contribution that way. So the structure was in place. The Grail was more of a supportive base for the kind of work that they were doing. However, many of the South Africans who could have provided leadership at that time were in exile because of the danger there, like Anne Hope.

It was quite a learning experience for me. We had not become politicized yet and it was very difficult because there was a terrific danger if Blacks and whites tried to do anything together. It was hard keeping up communication and the Grail people were all burned out. But now there's Jane Ngobese of South Africa who was a delegate to the 1993 International General Assembly at Grailville. The arrival of someone of her calibre is wonderful.

By the early 1990s, the Grail had been in Brazil for quite some time. I went there and fell in love with it. What a wonderful, earthy place. They sing the vision, they dance, they live it. Some of the Grail people who had come from other countries had come as professional people. There was not a lot of indigenous interaction, and most of the Brazilians I met at that time came from upper-class, privileged backgrounds.

And then there was a whole network of Americans who had gone to Brazil. I went there twice and it was the second time that all the liberation theology groups were under scrutiny and everything meaningful was underground; these were repressed people. I went into the interior to speak to a group of women because I really wanted to meet them.

So I gave a talk in English which was the only thing I could do. And when I finished they said, "Very good, very good." They had been taught to appreciate. This touched me. We also attended underground Masses. They were underground for two reasons: because the people were doing quite a bit of experimental liturgy, but also because the priests were suspect. They were doing the most innocent of things and the church was playing this fantastic role by helping to raise the consciousness of the people.

I don't know about the rest of the country. All I know is what my experiences were. One evening at a party that I attended I was warned that one of the men there was an agent. Subsequently about a year after that, some of our people were even in jail for a while. Later, when I went to northeast Brazil I was followed a long way by a man I knew was an agent and I was only able to lose him by going to the American Embassy.

Coming Home and Going Full Circle

In 1971, Simone Tagher from Egypt was elected at the International General Assembly to be the next International President of the Grail. The next few years for me were quite difficult. Within a few weeks of my return and Audrey Schomer's from overseas, Evelyn Pugh was diagnosed with cancer and we became her caregivers when she came home to New York. And when Evie died and we were getting ready to go to her funeral, I found out that my brother, who had a wife and two young children, had just been diagnosed with terminal cancer as well. So then Audrey and I plotted our course and she said she would, with me, be a primary caregiver.

It was out of this base that I started going to the United Nations. So there was a positive side to the coin in that the UN was the great outlet I wanted for my international experience. And it helped me to find my way again and to move into a profession and to be in that kind of a structured environment. But it was a heavy time because of the death of Evelyn and my brother's illness, so we were not upbeat characters. We were kind of down and out for a while, finding our way.

I encountered Barbara Wald at one point when she was working for the regional Women's Bureau for the Department of Labor in Kansas City. She told me there was a job opening in the U.S. Department of Labor in Chicago, the center for a six-state region similar to one in which she worked. I applied for the job and got it very easily. I think it was on the strength of what a fantastic performer Barbara was. They knew that this Grail prepared a woman for this kind of role.

So I moved to Chicago. I was regional administrator of the Women's Bureau, a job that required a lot of public speaking and meeting with groups of women. We could create the kinds of groups we wanted to work with. For example, there were a lot of Black women in Chicago who were cleaners and wanted to unionize. So we got all the appropriate journals and studied them in order to teach them how to organize. Also, Native American women in the area had been ignored by the Women's Bureau in the past, so I tried to do some things with them as well and got onto the reservations. So we reached out to different constituents. We made a trip to Grailville that I set up to get funds for a project for rural women. One time I was scheduled to debate Phyllis Schafly on the status of women, but she didn't show up.

I succeeded quite well at this job and it was liberating. Bringing all the best I knew from Grailness, that's what it was. I knew what I knew from a women's movement. But I really hated the Federal bureaucracy and I decided I wanted to come back to New York. I read in a New York newspaper about a Master's program in labor studies at Long Island University. I knew I would have to do a thesis but I thought if it's labor studies, I know the jargon. I wrote my thesis on women's non-compensated work as a global issue and I used a lot of United Nations material.

I started job-hunting again and that's how I wound up at the Pontifical Mission for Palestine. This was a fund-raising organization for Palestinian refugees. I had never worked for the institutional church before so it wasn't easy.

I got my competency in the Middle East by traveling the region and through all kinds of education. I knew a lot about the region and a lot about the NGO sector. We first went to Jordan. That was my first taste of the Arab world and then we did everything by land. There were places on these trips where women were excluded, including at the Wall in Jerusalem. By then I was so angry, I just pushed my way through the crowd and stuck my message in the wall.

My conclusion was that there had to be small dialogue groups of people not so embroiled on site. And that's what we did in developing the non-governmental sector. I built up the constituency to a couple of hundred non-governmental organizations on a worldwide basis. Sometimes we would meet in Geneva and sometimes we would meet here in New York. The support for the Palestine non-governmental sectors skyrocketed.

I went from there to the United Nations. One matter I worked on was the question of the Portuguese territories in Africa. There was an African woman who was the chair of an intergovernmental committee on this issue and I helped her in the drafting of the resolution about that. We included the language for the inclusion of the nongovernmental sector in rebuilding Portuguese territories and facilitating better communication between Portugal and the colonies. As a result of this work, I was invited by the Tanzanian ambassador to the UN to go to a meeting in Geneva.

Some Grail members are represented on UFER, the French acronym for the International Movement for Fraternal Union Among Races and People. The Grail also got NGO status in the United Nations before my time. However, I have worked very hard in the United Nations for us to keep that status because it is very helpful and valuable for Grail members from different parts of the world for the Grail to have this status when meetings are being held in their regions and we have Grail delegates, the Grail face. It gives us another platform to make global contacts for the Grail. But it is not the same as the level of status to work politically that we have with UFER. So some of us have insisted on still being UFER representatives rather than Grail representatives. Thus, we have the two categories.

At age 60, I had to retire, since that's the retirement age. Since then the UN has become a meeting place for women from all over the world. It's wonderful the kind of women who are coming and what they bring. This to me is feminism. It doesn't mean that we will ever leave behind the need for analysis, but what we have now is much more existential. It's a wonderful place for formation.

It is very exciting to see women bonding across the nations because such bonding was at first a very Western phenomenon. And now women in the West are discovering the plight of their sisters in different parts of the world and espousing those struggles and helping things to happen—and educating for that happening. This sisterhood around the United Nations is fantastic. Women come to these international conferences not so concerned about what's going to come out of it for the UN, but how women-power will get bonded, how they will feel the strength and be helped.

All that I had done was very rewarding. To be able to earn your bread around such significant issues and see changes happen and to have good relations with your colleagues, this was the most solidifying thing for me in reference to my Grail experience. And during these years I was able to travel back to South Africa three times to be in solidarity and do interviews with people concerning labor unions. Sometimes this was dangerous but I had to do it. It was my beloved place. It was so important.

Retirement

Although I still attend many sessions and events at the United Nations, since I retired I have devoted most of my energy to jobs in the Grail. I have been the national representative for the Liberation Task Force or network. It is much stronger here than anywhere else because of the kind of youth becoming Grail members and our access to the United Nations. We are keeping an international horizon in our work because of having access to all kinds of information.

I am also very committed to the US Grail International Team. We call this team USIT and we are fantastically united. Sometimes we meet at the UN cafeteria for lunch and analyze what's needed, what we need to be getting from the International Presidency Team in that area, and implementing that. I am so pleased to be involved in the Grail structure in this way since it is the first time since I have been back in the States that I get to bring my international skills to bear, to relativize things within the Grail.

What I find very inspiring is that so many women are seeking the spirit, their thirstiness, and that it's not out of style to honor that fact. For instance, twenty-five of us meet on a regular basis in this room in a politics and spirituality group.[39] There is a need for bonding among these women from various traditions regarding the feminine aspects of God, a theology of the Spirit, finding all the things we associate with women.

The Holy Spirit is the feminine in my book of life. This has been such a lesson. Here in the New York Grail Politics and Spirituality group are real feminists. Most of them have been very committed socially having come through the 60s, much more aggressive types of personalities than I am. So there's a certain political freedom while we attempt to make the spiritual integration, because we now see that the political by itself can be so draining and disillusioning if you don't have a faith life and your strategies don't come from a deeper perception of religious values. It's the juncture between the politics and the spirituality. Both strains are alive in these women at the different points in their lives. We have two retreats a year at Cornwall with silence, with ritual, with analysis of situations and discussions of our own futures.

I would say that the closest I have come to my ideal of retirement is being a member of the New York City Labor Chorus. My self-worth has always been linked to being productive, so I have had a hard time letting go and just enjoying retirement, but singing in this chorus for the past four years has been sacred. We have

---

39 In Eileen's apartment, in Stuyvesant Town, on the East Side of Manhattan, in New York City, U.S.A.

performed on picket lines and in Carnegie Hall. Our chorus was even a backdrop with children singing songs of the 1960s at a Peter, Paul and Mary reunion in Washington, D.C. It's especially wonderful for me because it is so diverse. I am finally making an authentic rerooting in the struggles of the working class. I love this kind of political activism. It's sacramental. It embodies what I believe in.

Ton Brouwer, location and date unknown

8

Antonia (Ton) Brouwer

The international character of the Grail ...
the belief that you have to use the talents you have ...
that as a community of women we have strength ...
this has been the light in my life.

A new wave of understanding of cultural identity and autonomy previously eclipsed by traditional approaches to overseas service and by colonialism strongly influenced Ton Brouwer's view of the changing role of lay missionary work. The time was ripe for the innovative styles of leadership that Ton exerted in her twenty-two years in Africa. Her conscious and deliberate efforts to empower indigenous women to exercise self-determination eventually resulted in the Africanization of the Grail.

Ton was born in 1932 in Delft, the Netherlands, and experienced at first hand hardships and oppression during her very formative years when she lived under the Nazi regime. Her teenage years in post-war Europe exposed her to a new climate of critical thinking which is reflected in the kind of decisions she made and her absolute perseverance in carrying them through. With her characteristic determination, she decided early in childhood that she wanted to go to Africa to be of service. In order to accomplish her ambition she followed her own instincts in a society where women were expected to grow up, marry, and have children; she did not want to marry and she did not want to become a nun.

Ton describes her childhood as a very happy one despite the suffering inflicted on her family as a result of the German occupation of World War II. There was no heat for homes, no schooling, and by 1944, her family, like many other Dutch people, were eating tulips. Her mother often told her seven children to go to bed to stave off hunger.

Traditional roles in the family were adhered to; Ton's mother raised the seven children (number eight was born in 1947 after the war) and kept house; her father owned a printing press. Her father also devoted a great deal of his time to helping the poor and less fortunate through volunteer work. His concern for economic justice likely had a great influence on Ton and her future goals since he was deeply concerned about the gap between the rich and the poor.

Ton's mother, though, also had a very strong influence on her life. Ton gives recognition and great praise to her mother and to Grail member Beatrice van Voorst tot Voorst, both of whom corresponded frequently with Ton for the twenty-two years after she left home. These correspondences allowed Ton the opportunity to mirror her personal feelings and concerns about what she was doing without fear of being judged.

Catholicism permeated the Brouwer home. There was regular attendance at Mass, special Sunday celebrations, daily prayer, and an awareness that both her mother and father prayed together each night for their children and others near and far. The Catholic atmosphere was further enhanced by attendance at parochial schools and involvement in other Catholic-sponsored activities beyond the home and school. When Ton was barely fifteen, she came in contact with a missionary training school in Ubbergen and five years later began her nurse's training so that she could go to Africa. While in training Ton met the Grail; her initial response to the Grail was somewhat indifferent. However, she felt the Grail might be the vehicle for achieving her goal—Africa.

Like many other young women who decided to work with the Grail overseas, Ton spent a year of preparation at the Tiltenberg in the Netherlands where she was exposed to all of Father van Ginneken's courses. She recalls today that the very visible elements of the Grail which van Ginneken put forth and were so integral to its work and presence in the world were demonstrated in everyday life at the Tiltenberg: the international character of the Grail; the shared work by everyone regardless of economic, social or educational background; the importance of each person developing and using her own talents; and the strength of women working together in community.

Although Ton became a Grail Nucleus member at a later time, in Africa, this early experience, particularly the international aspect, solidified her commitment to the Grail and its mission. In addition to the realization of the power within community, she remembers having a more sophisticated exposure to Bible study and liturgy. These became significant ways of broadening and deepening the religious and spiritual understandings she brought from her home life in Delft.

In keeping with the convention of the times, Ton's parents would have liked their daughter to enter a convent; it was safer and seemingly more secure than the Grail. Ton explained to them that she would never be rich but she wanted to go to Africa with or without the Grail. Their full support of her decision was revealed in an inscription in a prayer book given to Ton when she left for the Tiltenberg. It reads,

> With your youthful enthusiasm, you go there voluntarily. You are leaving us in order to give yourself to help others. We hope your ideals may be realized. Ton, a Brouwer goes on, she

never gives up. Keep going and don't be afraid of difficulties. And if they are there be sure we will accompany you with our daily prayers.

Papa and Mama
November 18, 1958

Eventually Ton's parents visited her in Africa, and she tells of her father at one time saying that although she had not had the easiest life of all his children, she was the luckiest one.

In 1958, Ton arrived in Usumbura, Burundi, to begin twenty-two years of work in three African countries.[40] With three other Grail members, she helped in the formation of church-sponsored clubs for women and children and in a family movement which had as one of its goals the encouragement of women's greater voice in the home and society—a very slow process.

A year later Ton's nursing skills would be challenged to their limits at a hospital in Kasongo in the former Belgian Congo. In the early morning hours of July 26, 1960, almost a month after independence, Ton and the other members of the Grail team who were working at the hospital escaped and began a two-day drive to Burundi just hours before the hospital was all but destroyed by government troops. The murder of a Grail member in Burundi while Ton was in the Netherlands on leave left the Grail team in even greater turmoil and uncertain about their future in that country.

Ton decided to go to Tanzania, where she joined the staff of a maternity dispensary and trained nurses. It was a fortuitous decision on Ton's part since it was in Tanzania that she met Imelda

---

40 Usumbura, now called Bujumbura, is the capital, largest city, and main port of Burundi. "Bujumbura," Wikipedia: The Free Encyclopedia, accessed November 18, 2016, https://en.wikipedia.org/wiki/Bujumbura.

Gaurwa.⁴¹ Gaurwa, with strong support and encouragement from Ton, and with the help of another Grail member, Honorata Mvungi,⁴² began the first Grail training center in Tanzania; this center was also the first started and developed by Africans.

During the next several years, while the Grail Center was under development, Ton stayed in the background, managing a bookstore in Moshi. She created a community by making the bookstore a place where people could gather for discussions and receive health care advice and information. Her simple lifestyle and her demonstrations of solidarity with the people and their customs gained her their trust and admiration.

By 1980, with the realization that the Grail Center was running well and the bookstore ought to be run by Africans, Ton responded to the request to return to help at the Tiltenberg. For the next eight years she assisted with programs at the Tiltenberg and was a member of the Dutch national Grail team.

The first years back in the Netherlands were difficult ones for Ton; she had to adjust to a church and country that had undergone profound changes and to a totally new lifestyle among people who had little understanding of her African experiences. The greatest adjustment was moving from a living community to a culture immersed in individualism.

Ton left the Tiltenberg in 1988 to begin a new life in Voorburg, living alone for the first time in her life. Her hopes of "doing something more with my experience in Africa" materialized in the next several years through her work with Caritas International, the confederation of Catholic relief, development, and social service organizations, and with the Council of Churches, where

---

41 See Chapter 15, 297-324.

42 See Chapter 16, 325-344.

she became an advocate for the problems of refugees and asylum seekers.

As she grows older, Ton no longer sees her role as one of starting a movement but one of responding in more individual and particular ways to the needs of others. She still has the same sensitivity and commitment she exercised when she encouraged Imelda Gaurwa in 1970 to begin the Tanzanian Grail. She spends her days helping older Grail members who have no immediate family to care for them in their old age; assisting friends who are suffering a health crisis or are coping with a death; helping to create family gatherings and celebrations. Whether participating in a Grail group, being with her family or an elderly Grail member, Ton considers her task now to be to continue to share "from the inside" who she is, to be an inspiration to others, and to support their needs and growth.

Interview

A Goal That Was Unshakable

When Rachel Donders, the International President of the Grail, asked me if I would join the Grail even if I were not allowed to go to Africa, I told her that my ambition could not change; I had longed to go since I was a child and there was no other way.

You see, I thought I was very lucky; I had a nice family, I received a lot, I had many opportunities, and I wanted to share what I had experienced. I really wanted the world to become a better place so that everybody could eat and drink and have a roof over their heads. Of the eight children in our family, I was the only one who had this idea.

Even though I consider myself more practical than intellectual, I knew that I had to study to reach my goal. So when I met the Grail, I had finished my nursing training. I was twenty-four by then and was at Ubbergen taking languages and cultural studies in preparation. When I found out that there were Grail teams all over Africa, I realized I did not have to do it alone, by myself, but I could work with a team.

It was really the international character of the Grail that attracted me. I was encouraged to go to Antwerp for a tropical medicine course since I intended to go to Zaire, which was then the Belgian Congo. After that I spent one year at the Tiltenberg.

The Beginnings of a Dream Fulfilled

In 1958 I finally left for Africa. I went first to Usumbura, Burundi, with a small Grail team consisting of Hilda Canters and Hanny Doesburg and two teachers from Burundi. It was quite new for the people there to work with three unmarried women who were also lay people. They, of course, had seen nuns and they had seen priests but they had no idea that we were living in celibacy. They always asked the same questions: do you have children? How many?

We worked with young girls, with married women, and with the family movement where we realized it was quite difficult for women to speak for themselves when men were around; they were very shy. We saw that it was too early to start with families; we had to start first with just the women. So we began by encouraging the women to talk, but they told us that their husbands were not happy; for the men, just talking was a waste of time.

So we began to teach the women some practical things to take home. We also talked about marriage, childbirth, the anatomy of the body, about different celebrations of Easter and Christmas. And then came the time when the women said they wanted to discuss things with their husbands. This moved very slowly but eventually we had meetings together.

An interesting experience I had was around language. I knew French but I needed a translator for the local language, Kirundi. When the African woman who was my translator agreed with what I had said, she just translated it. But if she thought it was wrong, she began by saying, "She said—" She didn't want to take responsibility.

Burundi is a beautiful country. We lived together in a more or less Dutch community, as well as with the two teachers from Burundi, Agnesi and Adele. Later I always lived with the Africans. Our surroundings were very lively with lots of noise and music. On one hand, I loved it, but to get some quiet we retreated for weekends to a Jesuit college.

After a year, Rachel came and said there was need for a nurse in the Congo right away. I was ready to go. I had already learned Swahili and I had all the credentials for the job, especially the medical work. I would also be in a hospital in Kasongo just three miles from a sanatorium where another Grail member, Sis de Klerk, was working.

The hospital I went to belonged to the Belgian government, and the White Fathers wanted the Grail to be in there to provide an entrée to the patients, so they could say Mass for them and give them the last sacraments. So in 1959, I became the matron of the hospital; there were three of us from the Grail and I was the youngest of the team and had never been in such a leadership position before. We made very good salaries, so the five of us, including the two Grail members who worked at the sanatorium, lived together and sent money to Burundi for their work. Knowing that we were helping in this way made my work easier.

Of course our work in Congo was very time-consuming and we had heavy responsibilities, so we did not even attempt to start a movement. We began each day with an hour of prayer and meditation, followed by Mass; then we started our work.

The hospital was very poor. People were lying around on mattresses without sheets, and food was served out of pails. We did not even have a phone; this was real bush country. We were very much with the African people. The five of us went to Mass together on Sundays and celebrated together. We were each other's support. The other Europeans were the real colonials with their own separate lives and their parties.

Things really went smoothly until one year later, June 30, 1960, which was the date of the independence of the Belgian Congo. At first we celebrated with the African staff in the hospital and felt that the time had come for them to take the responsibility. Then we heard the speech by Patrice Lumumba in which he said he was against the whites. We were very shaken. Here we were clapping for independence and looking at pictures of a new flag being raised while standing in the midst of blacks and being told that they should be against whites. They were against the whites and the colonials.

It was a disappointment, a disillusionment, and suddenly it was true, I had a white face. We just couldn't talk about it. Eventually the doctors told us that we should leave for the sake of our safety. There wasn't even an airport in Kasongo. When a plane landed at night, cars went to the landing strip and turned on their headlights so the pilot could see where to land. None of us in the Grail had any experience with revolts or uprising and we didn't know what to do. I felt terrible.

Then a white Belgian bishop came and asked us, "Are you here for the money, or are you here for the people?" That is just what we wanted to hear; we wanted to stay. Planes came and took the women and children and when the fifth and last one came, it left without the five of us. We stayed another month until the news came that things were much worse and then the bishop told us that we had better leave.

By then Rachel had sent us a telegram saying, "Please try to leave." And radio calls came from Hilda in Burundi; she was very frightened. At that time, I had never felt in such harmony with life and death. I thought, "I am not afraid to die; I am ready." The five of us were ready to give our lives at that moment. I don't know how to express it, but there was a certain feeling as though I have never felt so close to anyone as I was to those four people that last week in Kasongo.

Very early on July 26, taking very little with us, we left for Burundi in a small car that Hilda had sent us, along with a White Father and a White Brother. As we were leaving, people in the hospital asked us who would take care of them. We cried as we left.

I had never been in such a difficult situation in my life. We couldn't ask anyone's advice. We were taking responsibility at that moment, and we were taking the consequences. We spent two days on the road. When we arrived in Burundi, we met the bishop and doctors from Kasongo who told us that by ten o'clock on the morning we left, soldiers had come and ruined the hospital and people had been killed. They, themselves, had escaped by plane. Even though this kind of thing has happened more and more in the world, for us this was a first experience of it.

The Worst of Times Before the Best of Times

I took over the big Grail training center in Muranvya, Burundi, while Hilda Canters went home on leave. We lived together, five Africans and five Dutch people, while we shared life and responsibility for working with women and girls. We had a real community.

Together with two African girls, I also ran a radio program for women. I did the arranging and they did the talking about health issues, hygiene, nutrition ideas, the importance of planting gardens, how to celebrate the feast days, family prayer, and so forth. We became known through this program and as we went out in our little car to give one- or two-day courses as follow-up, people would recognize us because of the radio program.

We often slept in a school or at the mission. Our audiences were very eager. Hilda had passed on some strategies from the days of the Dutch Grail youth movement, but for me it was all new. A few African women helped with the training. They were both teachers and staff since they shared in the responsibility and got an education at the same time. Now we were trying to build a movement. But this didn't last for very long.

When Hilda returned, I went back to the Netherlands for my first leave. Three days after I left, Sis de Klerk was murdered. The person who killed her had to go right through my room to reach her. She was my best friend and the only girl child of her parents; she had only one brother. I had to phone her parents to tell them and then visit them in England. It was a very hard time.

However, I stayed a year in the Netherlands and helped introduce student nurses from Tanzania to Dutch culture. A Dutch doctor in Tanzania who wanted to build a hospital with good trained nurses had sent them. I met these nurses years later in Tanzania.

The center in Burundi was closed, but after a year I went back because I had this need to find out what really happened to Sis. The hardest part was that I never did find out. When the call came from Tanzania that a nurse was needed, I went.

Tanzania: "These Were the Most Important Years"

Magdalena Oberhoffer was International President at the time the bishop of the Tanzanian diocese of Moshi, Joseph Kilasara, told her that he wanted "all the flowers of the church," and therefore he wanted the Grail to come to the foot of Kilimanjaro. There were two others, Joke van Neerven and Imelda Gaurwa, a Tanzanian who had trained with the Grail in Uganda but had never had the chance to work with the Grail in her own country. This would be her first experience. We went to Rombo Mkuu to work in a dispensary and maternity ward where African nuns (nurses) who were not qualified had been working. There were no doctors.

Joke took care of the women's and maternity wards and I did the dispensary and the men's ward. Imelda started with the women, training them with classes and courses. We also trained young African women as nurses. We had twenty-four-hour a day duty, seven days a week. The three of us were living together and the door was always open, and often we were called in the middle of the night. If we had cases we couldn't treat, we sent them by bus or car to Moshi, sixty kilometers away. The doctor came once a month and she was very helpful. We learned a lot from her.

However, we had problems with the parish priest who first insisted we have an x-ray machine so that people could be charged a fee that would go toward his school. We did not agree with him. Then he wanted a permanent doctor to build up the hospital. The government told us that a hospital would be built three miles away and we would be a health center and also a training center for midwives. We loved this idea, but the priest did not agree. It was obvious we had to leave.

Magdalene asked all of us if we wanted to go to another country. And I said, "Magdalene, I want to stay in Tanzania because of Imelda." She had lots of contacts by now and I wanted to continue with her. If I had not stayed, she would have gone back to Uganda.

The White Fathers had already asked us to run a bookshop in Moshi. In a way, I was the person for the job; the White Fathers had already a bookshop in Tabora with its own printing press, and my father had a printing press and my whole family were business people. And so I said, "I am going to try it." I told Magdalene that

I would go to the bookstore just long enough for Imelda to get a position in her own country and until someone else was trained to take my place at the bookstore. I stayed seventeen years.

In 1965, Imelda and I went to the bookshop. She helped out in the mornings and in the afternoons she went out with the women and girls to start her training. For her the bookshop was a kind of entrance to her real work. And it provided us with a little more income. We got an apartment and a car.

People who came into the bookshop often saw me as a nurse and I could converse with them on their health problems in Swahili. But I was a complete blank concerning a bookshop. I love reading, so I started to read a lot. I went to different schools and asked for a syllabus and asked what books they needed. I went to different families to ask about books, especially for names of good authors, including those of children's books. I wrote to Beatrice van Voorst tot Voorst in the Netherlands, asking her to help me set up a bookkeeping system. So with all this help I managed to run the bookshop.

Before long, the shop became a local meeting place for providing information and observing people as they came into the shop and seeing how they were doing. How was their health, could they understand? And we would spend time talking. New people in town would ask for directions, where they could find so and so, where they could buy this or that—just about everything. And we always had coffee available.

Imelda continued in her work with women. The bishop was so pleased with what she was doing that he gave her extra financial support so that she could get out of the bookshop more. Then another person, Honorata Mvungi, was sent by the bishop to live with us. Honorata was looking for something and he thought she would be a good Grail member. She came to live with us and worked as a catechist.

We lived together, we ate together, we prayed together, we got together for Mass every day. Imelda told me her stories about what she was doing and about the women, and I told her my stories. But I made no interference whatsoever with her work. One of the biggest challenges for me in Africa was to allow others to use their talents—if there is nobody who can do this better at the moment, then I will do it, but if there is someone who can do it, I will let them do it.

The African Grail Belongs to the Africans

At a certain moment a Dutch bishop came to me and asked if I would come to his diocese to train young women in Kisekibaha. He felt they were not challenged enough and we could be a great influence. I was thrilled. Coming to this bookshop had not been in vain. This could be the official start of training for women in Tanzania. Now the bishop thought that I would come to his diocese but I told him that Imelda would come with Honorata; Honorata had been with us over half a year and Imelda was ready. They would start the training, I would go on with the bookshop. And the bishop agreed.

Imelda and Honorata went to Kisekibaha on May 10, 1970. It was the first time a center had been started by Africans. In the past, an American team or a Dutch team started a center and then it was Africanized. This one began at Kisekibaha with five young girls plus Imelda and Honorata.

I followed the growth of the center with great interest and went there on some weekends. I took part whenever they asked me to but never interfered or criticized or made remarks, even if I thought I would have done things in a different way—the Dutch way. I thought what I thought and never interfered. For instance, I would have prepared the whole center before the girls arrived for training. That was not their way. The girls came and certain things took years, such as getting mattresses for the beds, having storage space for girls to store their things, cutting the grass.

What I realized was that when the Grail was started from the outside, even though the women were doing their best, things seemed to go down. Then the Africans would take over and do things in their way and things would go up. Now with Kisekibaha there was a difference; things never went down, they went up from the very beginning. Since 1970 until now, it has always been their way, the African way, perhaps slow but always African. This has been very important and I learned from this.

Part of the Tanzanian Grail's uniqueness in Africa is that there is a strong Nucleus. In fact, in the beginning it was all Nucleus. Imelda felt that the culture with its lack of experience with lay people and especially unmarried women pointed to a need for a strong spiritual education for single women who did not want to be nuns. She thought they needed to be able to be together in community so they could live a religious life in one way or the other. The Tanzanian Grail cannot do without the church; it is so much a part of their life patterns. All things are done from within the church.

The training for the Nucleus lasted for three years and the ones who didn't feel at ease left. Those who left to marry did not keep in touch with Nucleus members since there was no place then for them as married women in the Tanzanian Grail and many of them felt they had failed. This has changed; there are now several married members in the Tanzanian Grail. In Kenya, nearly all the Grail members are married and in Uganda there are both married and Nucleus.

I became a Nucleus member while I was in Burundi. Rachel came and we drove to Uganda where I made my dedication in Dutch. I wanted a lifetime dedication; it fit with what I thought my vocation was and I saw my work in Africa as a lifetime fulfilment. Today things are changing and I don't see as much need for making any distinctions between those who are in the Nucleus and those who are not.

Another unique aspect about the African Grail is their sense of togetherness, their wholeness. Meetings never started at the appointed time; people spent time talking with one another, not only about who you are and what your work is, but getting involved in the background of each person, giving advice, sharing news about the harvest, becoming comfortable with something to drink and eat.

It is a more humane life. Emphasis is on the value of the person. We Europeans are so work-oriented. There it's people first and then your work. In West Africa, which is very capitalistic, the women are much more independent. But in East Africa, there is more socialism, more community, and for a long time there was no difference in Tanzania between the rich and the poor.

However, the women have a harder life. While I was there, we fought for a better life, not because of feminist theology but for more to eat and a better way of life and more education for their children. We worked for recognition of women's influence, but it was not until I returned to the Tiltenberg and was exposed to feminist theology that I became more conscious of women's issues.

At the same time, the Africans are not as critical as we are. They are so gentle. They live with simplicity and even the poor share what they have. I would love to have brought these values back to the Netherlands with me. I wanted a simple place but people kept telling me that I needed this and I needed that. And of course, you want to live life as a normal Dutch person.

During my time in East Africa I lost my father, my mother and one of my sisters. In that time it was not done to go back to the Netherlands for the funeral.

Culture Shock: The Netherlands Revisited

When I came back to the Netherlands in 1980, after realizing the bookshop needed to be Africanized, one of the hardest parts was hearing so much criticism and finding that the Tiltenberg, where I was asked to live, was not really a community. It was a conference center. There was not much of a Grail movement in Holland and, at first, I did not know many Dutch Grail members. Many changes in the church and in the Grail had taken place over the past years: the Vatican Council; many people had left the Grail; priests were marrying. The first year was very difficult—it has no comparison.

I stayed at the Tiltenberg until 1988 and was able to be a support to the older members who had given their lives to the Grail in the Netherlands. There was a strong Nucleus in the Netherlands without a strong movement. Those of us with the energy and training had gone out to other countries and the ones who stayed in the Netherlands were involved in professional life. By telling them about the growth of the Grail movement in Africa, they saw that their lives had not been in vain. They had made the expansion of the Grail a possibility.

It's because of them that I have never seen myself starting a Grail movement here. I saw all these old women around me and thought, well, they have given their lives. I want now to help them, to assist them. I want them to die in peace and know that their lives have not been in vain. This is my present involvement with the Grail in the Netherlands and I do my best. I also visit the elderly in nursing homes and hospitals. I am in the diaconate so I help with the prayers and do the readings. I also help with communion.

I became a member of the national team and we had to make decisions around the continuation of the Tiltenberg that I opposed for a time. But Mimi Maréchal, Carol White, and Trees van Voorst tot Voorst were really fighting to keep it. So I supported the decision of the national team to give them the chance and all the freedom they needed. However, I had the feeling that I was living in an ivory tower and that I was not really sharing my life with others, so I made the decision to leave the Tiltenberg. In January of 1988, I moved to Voorburg where I had my very first experience of living alone. My family loves to visit me here. They feel that it is my house and has a spirit reflecting my lifestyle. Since coming back I spend time with my five sisters. We meet every two months for a whole day together. I also got a paying job with Caritas, working with asylum seekers and refugees, so I was back in the international scene.

I also belong to the Eighth of May movement, working for change within the church.[43] If we wait for permission from Rome, things will never change. We need to be moving within the church. I am interested in other religions and I realize had I been born in Japan, I would have had another belief. But I was born in the Netherlands and I have to face this. However, I suffer from the church I love and sometimes I feel ashamed to be a Catholic. How can Rome do some of things they do? I do feel the importance of being a member of a community, to have good friends to talk to about your concerns, to have people with whom you are striving for a better world and for more justice.

I have been back several times to Tanzania and I have attended International General Assemblies where the Africans were as well. Things have changed. Early on, the Africans had less influence and they found the meetings hard; the discussions were too quick. Then I could identify and I felt more like an African.

---

43 The Eighth of May Movement was a Dutch Catholic reform movement, the formation of which was stimulated by the visit of Pope John Paul II to the Netherlands in 1985 and the silencing of feminist theologian Catharina Halkes. It was disbanded in 2003. "Eighth of May Movement," Wikipedia: The Free Encyclopedia, accesssed November 18, 2016, https://en.wikipedia.org/ wiki/Eighth_of_May_Movement.

When I was working with Caritas I heard for the first time of the trafficking of women and was confronted with one of the victims. I was shocked and proposed a plan of action to combat trafficking at an international Grail meeting in 1988. I was convinced that the Grail, as an international women's movement active in countries where the victims of trafficking were attracted under false pretences and in countries to which the victims were brought, should take international action.

I continued to do so at all the following international Grail meetings. But it was ignored; trafficking in the different Grail countries did not exist, or so it seemed. It was only in 2004 we had a Grail meeting in South Africa where I found a newspaper with pictures of girls found in a hotel being victims of trafficking. From then on trafficking was recognized in Kenya, Uganda, and other countries. In 2006 at an IGA in the U.S.A., Human Trafficking became an official Network of the International Grail. For twelve years I also worked as a volunteer on the pastoral team in the prison in Scheveningen with drug users who wanted to kick the habit. And when we got the new Grail house in Utrecht in 2004, the Secretariat of the International Grail that I had taken care of since 1988 was moved there.

The most difficult day in my life was the twenty-ninth of July 2008 when I had to bring Beatrice van Voorst tot Voorst to a nursing home here nearby. I go to see her twice a week and help her with the food. She is a nice-looking lady sitting in a wheelchair, well dressed, but not speaking anymore and not recognizing me.

I am grateful for each day I get up in the morning and my whole body is working. I thank the Lord and promise to do my best.

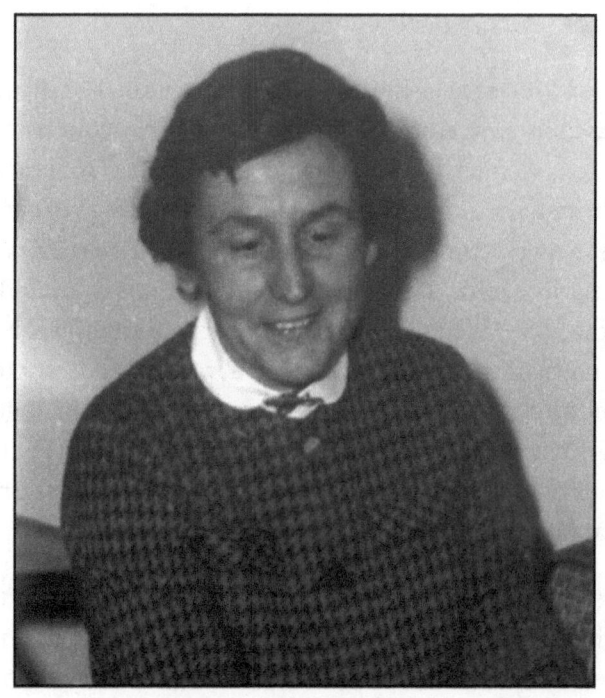

Magdalene Oberhoffer, Paris, 1963

9

Magdalene Oberhoffer

The creativity that comes out of community is very special. It's the character of the Grail. This is our strength.

Magdalene Oberhoffer, the first medical doctor to become a Grail member, was attracted to the Grail because of her desire for a more contemplative life. However, within a few weeks of making her dedication in the Nucleus of the Grail in 1954 she left Germany for Africa to become the medical director of a hospital in Kampala, Uganda. With specialized training in tropical medicine and obstetrics she was prepared to work with the most critical medical needs in that part of the world.

Because of the Grail's multi-pronged mandate, Magdalene became part of a growing community development team whose focus was on the education of local women and their families. So for the next several decades Magdalene committed herself to the needs of this expanding Grail community in Africa. Her talent for balancing dual roles, her affinity for the peoples of Uganda and her ability to work with Grail members from various professional backgrounds and cultures who were coming to work in Uganda, led to her appointment as the first national leader of the Ugandan Grail.

Magdalene's work in Africa was interrupted from 1961 to 1967, during and just after Vatican Council II, when she was the first non-Dutch member to serve as International President of the Grail. For these years she guided the Grail through its most difficult period, a time of both great upheaval and challenging new trends. After serving as president of the International Grail, she returned to Rubaga Hospital in Uganda, where she served until 1975. When she returned to Germany, Misereor, a German-based lay mission group, recognized her unique international background and invited her to work for them; Magdalene remained with Misereor until 1988.

Magdalene's sense of service, her adaptability and her willingness to risk certainty for the unknown had their roots in her childhood. She was born in Bonn, Germany, in 1923, the youngest of three children and she grew up during the Nazi era. She remembers those years as "a time of suppression—a most terrible time."

The war touched Magdalene's family and their lives in many ways. From the beginning, her parents were not supporters of the Nazi party. Her father was active in Zentrum, the Catholic party. He would not subscribe to Nazi newspapers and his refusal to join the Nazi party prevented him from receiving promotions in his profession as a high-school teacher of languages.

Magdalene realized that her father suffered for this. She recalled that at first her parents spoke French when they discussed politics around the table. When the children went to school and learned French, her parents started speaking in English. But as time went on, the children knew what was going on, so, as Magdalene said, "they had to live a double life." Later her brother who was a medical doctor had to go into the army. Her mother's brother, a priest, spent five years in concentration camps where many died, but he came out alive. She also lost a cousin in the war, another priest. "Two hundred young priest theologians were killed. A whole generation was lost," she recalled.

Despite the fear and hardship resulting from the war, Magdalene grew up in a home and community of friends surrounded by a sense of security. She, her brother and sister were able to sustain a sense of their own interior identities, a sense of who they were and what they could do. Since her family came originally from Trier, the oldest once-Roman city in Germany, they had a great interest in history.

Her father's profession of teaching languages also provided Magdalene and her siblings with what she described as an international outlook. She credited her parents for creating stability within the family by living out their own values and giving their children love and the confidence and freedom to make their own choices. She described them as two people "whose love stayed with them all of their lives." Her memories of childhood include the fun and humor they shared as a family.

Religion and religious practice were taken for granted. The children attended Catholic schools and daily Mass. A Catholic culture was integrated into the everyday life of the home. For instance, feast days, such as Christmas and Easter, were celebrated with special foods, decorating the house, lighting candles and much singing. Both her parents loved music and Magdalene says that she could sing before she could talk, a talent she developed and continued to share with others.

Magdalene was an avid reader when she was a child. She was especially fascinated by books about the life of Francis of Assisi and the writings of the mystics such as Teresa of Avila and Thérèse of Lisieux. By the time she was ten, her uncle, a priest, was giving her theology books from his library for her to read.

Early on Magdalene excelled as a student. Like her brother and sister, she decided on medicine as a career. Her decision to study medicine was influenced by the destruction of war and her desire to do something practical and close to human needs.

At the end of the war, the Allies took over the Oberhoffer home for fourteen days that extended to four years. So her family moved in with another family. This move brought about her meeting the Grail in 1946, just a year before she took her medical exams. A German Grail member, Alberta Lucker who lived in the house opposite to where the Oberhoffers were living, had joined the Grail in the 1930s and gone underground during the war. She saw that there were students living opposite her house and she invited them to her house for discussion and song.

Eventually the third floor of Alberta's house became the official Grail flat, hosting on-going meetings. This first post-war Grail group was called the "Kleine Kreis" or the "Small Circle," where young women who were searching for a greater meaning to their lives studied and discussed the works of Daniélou and other theologians whose thinking was influencing modern approaches to missionary work and reform in the church around the world. Often Alberta invited some of these well-known theologians to the flat and the women made retreats. It was here that Magdalene was exposed to international visitors hosted by Alberta who held positions with the Central Committee of the Catholic Church in Germany. in the Department of Foreign Relationships.

Although Alberta was not, according to Magdalene, in the "recruitment business," she brought many women to the Grail. She arranged for a dozen of these women to go to Holland in 1950 for a retreat at the Tiltenberg, the Grail's international center in the Netherlands. By now, Magdalene was working at the university hospital in Bonn but she made herself free for this trip. She was astonished that they did not meet any enmity in Holland despite the terrible suffering the Dutch had experienced during World War II as a result of the German occupation. Her visit to Holland and her stay at the Tiltenberg convinced her that she wanted to join the Grail Nucleus, the committed celibate core of the movement, despite earlier leanings toward marriage.

So a year later, since Germany did not have a Grail training center, Magdalene left Bonn for a year's training at the Tiltenberg. This time of spiritual formation in an international atmosphere that included silence, prayer, and Bible study and fasting, created a valuable and lasting foundation. Her initial aversion to organizations of any kind resulting from the Nazi regime was overcome by what she saw at the Tiltenberg as "the tremendous democratic principles" of shared work with "the free movement of women working together."

Shortly after this year, she and an American Grail member, Dolores Brien, were sent to Germany at the request of a mission institute whose leaders had heard about the Grail. Here they helped with the spiritual training for young persons preparing for medical and health professions and eventual work in the missions. Around this time, Grail leaders Lydwine van Kersbergen and Margaret van Gilse had returned from Africa and the Grail had been accepted by the White Fathers to work with them in Uganda. So, having completed three years of training, Magdalene became the first post-war German Nucleus member and a short time later was sent to Africa, an assignment she was very pleased to be given.

After thirty-four years of international service, Magdalene retired in 1988 and in 1993 moved back home to the Rhineland, to Königswinter, a small town across the Rhine River from Bonn where she grew up. She described the final decades of her life as a "marvellous new chance to be free and to do what I like and to shape my life—an opening." In many ways, retirement for her was a continuation, "a deepening and a widening" of what attracted her to the Grail in the first place, the opportunity for prayer and to have a more contemplative life.

Magdalene lived for almost a decade in Königswinter, continuing her lifelong involvement with the Grail and consulting with Misereor. But her life was more and more focused on silence and prayer. After several annual retreats with the Carmelite nuns at their convent near Dachau, the former concentration camp in

Bavaria, she moved there as a permanent guest in 2001. In June of 2008, while visiting her niece in Heidelberg, she suffered a heart thrombosis brought on by a treatment for kidney failure, and underwent several cardiac surgeries. By autumn, her condition had worsened, so she was unable to return to the Carmelite convent. On October 21, the Munich Grail group celebrated Magdalene's 85th birthday with her with a Mass in her hospital room.

Magdalene ended her days at the nursing home of the Sisters of Charity in Adelholzen, not far from Dachau. She died on December 2, 2008, surrounded by Grail women who had accompanied her on her journey as well as the prioress of the Carmelite convent. She is buried in the Carmelite cemetery at Dachau. Grail women from around the world mourned the loss of this vibrant woman of vision whose faithfulness to her convictions yielded a rich and meaningful life and continues to make a lasting contribution.

Interview

A Time of Decision

When Alberta Lucker organized a trip to Holland in 1950, she very cleverly combined it with a retreat. It was just after Easter and it was tulip season. We came to experience that famous Tiltenberg. It wasn't only a retreat; we were also shown the Grail Missionary Training Center at Ubergen that had been started in 1947 by the Grail.

I knew right away that I wanted to join these women in a more total way. I was interested in other countries and I had a desire to help people in some way. I was fascinated by the richer view these women had, their vision, and their internationality, that worldwide church. I certainly did not want to be organized since the Nazis had organized everything. When I met Rachel Donders I told her that I was not coming for activism but for the prayer life and for joining a group of women motivated for the sake of the kingdom of God.

On February 2, 1951, I went back to the Tiltenberg. It was not a difficult decision to make but it did mean "breaking bridges" since I had always thought I would marry. I left the work I had been doing as a physician in order to be available for the Grail. Our availability was really radical. After a year of spiritual formation, Delores Brien and I were sent to Germany to give spiritual training to young women going overseas mostly in professional capacities for mission work. They were not Grail people.

My African Experience

Then it was decided that I would go to Uganda. I prepared medically by coming back to the Netherlands for training in tropical medicine and obstetrics. On the twenty-second of July, 1954, the feast of Mary Magdalene, I made my dedication in the Nucleus of the Grail. By the beginning of August I was on the boat with Elizabeth Weigand, another German Grail member who was a health professional; we were bound for East Africa.

We worked with the first African bishop, Josef Kiwanuka. He and a Canadian, Archbishop Cabana, had invited us. Kiwanuka wanted to open a school but Cabana wanted us to develop his hospital in Rubaga, which had many outposts. There was not a doctor there when we came so I became the first residential doctor.

They also wanted us to begin a lay group to encourage and advance women. We later discovered that one of the greatest needs of the women in Uganda was to gain knowledge and self-esteem about their own possibilities and capacities in the household. So we had a very integrated approach.

Of course in the hospital we did nursing and laboratory training and eventually started a secondary school. But I was also the Grail leader and eventually the national leader of the Grail in Uganda. As such I had to do a great deal of travelling. Word about the Grail spread and bishops from Tanzania, from Burundi, and from the Congo who wanted the Grail to start in their countries asked me to visit. I also travelled to Kenya, South Africa, Egypt and Rwanda. And I had to travel to the medical outposts that we started. They were usually maternity dispensaries.

The hospital with its many outposts was our biggest project. I was the first residential doctor at this hospital that now [in 1998] has 300 beds. Misereor, the organization I later worked for, financed this hospital as one of their main projects and they continued to help. Before I came, an East Indian doctor, a Muslim, who had been in the country thirty years came twice a week without being paid. He attracted many Muslim patients to the hospital and they still come. He had great esteem for the White Sisters who had been managing the hospital. He was a very religious man who prayed before an operation and would pray to our common father, Abraham.

The other project was social work, which began with Joan Dilworth, from Scotland, who went into different dioceses. When she first started visiting the villages, one of the White Sisters would walk with her. A tremendous friendship grew between the White Sisters and us. Alice Dougan came later and discovered her talent for social work.

Joan and Alice helped develop a family movement and promoted better partnerships between husband and wife. It was adult education about womanhood. We always tried to combine this with a spiritual training by giving Christian symbols a practical application such as the relationship between the waters of baptism and water as used in everyday life.

Joan and Alice actually did community-development work with the women, forming hundreds of clubs, which laid the groundwork for the later introduction of primary, or community, health. The medical people coming from Europe were very patriarchal. Leadership was vertical with authority and information coming from the top down. In contrast, community development came from within. This was a tremendous breakthrough.

We then started the secondary school for girls, but not the way the British had been running them; we wanted to give it an agricultural base. So Josephine Drabek and Jessica Stuber arrived from Grailville with a tractor. The people of the village couldn't believe it, a woman driving a tractor. They marched behind the tractor—it made a lovely story.

And, of course, we tried to get these young women in the school interested in the Grail. That's how we got our first members who became nurses and teachers. Like Elizabeth Namaganda, they came from the secondary school.

Even though we did a lot of medical work and saved a lot of lives, I think the most important thing we did in Africa was the education of women, the adult education, the social work, and the secondary school. Many wonderful women have come out of these efforts. Although over thirty people from other countries came to work with us because the African women were not yet ready to take over, many of the local women were preparing as nurses and teachers. By nurturing their talents we were helping them to take over. At that time, especially in women's issues, we were pioneers. We were very well accepted in Africa. This, I am sure, was because of our approach, our immersing in the culture and respecting it, learning their language, listening to their needs and forming our work around these and not our assumptions.

Eventually those of us from Europe and the U.S. had to recede into the background, which is the modern approach. This is very Grail. There was a lot of theological thinking at the time about the future of mission work. Daniélou's theology of modern missionary work was that like John the Baptist you go, not for life, but you disappear when you see Christ coming. The White Fathers, too, wanted the Africans to become the African church and in my time we saw this happening.

Reflections on My African Experience

The political situation made our work difficult at times. When Uganda got independence and a military coup took over, it was very dangerous for the church. My African experience, though, helped me to recognize the merely relative importance of our own culture. I have seen the beauty of another culture and especially the depth of their faith. The African people I knew were amazing. I felt how naturally they were Christians. In some ways they were more Christian than we were. So this experience enriched me; it gave me another horizon for what was going on in the world and in the church.

Also, we were an international team: Americans, South Africans, British, Canadians, Dutch, Germans, Australians, French. This gave all of us a new horizon. Our approach as laypersons was quite different from the traditional missionary role. We came to help develop the church in Africa and not just serve in our professional capacities. This approach emphasized self-help rather than doing good works and giving aid. This was especially true for the work we were doing with women.

The second time I went back, after I had been International President of the Grail, it was not as medical director but to work on Africanizing the hospital in Rubaga that we had handed over to the African sisters. I also did a lot of Grail work. They wanted me to stay and did not understand why I needed to leave until I told them that I wanted to go back to Germany to take care of my widowed father. That they understood.

The Grail in Africa was by now building its own structures and Africanizing. I left Africa for the sake of Africanization. It was a sacrifice for me to let all of this go, but I knew it was the right time. When I went back to visit Uganda last year (1997), they had gone through a war in which many people died. And many had lost family members to AIDS, including Grail members.

Despite this, I think we are standing in a tremendous watershed. The strong European and American hold we, as Grail, have had is absolutely shifting in the Third World. The African women are speaking up which is a marvellous development. During the span of twenty years, from the mid-fifties until the mid-seventies, I have seen important developments taking place in Africa. The people of Africa, especially the women, became conscious of their own potential in society and the world at large.

It's not only in the Grail—we saw this in Beijing, we see it at the UN women's conferences. These women joining together, whether, they are Grail or not, would be a terrific power for good in the world. We could overcome war and the aggressions of men as they play games with war. Women have become important in bringing peace and justice to the world.

International President during Turbulent Times

In May, 1961, when I was on home leave from Africa, I was elected International President of the Grail. Grail leaders from every country were at the International General Assembly and did the voting. Although we didn't have a democratic process yet in the Grail, we did have the principle of national representation. I was the first person from outside of Holland and the first post-war member to have this position.[44]

---

44 Technically, what Magdalene says here is true; she was the first person from outside Holland to be the president of the International Grail. But this is the case, in part, because the Grail did not use the title "International President" until after World War II. The first head of the Women of Nazareth, the group that evolved into the International Grail was, in fact, a Belgian national, Margaret van Gilse. Van Gilse led the Women of Nazareth entirely from the Netherlands, however, and her title was "Mother Margaret," not "President." Donders, *History of the International Grail 1921-1979*, 6.

This was never my ambition. In fact, I wanted to go back to Africa. I was in tears. Couldn't they find somebody else? But this was the way we accepted responsibilities. A totally new phenomenon was implemented at this meeting. Two vice-presidents were elected—a French member, Benedicte Milcent, and an American, Dolores Brien, each from a different culture with different backgrounds and experiences. And previously the leader was called Leader; then it became President. This was the beginning of a much broader international structure.

One of our first decisions as a team was to move the headquarters of the Grail out of the Netherlands so that we could have more international influence and identity. The Dutch Grail not only gave full support to this first non-Dutch international leadership team, but showed great flexibility and openness to the move. The oldest Dutch members even started to learn English. Our founder, Van Ginneken, had insisted on this flexibility. "You have to be flexible. You may not give up your principles but in all other things you have to be open."

We chose a beautiful house in Paris, since Paris was so central a meeting place and seemed like a good place for entering the Mediterranean countries. At this time, I also worked to help the German Grail become a national entity with its own leadership structure. Until then all the German women went to Holland for training. We got a national center in Mulheim that became a training center for new people and for those going out to developing countries. Later the Grail developed a German profile with centers in Bonn, Münster and Munich.

By now the Vatican Council was under way. Everyone in the Grail was watching the Council and many Grail members were involved. Monsignor Willebrands, a friend of ours who later became a Cardinal, worked in the Secretariat of Christian Unity in Rome, and later became its head. He came to me and asked for two Grail members to assist him during the Council. I sent Corinna de Martini, an Italian who spoke several languages, and a Belgian, Josette Kersters. Dolores Brien attended the second session of the Council, and Alberta Lucker went to every session. Of course lay people were not allowed to attend the meetings with the bishops, and women certainly were not. We stayed very well informed, though. Alberta knew Karl Rahner, and she always got the latest press releases.

And then we started our *aggiornamento*[45] in the Grail. This had already begun for us as a result of the Council. We knew we had to adjust our concepts and our structures to the times. We needed more democratization. Rather than vertical structures and lines of authority, we needed to broaden. We need to listen to and hear the opinions of everyone. Previously, people could voice their opinions but it was the leadership who made the decisions. We began to introduce a new kind of decision-making, especially into the Nucleus.

It was a slow process since members didn't know what was meant by shared responsibility, a concept that came from the Council. And we, ourselves, were still insecure and the members didn't know what we meant. Sometimes the old ways seemed easier.

The Council declaration, "Lumen Gentium," which gave a new view of the church as the people of God in process, a people on their way, was very helpful. I know the Grail in Brazil worked for years with it. So, we were very much the Grail on the way. And we tried to apply this in our concepts of our community.

---

45 *Aggiornamento* is an Italian term meaning "bringing up to date" and used by Pope John XXIII to explain one of the purposes of Vatican Council II—to bring the Roman Catholic Church "up to date." "Aggiornamento," Wikipedia, the Free Encyclopedia, accessed October 28, 2016, https://en.wikipedia.org/wiki/Aggiornamento.

As part of our *aggiornamento*, we sent a questionnaire to the total membership, not just the Nucleus. This was a new step in the Grail. We asked everyone questions about what they valued in the Grail, what they saw as essential in our time, what is our task. The questions were under three headings: the conversion of the world, communion within the people of God, and Christian maturity.

When the questionnaires were returned, we sorted them out according to the themes, which were written up as "Guidelines of the Grail" and presented at the first International General Assembly of the Grail, held in 1965 at the Tiltenberg. The second International General Assembly affirmed this document in 1967.

The first one, conversion of the world, emphasized attentiveness to the signs of the times and actualizing proximate goals corresponding to the local situation. The value of involvement in secular as well as church structures was affirmed. Although the essential role of participation in a community was stressed throughout the document, individual commitments motivated by the common vision of the corporate Grail as a Eucharistic community were validated.

The stress on ecumenism was very strong and urgency was given to involvement in non-Western cultures. Communion within the people of God could be expressed in prayer, through quality of relationships, and through various forms of groups with respect for the individuality of each person and the value of her experience. International unity would be fostered by Grail groups being authentically rooted in the cultures to which they belonged and by the development of lateral relationships between countries.

Christian maturity, symbolized by the expression of charity in our lives, we said, involved a life-long process of growth in self-knowledge, the ability to relate to others and to respond to one's situation in the world with ultimate values. Different vocations in the Grail were seen as different expressions of the same commitment. Diversity and unity were the words. We had to provide a new structure. Within a few years we had entered ten different countries. How could we have unity without fragmentation? What was special about the Grail identity? The development of Christian community and Christian maturity through the developing of women's contribution to the life of the church and society were basic to developing new structures.

A second part of the document addressed the role of the Nucleus in the Grail as an identifiable group of women with a lifetime commitment in chosen celibacy. This part of the Guidelines was meant to give new life and vision to the Nucleus. The Vatican Council influenced a big wave of people to leave the Nucleus, beginning in 1964. One of the main reasons was that the Council updated and affirmed the value of marriage and the concept of celibacy became clearer.

I released sixty-six people from the Nucleus. I had a letter every day from someone requesting to be released. The reason was that most of them found that they didn't have a vocation to celibacy and they wanted to marry. We had a psychologist; we had some priests who were helping us. We had to meet with people, counsel them and give advice. It was another change in the times and in ways of seeing things, but these times were very hard on other members who didn't have the same insights. We saw the Nucleus dwindling like snow under the rays of the sun. Some who left were great friends. It didn't shock my faith in the Grail or my vocation or what I was doing, but it was a very hard time. It was tremendously difficult. It meant we also had to give support to those who did not leave the Nucleus. We survived and I think this was another sign of our maturity.

I think we have to remember that even though the Nucleus had had a leadership monopoly, historically they provided the continuity. During the Nazi time the youth movement disappeared and what survived was a group of Nucleus members because they had made a commitment for life. Although the women who had been in the youth movement maintained the spirituality of the Grail, the Nucleus members provided a permanence.

But recognizing the equal value of Nucleus and those who were not in the Nucleus was a tremendous step forward for the Grail. It was difficult for many people, especially in Europe. From the Americans, we got the idea of interaction, a totally new word to us. It meant that people of different callings within the Grail would enrich the Grail by interacting with one another. This was a great gift. America had a strong movement that Europe didn't have and we recognized that. I still feel that we need a Nucleus, a "fiery kernel" of one group committed for life. It may consist of married people. For spiritual reasons, I think we also need those women who choose celibacy.

I also did a lot of travelling as International President. I actually went around the world—to Indonesia, Malaysia, India, Japan, Brazil and Africa, and several times to the United States and Canada. It was a time when national groups were starting to shed the European identity and to get their own faith. I encouraged this, of course.

But this kind of opening up shook some people. It made them feel very insecure. We no longer had the strict rules; decision-making was more democratic; there were Protestants in the Grail. Things were changing. But we came through this time. I was open to change while trying to differentiate between all kinds of new ideas and discern what was essential for us, such as our faithfulness to the sacraments, to prayer and to friendship within the Grail. I think through all of this the Grail showed great flexibility.

Perhaps my greatest contribution while I was International President was my openness to change while still trying to keep the essentials. My main concern then was spiritual responsibility for Grail members in twenty-two countries, our common mission and how to live it in our time and situation. Sometimes it was like being in a big storm. However, I felt carried very much by the community and the many Grail people who were like-minded.

A Significant Turning Point

My meeting the Grail, my African experience, and the international presidency were all turning points for me in my life. Then in the late 1970s, after returning to Germany, I began another tremendously fruitful period of my life. I was invited to work for Misereor as a medical consultant. Misereor, the largest Catholic development organization in the world, was founded in Germany in 1957.

At first I was hesitant because I thought it would be a desk job, doing paper work. But it was quite different. It turned out to be a very significant time in my life. This was where I could use my past Grail experience in a very practical way and still learn a lot since it was a very human exchange. Until then, the emphasis in the church had been on giving money to the missions. However, Misereor developed the principle of people helping themselves, a policy of self-help.

Another principle was to work with the politicians to raise their consciousness as to what was happening in their countries. Rather than us going to countries and telling people what to do, people from the various countries submitted applications to us for funding of certain projects, many of them in primary health care and preventative medicine that were new at the time. People asked for health centers and for equipment such as x-ray machines. We supported the training of local village health workers and midwives, mostly women, about hygiene, clean water, and nutrition. I was in charge of the health department.

So as consultant, evaluator and advisor, I had to make the final decision from the perspective of a medical expert. Misereor was processing three hundred million marks a year and a great deal of money went over my desk into projects. I had to travel a lot and sometimes into problematic situations. We had to decide what kind of equipment was best for different areas and if people had the staff to operate it.

We also funded less technical projects such as community schools for children and for adults. And we made sure that the local people built things themselves so they would learn the skills. After careful evaluation, we funded some interesting herbal medicine projects. For instance we gave money to some Tibetan monks who had a great deal of experience in the medicine of plants and they launched a little industry.

We did this in other places, too. In one village I visited there were medicinal plants growing around the chapel so that when people came to pray they were instructed on how to use them. That's really integrated community health.

There were Grail projects funded by Misereor as well. For instance, Anne Hope and Sally Timmel wrote a very practical book on how to use the DELTA method in development work that was financed in large part by Misereor.[46] They also funded Grail member Pearl Drego's work with women in India.

---

46 DELTA stands for Development Education and Leadership Teams for Action. DELTA was the training of community leaders in participatory methods of enabling communities to read their reality and write their own history. The training of trainers program included Paulo Freire's methods of critical consciousness, simple economics, gender analysis, group processes, spiritual grounding of the work for long term commitment, organizational development, and strategic planning. Anne and Sally put this work into practice for seven years in Kenya, and then in the early 1980s in Zimbabwe. The handbooks that they used were eventually published as the three-volume *Training for Transformation*, published originally by Mambo Press, Zimbabwe. (Sally Timmel, email to Marian Ronan, November 19, 2016).

A New Focus

I returned to Germany upon retirement in 1988 and have remained as a medical consultant to Misereor's development work. Since then they have even done gender training for their whole staff. I also spent a year in Mulheim helping with decisions about what the Grail would do there. Early on I told you that I came to the Grail many years ago with the desire for more prayer and contemplation in my life, and now as an older person, it has been my wish to give this desire priority.

Prayer has deepened and simplified for me. I don't have as much formal prayer; it's more just being in God's presence. I believe in praying for others and this is also my task. The whole of the Grail is so active; we need personally and as a group to be rooted in an intense spiritual life. And for that we need prayer. Van Ginneken said that without this interior life of prayer we would lose our spirituality, since the Grail is not just a Catholic action movement—it is, first, a spiritual movement.

My happiest moments in the Grail have been in sharing with others in beautiful liturgies—with the community celebrating together. The experience of belonging to such a warm-hearted, deeply motivated international family like the Grail always fills me with joy and gratitude. That is one of our strengths that I have never found in other communities, and we should keep that intensity.

For my spiritual life, Christ is central as the human face of God. For me, God has always been a loving father. Having such faith has been easy because I had the experience of a loving family. My spirituality is also bringing me to a new kind of asceticism as I age. The physical diminishments come along in different ways than we expect. I think that as Grail we just have to be open to recognize them for what they are, and then be willing to give up certain things we were able to do in the past. This means leaving things, too, letting go. This is in a way preparing for the process of dying. This is not true only in the last stage but actually the whole of life is a process of letting go. But I think in old age we are also receiving, receiving a lot of friendship.

You also feel freer to be yourself. You have a rich harvest with many fruits to share. At the same time, you realize that life is a gift. I think older people have a certain wisdom that comes with age and this can be shared with younger women. We can learn from one another. A wider exchange between people of all ages is important. I see this happening in the Grail in many ways. Today I realize our international challenges in the Grail are different. The problems of globalization, world peace, and protecting the environment are areas where women have the potential for bringing about change, particularly if we recognize our talents and work, not just as individuals, but together.

On the political level we have come to realize that women in higher positions in society have had to imitate men. They have had to be twice as clever and work like them. This is not what we want. In the long run, we, as women, have to create another culture of working with each other. Even though it's far from being a reality, something will come even though we don't know how. I would say, "Be open to the Spirit." I think the creativity that comes out of community is very special and this is more visible now. This is our strength and it's the character of the Grail.

PART - III

The Vision Burned
(1953-1970)

Teresa Santa Clara Gomes, location and date unknown

10

(Maria) Teresa Santa Clara Gomes

*There is a Presence of the unknown,
of the ineffable that goes beyond images,
and crosses the barriers of language.*

Very often, members from afar brought the Grail to a new country. But occasionally, the women of the country themselves started the Grail. Teresa Santa Clara Gomes and her Portuguese collaborator, Maria de Lourdes Pintasilgo, were two such women. Teresa Santa Clara and Maria de Lourdes both became involved with the Grail as students in Lisbon during the mid-1950s, when Catholic Action was very much alive in universities in Portugal. [47]

---

[47] Catholic Action was the name of many groups of lay Catholics who, beginning in the nineteenth century, attempted to encourage a Catholic influence on society. "Catholic Action," Wikipedia: The Free Encyclopedia, accessed July 13, 2016, https://en.wikipedia.org/wiki/Catholic_Action. See also 2016 Introduction, vii-xxviii.

For Teresa Santa Clara, the intellectual vitality of the Catholic Action movement, with its emphasis on new ideas and new forms of community, provided a contrast to the specialization of university academic studies. She described herself as a person who never planned the future but was always open to new possibilities. She was especially drawn to the concept of the lay apostolate, with its emphasis on a lay spirituality. She credited her involvement in this movement with receiving high grades while at university, because in Catholic Action groups she learned to think for herself and take a critical approach to society.

Born in Lisbon in 1936 to parents who had emigrated from the Madeira Islands, Teresa Santa Clara grew up in a traditional Catholic home. Regular attendance at church, at Catholic schools, and in parish groups was considered a way of protecting the young, and especially girls. Teresa Santa Clara felt that the influences of her early years were formative but "only one way of being Christian."

Teresa Santa Clara's mother, a homemaker and caregiver, provided security for her eight children; her father, an engineer, encouraged his children to study. This blending of a protective milieu with intellectual challenge had a significant influence on Teresa Santa Clara's life; it contributed to her strong sense of trust in herself, enabling her to be open to the many risks she would take in the future.

As president of the university Catholic Action movement in Lisbon, Teresa Santa Clara eventually accompanied Maria de Lourdes Pintasilgo, then president of the international movement of Christian students, Pax Romana, to meetings in Austria, Switzerland, and Latin America. In the summer of 1957, on their way back from a conference in El Salvador, she and Maria de Lourdes stopped at Grailville, the national center of the Grail in the United States. Maria de Lourdes stayed a few days; Teresa Santa Clara stayed for two months.

While the Catholic Action movement had given Teresa Santa Clara a strong foundation, she was by now looking for more meaning in life. She was impressed at Grailville by this group of women from many different countries not only working together but also striving to live together in a Christian way. This was new to her. She was especially affected by the attention given to the integration of the liturgy and arts in all aspects of daily life and work.

It was at Grailville that Teresa Santa Clara was able to "capture the spirit of the Grail." She realized that through the Grail she could do something meaningful with her life. The fact that the Grail was a women's movement was not the reason for her initial attraction, but she did believe that by women combining their energy and power, they could help to transform unjust conditions in the world and create a more humane society. This was the challenge and the reward for Teresa Santa Clara and the source of her commitment to the Grail. Along with Maria de Lourdes Pintasilgo, Teresa Santa Clara made her dedication in the Nucleus of the Grail at the Tiltenberg, the international Grail center in the Netherlands, on March 25, 1961, the feast of the Annunciation.

When Teresa Santa Clara returned to Portugal as an assistant professor of the history of Germanic culture, she worked with Maria de Lourdes to start the Grail movement at the university. There was a real desire among university students to study the roots of their faith, which, according to Teresa Santa Clara, had not previously been connected to daily life or social concerns. So she and Maria de Lourdes began by forming small discussion groups for exploring contemporary issues and concerns.

Some of the discussions focused on the role of lay missionaries, a new idea in Portugal. These discussions also attracted students from other countries. The success of these beginnings had a great deal to do with the reputation both Teresa Santa Clara and Maria de Lourdes already had. They were well known and respected through their previous leadership roles in Catholic Action. Also, they found a great readiness among the young women students for the ideas the Grail was putting forth.

As the Grail grew in Lisbon, there was fear among the clergy about the emancipation of women and apprehension concerning the Grail's lack of visible connection with the official church. The Cardinal of Lisbon told Teresa Santa Clara and Maria de Lourdes bluntly that he did not think Portuguese women were culturally prepared to accept the Grail. He also told them that future Grail activities could not continue under his auspices. Therefore, they started the Grail in two other dioceses, Coimbra and Portalegre. From that time until the late 1970s, the work of the Grail in Portugal expanded beyond the university to programs with rural women. As needs and resources evolved, the emphasis also focused on professional women in more urban areas.

Teresa Santa Clara identified her return visit to Grailville in 1964 as a very significant time in her personal history. She stayed for six months and was much influenced by the ecumenical dimensions of the United States Grail. Her exposure to the thinking of Protestant theologians opened her to an expanded way of viewing other traditions and an acceptance of different ways of expressing the Spirit.

A year later, in 1967, at the age of thirty-one, Teresa Santa Clara was elected to the International Board of the Grail, a position she held until 1971. As a member of this Board she was influential in guiding the international Grail through the years of implementing new structures and guidelines produced by the *aggiornamento* meetings after Vatican II.

At the same time, Teresa Santa Clara remained active in the development of the Grail in Portugal as it, too, went through a time of redefining its mission and direction after the Portuguese revolution of 1974.[48] The political parties of the country at that time were seeking stability. In the early 1980s, because she was non-partisan, Teresa Santa Clara was one of the few people invited to put her name on the lists of the socialist party even though she was not a party member. As a result, she was elected to Parliament representing what were called the "progressive Catholics."

As a member of Parliament, Teresa Santa Clara worked on several commissions including the Commission for the Participation of Women in Society and the Commission for Foreign Affairs. Her participation in politics expanded her knowledge of the needs of Portugal. It also made her aware of the growth of nationalism throughout Europe and the world.

In 1988, when Teresa Santa Clara was one of three women elected to the International Presidency Team of the Grail, she brought a rich background from her career as well as her previous international experience in the Grail. In this new role, she was instrumental in helping the Grail acknowledge and work creatively with the increasing diversity in society and in the Grail. She was particularly concerned with attracting new and younger women to the movement. Her encouragement of honest and open dialogue and her willingness to take the risks of breaking new ground helped to build a bridge between tradition and new initiatives. The documents she helped to prepare for the 1993 International General Assembly of the Grail delineate a global vision that speaks to the most pressing issues of the time.

When Teresa Santa Clara found out in the winter of 1994 that she had bone cancer, her response was to continue her work in

---

48 The "Carnation Revolution" of 1974 replaced the longstanding Portuguese dictatorship with a democratically elected government. "The Carnation Revolution," The Association for Diplomatic Studies and Training, accessed November 18, 2016, http://adst.org/2015/ 04/the-carnation-revolution-a-peaceful-coup-in-portugal/ .

government and in the Grail. She talked in the interview below about her growth in the awareness that her own strength had never been enough to sustain her; she was a community-minded person, conscious that her strength came through interaction with others. She remarked that she was not as discouraged by her illness as she could have been; that in fact, she had accepted it quite well because of the outpouring of sincere love and concern from so many friends. It was through these many signs of love that she felt God was being revealed to her.

All of her adult life Teresa Santa Clara believed that life was permeated by the spirit of God that is manifested through humans, through nature, and through organizing and working for justice and quality of life. All of these efforts she believed are "somehow a kind of energy that reaches out into the universe, and that's what sustains us."

Shortly after Teresa Santa Clara's death on October 4, 1996, at a Mass celebrated in her honor in Portugal, a copy of a poem she wrote was shared. The last verse of this poem, "Paradise," speaks to her experience of the mystery of God: "Today? An intimate lure of soul, a sweet touch of tranquillity, the 'unbearable lightness' of experiencing/being entire—in time, in the universe, in myself, in God."

Interview

Grail Beginnings in Portugal

Although all of our work since our beginnings in Portugal has drawn from the international dimension of the Grail, we were one of the first countries where the Grail has been developed by the women of that country. We were inspired by other Grail groups and especially by Rachel Donders, who brought to us what I call the "Grail culture," and who at the same time encouraged us to develop and create our own reality.

The initial stage of the Grail in my country was to help a small group of women students who were living at our Lisbon center create an alternative lifestyle. They were taken by a cause and had a deep sense of doing something worthwhile. Maria de Lourdes and I had brought back from Grailville the idea of integrating faith into all realms of life through community living and group experiences. Therefore community building, rooted in the Christian faith and tradition, was very important. Community meant relationships; it meant exploring things together, and it implied a deepening of the very meaning of the Christian faith and its expression in our lives.

Although we had reflection groups and Bible study, lectures and common prayer, the main source of formation was our lifestyle of working and celebrating together. Symbolic language became very important in our liturgical celebrations, especially during Holy Week, as we reflected on the social problems around us. We used poetry and art appropriate to the occasion. We even chose flowers according to the liturgical seasons. We took great care for these details.

Along with building our own communities, we saw the need to open the students to other dimensions, especially for them to know their own country and its needs. To start, three of the women went to the rural area of Portalegre. The team developed a project to animate circles of women by working with them from their own needs and aspirations. Few of these women had any decision-making power outside the home. We wanted to connect human development and Christian development so that women would realize that being a Christian also meant working for their own needs and rights. It meant getting more involved socially and having a voice in their own communities.

It was a very slow work. Eventually the women organized cooperatives and later they were able to articulate that being part of a Grail circle was a decisive turning point in their lives. Many of them pointed out that the way they related to people had changed since their own sense of self-esteem had developed. They had always considered themselves inferior but through these circles they could participate in something new; they could discover themselves in new ways. They began to speak out more. One woman who had never been able to express what she had on her mind, said, "I was mute and there I learned to speak." This newfound ability had an impact on how she and other women related to their husbands, to their children, and to their communities.

What we did in the 1960s was quite pioneering; bringing the social, the cultural, and the religious into a rural area was very new. Many university students participated in the fieldwork, spending their holidays with our teams, so there was a lot of interaction that benefited everyone's growth.

This work was mostly for self-development of the women as individuals. However, in the late 1960s, we began a *conscientization* program modelled after Paulo Freire's work in Brazil.[49] These people were in situations in which they were suffering as victims of exploitation. We formed teams in both rural and urban settings to help the people identify key themes that would touch the core of their oppression.

The literacy program taught people to read and write by building on these themes. They would start with personal and local concerns and gradually, as they analyzed these problems, they would begin to grasp the political causes that were at the very roots of their situations. We had to do this work with great care and discretion because of the political regime that at that time was very

---

49 Grail teams in many countries around the world have used Paulo Freire's method of teaching literacy, based on learners identifying their own sources of social, political and economic oppression. "Pedagogy of the Oppressed," Wikipedia: The Free Encyclopedia, accessed July 17, 2016, https://en.wikipedia.org/wiki/Pedagogy_of_the_Oppressed.

totalitarian.⁵⁰ People were not used to expressing themselves and fighting for their rights. The police were following all the political and social steps we were taking. As a result of *conscientization*, some of the people became very active in the underground movements and were ready to become a part of the political change in 1974. So although we, as Grail, did not have political involvement up to the time of the revolution, our social work did have political implications.

The Grail After the Portuguese Revolution

After the revolution, there was a lot of social instability—everybody was pulled in different directions that caused a disintegration of many group efforts. People were asking, "Where am I? What is this country going to become?" We, in the Grail, had to rethink and restructure where we were going to put our energies. Even though we did not have clear social models for a socialist society, we were very idealistic. We knew we wanted justice, we wanted freedom, we wanted equal access for all.

We were studying alternative models from the political systems and experiences of other countries and we were very strong in condemning capitalism. It was during this period that we again tried to connect the Gospel to our present reality through mobile teams travelling in new areas as well as in areas where we had worked before. Through parishes and other organizations, we helped to create spaces where women could meet and talk about their role in the changing structure of the country. One of the works I was personally involved with was that of the Bible circles. Each week a Bible reflection relating to a main event in the country

---

50 This regime was the conservative Second Portuguese Republic, led by the dictator Antonio de Oliveira Salazar; in 1974, a military coup, led by military officers, ended the regime. "Estado Novo," Wikipedia, The Free Encyclopedia, accessed July 17, 2016, https://en.wikipedia.org/wiki/Estado_Novo_(Portugal).

came out for discussion. This was an attempt to connect life with the Christian faith. I think it was very successful because we used a language that spoke to both Grail women whose formation was more intellectual and with groups of women who had very little education.

As the country stabilized, our programs became more structured and institutionalized. We began to get funding from different organizations so we could have programs we had never had before. At this time, we felt that the formation of women needed more of a framework. Since many women were concerned about what to do with their children, we started a children's pre-school education program. We trained young women for two months, who then went into the communities to work with parents and relatives. By reflecting on what they could do with their children, the mothers were also led to think about their own self-development.

Some of the women who came to the Grail came through these efforts but did not live together as we had done in the past. Also, we experienced a change from our previous orientation. Our discussions were more focused on the specific situation of women in society rather than on the overall economic and social conditions. We began to analyze the sources of oppression for women. Gradually this became more and more an important part of the work of the Grail in Portugal.

There was not as much need for the kinds of pilot projects we had done in the past, so when Portugal became part of the European Union in 1985 and we had access to resources for giving shape to new projects, we developed some cultural and social programs. In Lisbon we opened the Cultural Center where people could meet and create a forum for exchange on national and international issues.

Through this forum, the woman question became more apparent and in 1989, we formed a project called Network Women 2000 that is about women's identity and change. The Network is made up mostly of professional women. It is still very alive and one of the more visible expressions of the Grail in recent years. The program is funded by the European Community for Professional Training. I am responsible for the planning of the projects. We also have women who are paid to organize and do the work.

A core group of twenty-five or thirty women meets regularly to discuss a pre-planned topic. We listen to one another, we share information and talk about what we have been doing; we take away some kind of action which usually has to do with planning seminars for other women. In 1993, we had a program, "Women and Structural Change," and in 1994, "Women and Decision-Making." This latter topic is part of a European program of consciousness-raising for women about what is called the "democratic deficit" that exists in society when women are not adequately represented in social and political institutions.

There has been a good response to these programs. About eighty to one hundred women participate. We have been gathering ideas from all over the world. What is new about these groups is that we go beyond issues of women's rights to issues of structural change. We want to make the connection between women's identity and social change by exploring how women can influence change to shape a different kind of society, not just for themselves but for everyone. We want to question what we can do and how we can reverse what is happening in society.

We have also developed a program called, "Cultural Exchanges: Currents of a Common Future," drawing women from all over Europe. About twenty women, mostly from Central Europe, have come together each summer to reflect on common trends. These meetings have connected women who want to go beyond discussions of the economic, political, and cultural dimensions of the unification of Europe. They have an interest in exploring together the meaning of their lives, the spiritual side of these realities. Although this is not a Grail network, we have taken on the organizing. These meetings have resulted in the beginnings of a Grail group of young women in Sweden. We are investing a great deal of effort in this young women's network. We may never know all the results of these efforts but I would like to see the impact the Grail has had on women, if meeting the Grail has been a turning point in their lives, whether they are part of the Grail or not.

The idea of women realizing their potential to make a specific contribution to society comes from Father van Ginneken. So for me it is interesting that this terminology speaks to us today. We are not necessarily finding answers but we are at least searching in the direction of women's power that can lead to new ways of viewing global problems, bringing about some kind of change in society.

Change has to begin through more exploration of the meaning of identity. We belong to groups but we are different individuals. Society can be enriched by these differences. For instance, the very view of faith has changed. Now people speak more of a spiritual search. We can say that in Portugal we are a microcosm of these perspectives as they are experienced differently by different people. In such a small country as Portugal, it's interesting to see the great diversity in the way women have come to the Grail, a diversity in our temperaments, ways of living and looking at our Christian roots. There are those women who are still connected to the church and others who aren't, but all identify with the Grail and with the expressions of faith that the Grail creates.

We are also aware that when we come together as women we influence one another. Personal transformation is important but we also have to acknowledge the need to bring about social change. There is a crisis in our civilization. We realize more and more that the existing model has gotten into a deadlock. It is important that new elements are injected into our societies and women have a special potential for introducing change.

International Grail and Government Experiences

In 1965 I was elected a member of the International Board of the Grail.[51] I helped to plan the 1967 and 1971 International General Assemblies. In 1968 we were going through the *aggiornamento* process, a painful time of trying to define who we were and where we were going. As the youngest member of the Board, I was faced with a great deal of complexity as we searched for continuity in the Grail.

However, the 1971 IGA was very affirming. I drafted the document, which came from this meeting, and all the countries present proposed that I be on the International Presidency Team. I didn't accept the invitation because I did not have enough experience. But I felt the vitality at this meeting and I realized how much international meetings mean in terms of giving new breadth and new dynamism to all of us. These IGAs have been marvelous experiences of seeing how women with such diversity of roots and cultural backgrounds and personal histories can come together and affirm one another.

By 1979 I was involved in Portuguese politics and so had less time for involvement in the Grail IGA occurring that year. Since being elected to Parliament I have been on several Commissions having to do with women, culture, and foreign affairs. As a member of Parliament, I have been able to combine my Grail work with political work, since my role on the Commissions have kept me in close touch with the real problems of citizens both in Portugal and in the rest of Europe.

---

51 The International Board of the Grail was not established until 1967, at an assembly in Amsterdam. It is likely that Teresa Santa Clara had, however, been involved in International Grail decisions from 1965. (Email to Marian Ronan from Australian Grail member Alison Healey, July 13, 2016.)

Even though this experience has revealed to me the limits of political institutions, I believe that it is very important for women to be involved in political decision-making. As a women's movement the Grail has gained a place in Portuguese society, not just as a church organization but also as one having a voice in the larger society, a voice for creating an alternative culture. This is unique. There are no other Christian groups that combine the elements that the Grail does or that have the same kind of presence in society.

It was in this context that I was elected to the International Presidency Team (IPT) in 1988. The challenge for me was to be able to connect my Grail experiences with those I brought from government. I was aware that nationalism was growing and that it was important to develop an international awareness in the Grail that went beyond nationalism toward greater inclusiveness. I was concerned that the Grail seemed to have reached a certain point of stability without enough effort toward developing new groups and increasing diversity. Differences can enrich rather than hinder. I knew that in the Grail this enrichment is possible because the bonds between people go much deeper than national awareness.

To deepen the cultural awareness of the Grail, we had two subcouncil meetings, one in Kenya and one in Manila, each using sensitive group processes. We really interacted and expressed our feelings, our images and our fears about one another. We discussed the differences in the ways we prayed and celebrated Eucharist, different kinds of commitment to social issues, different levels of community life, different sexual orientations, and different ways in which sexuality is discussed. We also shared memories about the images we had from our mothers and grandmothers, the kinds of women they were and how differently we experience the younger generations.

We came to realize that one thing that binds us is the common experiences we have shared in the past. Our international life is not shaped just by exchanging ideas but by experiencing things together, which is more substantial. Once we went beyond the intellectual search, we could find each other. We were affirmed in the concern for both the transcendent dimension and the presence of the spirit in our lives. The spirit is the binding force. When you go to Africa, for instance, you find women living a very orthodox Christianity that may be quite different from your own expressions. But the fact of acknowledging this diversity has not split us; this shows a great spiritual strength.

All of this was a great help to the IPT in planning for the 1993 IGA with the input of members through their representatives from different countries. That's how we came to the title of the meeting: "Women Shaping the Future: Building Justice and Solidarity, Facing Cultural Change and Contributing to the Survival of the Planet." These themes had been stated in the 1992 faith document and mission statement of the last IGA. Both have to do with our roots in the Spirit. Although the word "Christian" is not used often, there is a spiritual dynamism in those documents that binds people together. On another level we expressed our belief that planetary awareness and human rights are inclusive of all of the global problems of injustice—of the growing gaps between the rich and poor nations and the lack of basic goods that prevent people from living with dignity. We asked ourselves what we are doing to perpetuate the ways in which international trade is structured and consumption models are imposed. At the IGA we could see the Grail as a real microcosm of the world: women who came from rural areas of the world just now being touched by western consumption patterns, together with women from the sophisticated cities of the First World.

It was a rich international experience. We somehow went beyond the barrier of thinking that differences had to be answered in terms of yes or no. We really moved forward with a sense of mission, a sense that we, as women, have something to bring to the world today, a sense that the Grail is still alive with a future. The meeting brought people together with a great respect for one another. This Assembly, and my whole experience on the Presidency Team, went beyond my expectations.

I think the difference between the climate of the previous IGAs and this last one was a good barometer to measure the progress we had all made in functioning as a diverse group. It was a time of overcoming fears and resentments and really being open to the Spirit as it speaks to us in our time. The 1993 meeting brought a new trust into the Grail, trust in the future as worthwhile, trust that there is room and there are enough challenges for new people to be incorporated. That's very important. Otherwise we were just a surviving institution, and that was not what we wanted.

It was a privilege to be part of this historic moment where this diversity was confronted and collectively faced. We could say how much we could encompass while making the effort to remain as open as possible. We especially had to affirm what we had in common without levelling our differences, without wanting everyone to do or live in the same way.

These issues were very alive while I was on the IPT. I think I helped maintain the openness and encouraged the inclusion of different trends. I helped develop two trends reflected in the 1993 IGA. First, that the Grail is not just living from the past—there is a future. Outreach and expansion, something we could hardly speak about a few years ago—gained a new impetus. Secondly, this future is not going to be a uniform, predictable reality but will be open in many ways. We just have to let ourselves be transformed by what we live. It is good to see that these seeds are developing. And that is the result of the new wave of spirit in the Grail. We have new groups coming in with their own cultures and personalities.

Another Turning Point

All of this has given my life continuity——the human bonds with the international people I have worked with and my history with the Grail in Portugal. I have a deep loyalty to this group that has formed me. The other has been my fidelity to my Christian roots; they are so deep down, I can say that I drank them with my mother's milk.

My identity comes from that rootedness in the Christian tradition. My life expression has come from the message of the Grail. For me this personal faithfulness to life, of accepting it and feeling gratitude, is very important, especially now when I am so aware of the limits of life.

I want to get acquainted with death in a new way, as a natural part of life rather than the end. I want now to be prepared for a new stage. I'm leaving my political life and my professional life in one year. Then what? How am I going to use my energies? I don't know what's coming, but this phase of my life is a passage. I have been giving the whole idea of separation a great deal of thought. What will my next stage of life in the Grail be?

I have been on the "doing" side of things in the Grail—providing, organizing, helping. A lot of people depended on me. I was in the Grail in Portugal, so my presence was important for getting things done, for keeping people together, for a certain sense of being useful. I liked that or I wouldn't have done it, but at times it has been a burden to always have the responsibility for the administration of projects.

I'd like to have another kind of experience in the future that would have less tension. I really feel I'm at my last stage and the fact that I got sick makes this more concrete. There are demands that come through this kind of work that have been structured by life. Once these are not there, I may have a feeling of freedom.

This is a major turning point for me; I don't know where it will lead me, that notion of the definitive, the limits of life and facing death. I've never predicted or anticipated my future; I have not been a person to make plans. I have always been open to what life is at the moment. Therefore, I have never thought very seriously about death.

Now I am more aware. I want to get acquainted with death in a new way. I want to look at it as natural, as a fact of life, as a part of life rather than just the end. I think we have to live life as long as we can. Life is a gift as long as we are alive, so it's that gift we are called to live. It's not to concentrate on death. It is just being more receptive to the idea that we are trying to live it and at the same time know that life will have an end that may be soon. You need to have a reason to be alive, that's very important. After you have more of a sense of the end, you need to have a reason that sustains or leads you into life.

This is a letting go and at the same time I am so aware of life as a gift. What I am experiencing strongly at this moment is a feeling, an awareness of the goodness of God. I find it's a miracle that we are alive.

Many things I just did not see; I have taken a lot for granted. Now having friends, having people who support me, this is an enormous gift. After my operation I realized I was born again to many things. Just breathing the spring air and receiving flowers from my friends, receiving all those signs of generosity and deep friendship from so many people was a fantastic experience.

Through this I became more aware of the goodness of God. I have experienced many important things I cannot put into words. There is a presence of God who sustains, God who nourishes. I sense this presence very strongly at the moment. The signs of deep friendship from so many people have overwhelmed me.

This recognition has extended to all expressions of my life. I am looking at the suffering and goodness of people with new eyes. I see the goodness of people better than I did before. At the same time I see more clearly the solitude and suffering of others. We can speak of charity but until I had the real experience of dependency, these words did not mean the same for me.

There was a time when I was more Gospel-orientated and now my awareness is of the presence of God, of Spirit, of the unknown. We can use images but this is really about images beyond words; I have experienced this presence of God in many ways.

Today there is a tendency to find inspiration in other religious traditions that speak to the presence of God, each one in its own way. Young people today are looking for something; there is a wealth in the Christian tradition, not just the tradition as it has been lived in the recent past but what has not been explored. The Grail could probe this richness and create possibilities, not being afraid to create new models. I think the prophetic tradition is key when we speak of young people and new ways because young people also have to find the freedom and the openness to do it in their own way. That's not always easy for the older ones like us. What is needed is a real authenticity in the search. New generations are prepared, I think, to be original and authentic in their expressions. If people are authentic when they are searching for God, I think new ways will come.

I also think that women, when facing the complexity of the world, have a more holistic approach, knowing that there are no specific answers to problems, but everything is related. For instance, women generally are more aware of the exploitation of nature, the harmony of all living beings, the way that everything affects everything else in life. They tend to have a sense of the sacred, recognizing that the energy of the spirit renews and transforms life. I would say to younger women, then, be authentic, be true to yourselves; no matter what religious expressions you use, be open to the Spirit and make this Spirit visible in the world.

Mimi Maréchal, location and date unknown

11

Marie Elizabeth (Mimi) Maréchal

The universe does not stop at the horizon of what I can see—there is something beyond.

Mimi Maréchal left the Netherlands for Japan in 1962 with two other Grail members in the hope of starting a Grail movement among Japanese women. Although this goal was not achieved, meeting Zen Buddhism in Japan radically changed her life and eventually influenced the character of the Tiltenberg and her work in Holland.

Like that of most Grail members, Mimi's spirituality in adult life and her unique contribution to the Grail had their roots in childhood. She was born the eldest of six children in the historic city of Bruges, Belgium, on February 2, 1937, to parents whose religious thinking and practice were extraordinary for that time. Gerard and Emma Maréchal were deeply committed to new trends in the Belgian Catholic Church, in particular, the liturgical renewal and the Jocist (Young Christian Workers) movement, led by a Belgian priest (and later Cardinal), Joseph Leo Cardijn.

The Catholic movement for liturgical renewal was launched in Belgium at a National Congress of Catholic Action in Malines, in 1909, where Dom Lambert Bauduin called for the participation of the laity in the "dialogue Mass." To make this change possible, he also called for the publication of missals with the parts of the Mass in Latin as well as in the vernacular to facilitate lay participation. The St. Andrew's Missal was one of the first such missals, and it was edited and published by members of Mimi's family.

Daily dialogue Mass was the core of Maréchal family life. The St. Andrew's Missal fascinated Mimi with its prayers in the vernacular. As soon as she could read she began comparing the French and Flemish versions. Even her parents' wedding in 1935 was celebrated at a dialogue Mass, a unique practice at the time. Everyone joined in the dialogue at the wedding, a practice so revolutionary that it required special permission. Growing up in a family where religious expression in the home revolved around the liturgical revival influenced Mimi's sense of religion and spirituality profoundly. A complete modern Catholicism, fostered by her parents, was integral to what she called her "very religious upbringing."

At an early age, Mimi's parents introduced her to images of God through the French and Flemish art in the ancient churches of Bruges. They encouraged her to reflect on these paintings as they took her to the twelfth century cathedral in Bruges and to the rich collections in the local museum. She describes these experiences of sitting in front of the art of painters such as Hans Memling and Hubert and Jan van Eyck as mystical, involving all of her senses and rooting her as a child in an awareness of "something mysterious beyond the immediate." It was in these churches that she also heard the music of Orlando de Lassus and other great Flemish composers. These works became, as she said, "part of my religion." She later realized that it was this art and this music that had "something to do with spirituality," something akin to the mysticism she found in Zen Buddhism.

Mimi's parents encouraged her curiosity and motivated her to use her time and energy more for study and reading than for play. Her mother was especially strict in her belief that her children should use their talents well. Even in married life Emma Maréchal had rejected the traditional housewife role. Her parents had not allowed her to study medicine so she became a nurse and at the age of twenty-eight helped start a nurses' training school from which she herself later received a diploma. She was especially interested in homeopathy and was consulted by many people, including doctors, who could find no solution to certain illnesses.

Mimi maintained that her mother had to have strong convictions to marry a man like her father who, as a young man, was "the right hand" of Canon Joseph Leo Cardijn in his Young Christian Workers' movement. As an insurance broker, her father was able to assist people through financial advice and other kinds of support in building their lives. Mimi described him as a person with a social conscience, a humble and well-respected man, always ready to help others. According to Mimi, her parents' influence was instrumental in her development of a sense of freedom and willingness to take risks, to move ahead with the unusual. She expressed gratitude for the kind of education they had given her and credits their convictions with helping her form her own creative approach to life, especially her faith in the Grail vision and its potential for growth.

Growing up in a non-traditional household did have its limitations. With parental emphasis on doing "worthwhile things," and especially her mother's admonitions not to think about parties and boys, resulted in Mimi feeling isolated from her peers as a teenager. Her education had been in Catholic schools run by nuns. She liked her studies and later chose to go into a special teachers' training college at the University of Louvain that emphasized psychology and pedagogy. Already fluent in French and Flemish, Mimi also studied German, Dutch, and English, languages she learned to speak well. The summer she was eighteen she had her first opportunity to leave home, going to Bonn, Germany, to study. There she formed a friendship with a young man whom she thought she might eventually marry.

But while attending a summer course in English at the University of Edinburgh a few years later, Mimi met the Grail. Her mother had made arrangements through a friend for her to stay at the Grail Center in Edinburgh, thinking that this would be a safe place for her daughter. Mimi arrived during an international meeting of the Grail, a five-week gathering that had brought women from all over the world. She recalled that she had hardly taken off her raincoat when she said to herself, "This is the place for me." It was the international dimension of the Grail that impressed Mimi so quickly and so deeply that she soon realized that the Grail was what she really wanted for her life

The following fall she joined the formation program at the Tiltenberg in the Netherlands, the Grail's international training center. Here she again met women from every corner of the globe and from a variety of backgrounds. Many of them had professions and were preparing for work overseas. Training consisted of a disciplined schedule of meditation, prayer, and study.

Mimi remembered life at the Tiltenberg as being very strict. During this time she was asked to go to Munich as an interpreter for a catechetical congress. There she met Japanese bishops. Although she had never planned to go to the missions as a layperson, her interest in this possibility began to grow. When Akiko Morishita, a Japanese Grail member, asked her to go to Japan she accepted this invitation rather than one to help establish the Grail in France.

In 1962 Mimi, Akiko, and Rachel Donders arrived in Japan to start a movement of women. In the excerpts that follow, Mimi discusses in some detail why their attempts at starting the Grail in Japan did not succeed. Her words also take us into the world of

Zen and the lasting influence Zen was to have on her life and her work.

Mimi returned to the Netherlands in 1973. She spent the next twenty-two years of her life at the Tiltenberg where she helped establish a tradition of Zen practice. Her growing commitment to feminism and to Zen Buddhism allowed her to speak to a generation of young women who were defining themselves in new ways.

In June of 1992, Mimi was diagnosed with incurable cancer. When an experimental drug added a few more years to her life, she found that "it was easier to prepare for death than to prepare for life again." With great courage and with her characteristic determination, she continued for the next few years to contribute to what gave her life its greatest purpose and meaning: The Grail, the Tiltenberg, and Zen. She died at the Tiltenberg on March 27, 1995, surrounded by family and friends. A few days after her death, her close friend and colleague of many years, Carol White, sent a letter to Mimi's friends around the world. She wrote that Mimi "mastered the Japanese language and then returned to Europe with Zen wisdom—together with others she helped develop the Grail's own 'women's spirituality.'"

Interview

New Horizons: On a Mission to Japan

Discovering the Grail definitely changed my life. I like to use the image of growing beyond the horizon. The Grail made it possible for me to integrate all aspects of the social, the cultural, and the religious, and to continue to grow, to stretch, always to look further. I recognize this all the time in my spiritual life; it is something I have gotten from the Grail and it is the Grail that sustains me. Although my parents had a profound and positive influence on me, I felt a need during my university years to break away from their religious ideology. Then I met the Grail and suddenly I came back to the realization that it was good to be in touch with God, with something beyond the immediate. But this vision was much broader than what I had previously experienced. Whereas my parents had tried to shield me from the secular world, what I found in the Grail was both an international meeting place of women from all over the globe and an open worldview that brought together the spiritual and the secular. Just to be in touch with these laywomen who were not pious revealed a new kind of world to me. This broader perspective was fascinating. And because of it, I joined the Grail.

My growing interest in the international dimensions of the Grail was affirmed when I was asked to go to Japan. A request had come from Sophia University for some Grail people to come to work at the university and start something with women. I was very excited. I had already heard a great deal about Japan from my family and from Akiko, so I felt drawn to that country. According to my diploma, I could teach English, German, and Dutch but I was told to first learn Japanese. In preparation, I went to the Japanology Institute at Leiden University to study the language and to learn about Japanese culture. One of the first things I heard there was that my name, "Mimi," means "here" in Japanese. So, I made that my motto as a reminder again and again that I was called there.

For the first few years we were in Japan, I taught French at Sophia University, studied Japanese, and was preparing to take an examination at the French embassy. I can't believe now how I did all of this.

In addition, of course, I made contacts with women. We organized small meetings and eventually found a house that would accommodate twenty people. There we worked with many women; we had weekend courses for them, invited priest friends to speak and we did some Bible studies. We were trying to start a movement. We had hoped there would be enough Japanese women responding that we could start a group. There were some interested women who lived with us for a while, some for a few months, some for a year. We had hoped that they would become Grail members, but we soon discovered that developing groups was impossible. Mixing all these people together just didn't work.

The Japanese collective mentality constructed around family and class was completely different from our individualistic way of bringing together women from all walks of life. People didn't want to be mixed according to our ideal of including everyone. In Japan in the 1960s, women were in an inferior place in society. Marriages were often arranged; women were supposed to stay home and take care of the children. The women wanted it that way. Although they did have some power within the family (and that is quite a position) the woman was the one to serve.

The education of women was to reinforce submissiveness toward this collective model. There were few professional opportunities with any status for women, even for those who went to college. However, in the academic field, women who chose not to marry could succeed. Again the class structure: some women were in the top-level universities. Society had a lot of respect for women who have achieved this position.

I actually tried to be in three different universities to make contacts with some of these women, but this was a very Western way of thinking. We were continually in dialogue with the women to find out what was essential, but we could not ask, "How do you feel?" or "What is the difference between you and us?" That was too rational, too intellectual. Japanese "politeness" was a very delicate thing, very much on the intuitive level. We did have a hard time adapting but we learned to live in this Japanese mentality. There are some people in Japan who know what Western thinking is and how it works, but only a few.

We tried everything but it gradually became clear that the Grail was not suitable for Japan. We were not able to find a way, sociologically speaking, to insert ourselves. Perhaps we could have been more flexible about our individualism and our emphasis on personal decision making; Japanese converts to Christianity were used to a hierarchy that also existed for women in society and marriage. Some people say that now it would be much easier. I don't know that for sure. Although the idea of the conversion of the world was weakening by the time I went to Japan, we still had a very missionary attitude.

Even before I went, I had my fears and doubts about our Western mentality. After I had been in Japan awhile, I saw that Japanese congregations, convents, and monasteries under Western leadership had been able to adapt to the Western way of thinking. We realized that the Japanese people did not have a feeling for this and therefore they suffered a great deal. I began to ask myself, "What are we doing here? We should not be telling these beautiful people that our way of thinking is better. They have so much to give us."

Also, early on we realized that there was no point in bringing Christianity to Japan. Secularization in Japan is different than it is in Europe. We knew many Japanese people not closely connected with Buddhism who wanted to rent a Christian church for marriage but wanted to be buried from a Buddhist temple. The Bible was the number one best seller in Japan; they found it inspiring but less than one percent of the Japanese were Christian. They were not attracted to the laws and directions of the church. They welcomed us, they were open, they liked Christianity—but there was not the kind of attitude that says, "I believe" or "I don't believe." That was simply not there. Missionaries, Catholics and Protestants, did their utmost, but to no avail.

However, I think I was well accepted; my Japanese was good and I worked very hard at educating myself. As a result, I could enjoy conversation. I think I could also understand the Japanese mentality quite well and probably I didn't make too many mistakes that could cause misconceptions. So despite everything, I really experienced quite a bit of mutual understanding.

I am extremely grateful to Akiko. If she had not constantly pressured us to adapt, I might have just passed through Japan like so many other foreigners without going deeply into the language and the culture. Because of the friendships I made, I don't feel cut off from Japan even though I left in 1973. I still stay in touch with many people and some have come here to visit. That was our contribution to Japan. There are friends who really got to appreciate our kind of adaptive Western way of linking up with others.

It's Japanese also to remain faithful to the end of life. So if you establish a good friendship, it will last. But I think there was also an appreciation of our way of reaching out, of getting in touch with one another and not considering one way more important than another. And since I taught French, there are more people in Japan who can speak it. I feel like the gardener who can make flowers grow in your garden; it is a contribution but of another kind.

I Discover Zen

Although we did not accomplish in Japan what we had gone for, it was there that Zen came across my path. Later I was the leader in bringing Zen to the Netherlands and to the Tiltenberg. My stay in Japan meant that I was getting introduced to this very precious meditation. That's when the language and all the contacts we had made with the Japanese people came together and just clicked.

While I was at Sophia University I met William Johnston, the Jesuit priest who was doing his doctoral thesis on a comparison between Irish mysticism and Zen Buddhism. He was getting more and more interested in Zen and invited me to come and meditate with him and several students, mostly Japanese. There were also some Western Jesuits who would join us a few evenings a week.

In its essence, Zen is a monastic form; however, there are lay people who do Zen. Zen Buddhism is one of the world religions. It can be compared with the contemplative tradition in Catholicism. Dialogue between Zen and Christianity brings out many parallels that are mutually enriching, especially the thread of mysticism that runs through both traditions. I have taken part in dialogues between Eastern and Western monks and have found that the Western monks can learn how to be truly contemplative again and the Eastern monks can learn from the Christian prophetic perspective. Christians sometimes realize the reason why they feel so at home in Zen: there is something in their own background, embedded in Christianity, that has prepared them. Zen is not dogmatic; it does not say this is the truth and you must believe it. The practice of Zen is meditation. It is a way of letting go, of getting rid of turmoil in the mind. It is not just an exterior silence, but a silencing of the mind and the senses. It is an extremely silent way of meditating, of coming to a very deep silence.

After meditating for a while I found that Zen practice was feeding my spiritual life in a new and healthy way. I was finding the mystical thread I had been introduced to as a child and which Christianity had lost. Eventually I found a teacher and then I joined a school of Zen combining Soto and Rinzai traditions that uses the koan. The koan is a riddle given to you by your teacher that cannot be solved rationally. This non-rational work helps in the silencing of the mind. It helps you to go more deeply. You meditate by just repeating the koan while you are breathing without trying to find a logical answer. You repeat this practice until the koan is "sitting in your body," so to speak. The teacher who is skilful can see how you are doing, but it is not a question of achieving anything.

It was during this time that the greatest change in my perception of God occurred. I began to let go of that longing for the kind of security the Church had taught me to seek. For me, this also meant not searching for images of God, which can be very limiting. That was both easy and difficult. I had to think to be really aware of what I needed, who I was, what I ought to be.

Even though I am not connected with the Church structure as much as in the past, I have never made a break with religion. I was strongly educated in the Catholic tradition. I try to take a free stand and a free attitude. When a Buddhist tells me something, that is just as important as when a Catholic theologian has something to share. I know there is something greater than myself and the world, this tangible visible world that I can never understand completely. I know that we are all in a presence; we are part of the whole creation of the cosmos. Thanks to my Zen training, little by little I realized that this insight has to do with spirituality. Everyone has to go through her own personal spiritual process. Zen helped me in this respect. Zen has had a profound influence on my life; I am now a real Zen person.

Of course when I was in Japan, my relationship to Zen started very slowly. We, who were connected with the Catholic Church and Christianity, now were saying that Zen Buddhism had something wonderful to give to us. It was very confusing to Japanese converts who for centuries had been encouraged to leave all of their own traditions behind. Sometimes Japanese Christians felt that they were losing their Christian roots if they even visited a Buddhist monastery.

Now there are Christian abbeys in Europe and the States where Zen is practised because even in contemplative monasteries there has often been a real lack of a contemplative life. I think for lay people, too, Zen began to answer a spiritual need, a longing for spiritual deepening, for a spiritual dimension to life which churches in the West were not responding to.

Bringing Zen to Holland

Because of the hierarchy in Zen, which is patriarchal, I have never trained to become a Zen teacher. In the beginning, at the Tiltenberg, I invited Zen masters especially from Japan. William Johnston came several times. This was quite daring; I wasn't Dutch, Johnston was Irish, we had both lived in Japan for so many years. We didn't know about the interests of Dutch people, but Johnston wanted to let Westerners know about Zen.

It worked very well. Father Enomiya Lassalle, the well-known Jesuit Zen scholar and practitioner, also came twice a year to give courses at the Tiltenberg. Over time, the Tiltenberg has become a Zen center well known beyond the borders of Holland. Thousands of people have come here from all over Europe.

For a long time we focused on the meditation practice called sesshin.[52] Later we decided to work with comparative studies and have had study weekends with different Buddhologists, as well as Buddhist and Christian dialogues. These discussions have had nothing to do with practice, so lately we sometimes combine the intellectual work with meditation. Since people are ready for this kind of experience, these undertakings have been very successful.

Adapting Zen to the West is a continual challenge. We know that adaptation does not come by studying the tradition of the East and then applying it to the West. In these postmodern times, Zen has to become something that is more universal. Basically Zen is universal, so we should not try to make it Dutch or German or whatever.

---

52 Sesshin is an intensive period of meditation conducted in a Zen monastery but, obviously, elsewhere as well. "Sesshin," Wikipedia: The Free Encyclopedia, accessed July 14, 2016, https://en.wikipedia.org/wiki/Sesshin.

However, there is a hierarchy in Buddhism, just as in Christianity, which is quite patriarchal and authoritarian. In Japan, where women are considered inferior, more men practice Zen than women. This, of course, has an effect on women since our experiences are so different from those of men.

Because of these differences, we try together to adapt Zen practice to the world of women, discerning what is essential, what is good to keep for women here in the West. We keep asking, "Where does this line of patriarchy start, where does it show?" Through our study, reading, and questioning, we attempt to apply our Western feminist insights. Thus far, we have had two conferences here at the Tiltenberg on women and Buddhism. At the last one, which was international in scope, we initiated a network for women involved in Buddhism so that we can find our way as women in the modern Western world. I can truly say that discovering Zen, and bringing Zen to Europe, has indeed changed my life. In Japan I was a teacher, educating young people. Bringing this spiritual tradition to the West has been quite different; it has been like teaching in some ways, but goes beyond that.

A Zen Person Preparing for Death

During the past two years, I experienced another turning point in my life which has helped me in my Zen practice—that of preparing for death. Friends, family members, members of the Grail, and friends from the Zen world have written, have come. Some come out of politeness, but the kindness of people is not just kindness in words. They cannot just say beautiful things any more, it's the beautiful things they do. All pretence is dropped.

We cry a lot in saying goodbye forever, we touch, and we do things we wouldn't have done so easily before. There has been a special bonding, a sense that we are doing this together, which has been very helpful. Also, in Zen we talk about death, about dropping the ego, dropping attachments, letting go. From my personal experience, I know this has to be done, for whatever talents and the powers you have when you are healthy fall away when you are about to die. Then you have to detach yourself from your own life, from everything you are and everything you have. This is a very concrete way of practising Zen. It's something that indeed you are supposed to do when you are practising your meditation, but you cannot literally make yourself die. Zen has always been a help, but in this crisis I was suddenly discovering what a very great help it was.

My struggle now is to start living again. I'm in a much more confusing situation than before. To prepare for death is easier because there is much concern in society about helping the dying; many people are there to help you. But there are no books to tell me how to start living again. When I thought I was living through my last summer and had stopped the painful treatment, I thought that at least I would have a nice summer and that would be the end.

But meanwhile, another autumn, winter, and spring have passed and now another summer is coming up, and I am better. It is not the same life as before my sickness; I certainly remain ill, but I am changed, I am sure. I think that the letting go, the detachment, is stronger now and influences me in different ways. I feel it: I'm more able to detach myself from things that I was hoping for, that I was running after before. For me now life and death go beyond that dualism which I learned early in life, namely that we are born only to reach eternal life. That is no longer my spirituality. Buddhism has inspired me with the realization that in everyone at every moment there is some death. What is spirituality then? It is dealing with life and death together as one.

It is also good that I live to prepare others a bit better for continuing what I started in my immediate world of the Grail, Zen, and the Tiltenberg. My desire to accomplish this is not so much for my own sake but because I believe so deeply in the possibilities for all of these. I have great hope that they will continue.

I was so sick before that I couldn't prepare people well enough to take over. That is something I can do now. Sometimes this is hard because I am not well enough to put much energy into it. Yet at the same time, I am concerned; this is my work to do now. Since I live here, I identify so much with the Tiltenberg, the Grail, and Zen that staying in this world is where my personal tasks lie. If I am better now, it is probably thanks to the fact I have stayed here, so there must be other work for me to do. Some people advised me when I was first taken ill that I should take time now for myself, stay in my apartment, listen to music, read, but that is so much more passive than what is happening to me.

Even when I was sick, very sick, people would consult with me about what could be done about this or that. On my sickbed, I was also thinking of possibilities, of programs. That put some life into me. Even though I was very sick for quite a while, as soon as I was well enough to get up and do something in connection with the Tiltenberg, I did it. For me, it's all connected—these tasks, my own life, and my own cure.

Concretely speaking, I have the opportunity now to help people in their thirties because they are already here. This requires an individual approach since there is great diversity. Some are Catholics and some Protestants; some have left behind the religion given to them by their parents. They come; we work together. They are people who have already found a certain orientation; they have found Zen. We work together with a Zen approach, inspiring each other in mutual ways.

My commitment has become to ensure that the Grail in Europe will not come to an end. We need new ways of defining what belonging to the Grail means by considering spirituality in a broader sense. The contribution of Father van Ginneken's vision, that we as women have something to give to the world, has adapted to our time.

We must go back to the roots of the Grail, its essence, so that we do not lose it. We must continue to discover what is no longer alive and to explore how new life can unfold in the Grail. I am convinced that because we exist as a women's group we must join with other women, bond with other feminists in their struggle for their rights. We must also work in solidarity with people of different cultures, of different races, of different religions, from all walks of life and all lifestyles. This movement, this vision of spirituality and oneness with women, I think is the same vision we have always had but it is opening up more now. We all contribute to the movement. It takes great effort to incorporate the diversity, but if we can manage this, it will be an enriching experience.

We are already seeing results. What we called conversion in the early days is now transformation. That is what is happening right now with new people, the new generations who are interested in the Grail and the Tiltenberg. That same urge to bring about change, which was essential to young women in the early days of the Grail, is still alive. For the younger women today spirituality is the important thing, a turning away from consumerism and materialism. It is a solid surge, a reaching out in a serious way to bring a spiritual dimension, that transformation, to the world. To be inspired by that other dimension, that going beyond the horizon of my own ego and my own understanding, has indeed changed my life. There is something beyond.

Postscript

Several months after the doctors told Mimi that her cancer had stopped spreading, she wrote a letter to her friends describing her experience of moving from preparing for death to preparing to live again. Although some of her struggle is recorded in the previous text, the following excerpts from her letter written in early 1994 give further insights into Mimi's personal reflections on this, one of the most challenging of life's turning points.

> Something rare has happened to me. I had been preparing myself for death for many months here at the Tiltenberg. Workers, Grail members, relatives, and friends, especially from the Zen world have accompanied me—all of us preparing for this definite separation. I received a lot of visitors (sometimes too many), moving letters, cards (kilos of them), continuous attention, care, compassion, good counsel of different kinds. Drawn into the depths of our being, there was an intimacy that cannot be brought forth in other times. I think of one friend crying when I had to lose my hair for the second time, and a young man who wrote that he would like to take me into his arms—something he never would say otherwise. All pretence is gone, all attempts to make a good impression drop away. What remains are feelings of gratitude, even joy, because in spite of all the sorrow, in spite of the shock, in spite of the difficulty of acceptance, there is so much unity, so much touching of hearts.
>
> Now there is a change for me: I may live again. Though I am not cured, the disease has stopped spreading. My oncologist is completely surprised. "How lucky you are, how lucky you are," he keeps saying. I had crept through the very small eye of a very thin needle. I *must* start living again. I use these words intentionally: I must *learn to live* again, for it is not the same life as before my sickness. The intensity of life in those months supposed to be my last ones is now disappearing. Certainly I remain ill with cancer and cannot do everything as I used to. But I am no longer thinking daily about the approach of death. I am allowed to live still for some time, I *must* still live for some time. And I choose it; I want to go on with you all for some time. Marvelous on the one hand, but confusing,

too. The cautious steps I took towards death, supported by so many dear people, the process of learning to die, does not necessarily find a parallel in learning to live again.

I am happy with what I am able to do again, with my new possibilities, but in fact it is so different from what I had foreseen. Just like I had to learn to let go in the time I was preparing for death—letting go of my attachments, letting go of life itself—so now I have to let go of the important task of preparing for death. Now I have to take part again in life, the life of everything and everyone around me. It is a mystery. I have known two persons who fell ill with cancer at about the same time as I did; they have since died. Why can I, must I, continue to live while they had to die? Amazing, mysterious! Is there a reason?

In the course of human history all sorts of answers have been found to the great questions of life and death—God's will, Providence, the best course for us in God's plan. What I try is to move in the "zone of the Spirit," in gratitude, and feeling carried by the Presence permeating the whole of life.

Mimi died at the Tiltenberg in March of 1995, almost three years after her initial diagnosis.

Rebecca Nebrida, The Philippines, date unknown

12

Rebecca Nebrida

Our efforts in the Philippines
should be toward the elevation of
our poor sisters.

Rebecca Nebrida was born in the Philippines on August 8, 1927. For her, teaching—and learning—were fully in keeping with her family's tradition. Both of her parents were educators, and of the seven children in her family, three taught at one time or another, either in a high school or university.

Rebecca's father was a public servant: this did not make the family rich, but he told his children that the gift he was proudest to give them was education. They all went to the best schools in Manila. At one point, he had been sent for two years to study pedagogy at Columbia University, a distinguished academic institution in New York City (USA). His specialty was writing textbooks for children. At the time, all the textbooks being used were geared toward American children: "Run, Dick, run." Rebecca's father changed this to "Run, Ramon and Recita." However, the textbooks remained in English which, Rebecca conceded, was probably for the best since English is an international language whether Filipinos like it or not.

Rebecca's family was deeply religious. All of her education was in Catholic schools. Her parents had great devotion to Our Lady and the saints. Rebecca herself intended to become a Catholic sister, but an American priest (who later became a bishop) suggested the Grail to her. When she didn't bite, he urged her to do graduate work in theology and liturgy at the University of Notre Dame. At Notre Dame she met U.S. Grail member Audrey Sorrento, also a liturgy student, and ended up enrolling in the Year's School at Grailville. Like many other women, she was deeply influenced by the music at Grailville, especially the chant. By the time she returned to Notre Dame, and then to the Philippines, in 1963, she had developed an entirely new theology: that God is a God of love, not punishment. Rebecca taught theology at the college level for twenty-five years, serving also as head of her department and academic dean of the college. Then, just as she was about to be appointed academic dean of the university, with its three thousand students, Rebecca chose instead to become head of a high-school-level adult education program that served poor people. The program eventually enrolled a thousand students.

Changes in the Grail, and disappointments, were also part of Rebecca's education. Rebecca had wanted to join the Nucleus, but much changed in the Grail in the years after Vatican II, with many Nucleus members, including Rebecca's own mentors, leaving the Nucleus and even the Grail. In response to her inquiries about the Nucleus, leaders suggested that it wasn't a good time to join. Nonetheless, in 1975, during Simone Tagher's term as International President, the International Grail recognized the Grail in the Philippines as a national entity, fulfilling a dream Rebecca had had since her years in the U.S. And her leadership in the Grail went well beyond the Philippines: with Marita Estor of Germany and Teresa Santa Clara Gomes of Portugal, she served from 1988 to 1993 on the International Presidency Team. But during the twenty-five years of Rebecca's leadership in the

Philippines and internationally, a number of her requests for financial support for new initiatives were denied.

In 2000, the twenty-fifth anniversary of the Grail in the Philippines, a three-woman National Leadership Team took over; Rebecca had been in national leadership since 1975, when the Philippines had been officially recognized as part of the Grail. In 2001, Rebecca wanted to get funding from the Dutch Grail to continue the leadership seminar series for regional women in the Philippines begun in 1987. However, she did this on her own and the NLT had reservations about her individual initiative. This led, in early 2001, to Rebecca's taking an indefinite leave of absence from the Grail in the Philippines.

Despite this, there were friendly relations between Rebecca and some Grail team members. While on her own living in Antipolo, near Manila, she continued to embody the Grail vision. She began a preschool for children in the neighborhood, soliciting funds from family and friends. She started a traditional Christmas luncheon and gathering for tricycle drivers in her community and Rebecca would regularly lead the group to church or market.[53]

Rebecca continued to employ a woman to sew bags for her, to be sent, for the most part, to Grailville for sale, to augment her income. On her birthday, Rebecca would host parties attended by friends, family, and Grail members. Jeanette Loanzon would take prospective Grail members for visits with her as well, and Luz Silvestre-Galang would come from Apalit, Pampanga, to visit Rebecca.

---

53 Motorized tricycles, or simply tricycles, are an indigenous form of auto rickshaw and are a common means of public transportation in the Philippines. They are the most popular means of transportation in small towns and cities, especially in rural areas. "Motorized tricycle (Philippines)," Wikipedia: The Free Encyclopedia, accessed July 7, 2016, https://en.wikipedia.org/wiki/Motorized_tricycle_(Philippines).

In 2006, during the visit of Rosaurora Espinosa of Mexico, then a member of the International Leadership Team,[54] Rebecca gave a final preparation seminar to three prospective Grail members in Cagayan de Oro, Northern Mindanao, effectively ending her "leave of absence" that began in 2001. Then, in Advent of 2009, three new Filipino Grail members made their commitments at Rebecca's Antipolo residence. She took special delight in Jeana Costuna, a new Grail member from Taft, Eastern Samar.

In 2009, during the Asia-Pacific Forum held at Miriam College in Metro Manila, fifteen years after the Beijing Conference on Women, Sheila Hawthorn and Mary Robertson from Australia and Papua New Guinean Grail member Albina Namuesh visited Rebecca. In 2010, during the thirty-fifth anniversary of the Grail in the Philippines, Christa Werner of the International Leadership Team and Joke van Neerven of the Netherlands visited her as well.

On August 6, 2011, on the feast of the Transfiguration, two days before her eighty-fifth birthday, Rebecca died peacefully in her home in Anitpolo. Her Grail sisters attended her wake and organized the funeral Mass for her; most of the Metro Manila and Luzon Grail attended. The Grail also celebrated the ninth day of her passage into eternal life in Apalit, Pampanga, Central Luzon, with Bishop Federico Escaler, S.J., as celebrant. Bishop Escaler was a friend of Rebecca and her family; two of her sisters knew the bishop very well as he had served as Jesuit head of two schools in Southern and Northern Mindanao. Likewise, on the 40th day after Rebecca's death, the Grail celebrated the Eucharist at her Antipolo home with Monsignor Pepe Quitorio from Eastern Samar as celebrant. Msgr. Quitorio was in the late 1980s

---

54 The International Leadership Team was previously called the International Presidency Team.

and 1990s an active supporter of Grail projects in Rebecca's home region.[55]

Rebecca left behind thirty-plus Filipino Grail members with whom she had shared her deep and generous commitment to the Grail vision and mission. In 2015 the Grail conducted seminar/workshops for young women leaders in East Samar, the site of devastating typhoons in 2013 and 2014; three participants subsequently launched a feeding program for street children. Participants from an earlier seminar taught soap making to women from three needy villages. Rebecca left the Grail in the Philippines with deep roots and thanks to leadership by her and her Grail sisters, Grail women there have become more fulfilled in their search for the Grail cup, especially in their work with their sisters.

Interview

In the Beginning

I had a desire to help people and thought seriously about becoming a nun. When people asked me, "What do you like about the convent?" I would tell them I liked praying. I said if I entered the convent I would have more time to pray because at that time I was so active in my parish. I was coordinator of all the activities. So I was thinking that for my lifetime, maybe I should be a sister, a nun. All my education was Catholic, from elementary school right through university. We had European nuns for teachers and I went to a university run by the Dominicans. Of course, in my family everyone went to Mass on Sunday and we said the rosary on our own. My family had a strong devotion to Saint Anthony, which I still have. My mother even wore the dark

---

55 The ninth and fortieth days after a death are considered important in Filipino culture.

brown and white cord, the uniform of those who had devotion to Saint Anthony. The convent school reinforced all these duties, the responsibilities of being a Catholic.

I was also very devoted to Our Lady and when I was about ten years old I made a promise that I would imitate her virtues and be modest in my clothing. In fact, I wore white with a blue sash, the symbol of this devotion and promise. I still have a great devotion to Our Lady. Of course, I do not wear the white dress with the blue sash. At one point, I made the excuse that it is too hard to keep the white clean. But I never fail to pray to Our Lady every day. Sometimes I miss saying the rosary, but I never fail to pray to her. She keeps me charged and fueled: that's really engrained in me.

While I was looking for a convent, my parish priest, Father Francis McSorley,[56] who eventually became a famous bishop, said, "Stop shopping for a convent." He had the foresight that this was to be the age of lay people. "I know a group of lay people," he told me, "and you will really like them." His sister had gone to Grailville, but when I looked at the pictures of Grailville he showed me, I was not so enthralled. The pictures were not too attractive. The life seemed good but those pictures …

Meanwhile, I was in charge of the parish catechetical program and I felt very inadequate. I was not happy with the way our religion was taught but I knew very little about content and methodology. I felt I should learn more. McSorley advised me to go to the University of Notre Dame in the United States where they taught the latest Catholic liturgy and theology. I really wanted to teach theology in a college. So I came.

While I was at Notre Dame, someone said that she had heard I was interested in the Grail and there was someone from the Grail

---

56 "Bishop Francis McSorley," The Catholic Hierarchy, accessed July 14, 2016., http://www.catholic-hierarchy.org/bishop/bmcsorley.html.

in the same boarding house I was in—Audrey Sorrento. So I looked for her and told her I would like to know more about the movement. She invited me to go with her to Grailville after the summer session at Notre Dame was finished. This was in 1957.

Then I had to choose whether to return to Notre Dame to finish the M.A. degree or participate in the year's program of formation at Grailville. I chose the year's program of formation. So I spent one year at Grailville and another year at Super Flumina.[57] Then I stayed for a third year at Gabriel House[58] working with international students. Before I left, I was able to attend the last Grailville course given by Lydwine.[59]

One of the things I found hard about Grailville was that it was so cold in the fall and winter. I came from the east and was not used to the weather. I also had to walk to Mass although I did not complain; this was just a sacrifice. And I was quite shy when I first came, so I liked the silent meals during Advent and Lent.

Lydwine thought I was a weakling so she was rather hard on me. However, I really benefited from the training there. Grailville always impressed me with the new thinking and the exposure to the latest books. I remember Daniélou, Gerald Vann, Bede Griffith, Christopher Dawson, Bernard Cook, Joseph Goldbrunner. Goldbrunner had a very strong influence on me. We read his

---

57 Super Flumina was a small Grail center in Morrow, Ohio, not far from Grailville, the national center of the U.S. Grail, and was used for intensive spiritual formation.

58 Gabriel House, in Cincinnati, Ohio, was one of the several Grail city centers that existed at that time in the United States for residential programs for professional women and for outreach programs to local women.

59 Lydwine van Kersbergen, co-founder of the Grail in the U.S. See Chapter 1, 1-20.

book, *Holiness Is Wholeness*.[60] It was about personalism. These people would come to give us courses.

And the day began with Lauds and Mass, and then a silent breakfast. In the afternoon, we did project work for the whole community. On Saturday evenings we had Mass preparation for the next day's Sunday Mass. This was very important, since we read and talked about the text for the following day and interpreted what it meant to us. We also got to know families and other people in the community, so Grailville was not exclusive. Occasionally I would give a talk about the Philippines.

Eleanor Walker and Jeanne Plante were my spiritual mentors. What I treasure most was learning Gregorian chant. I joined the music family and Eleanor was our housemother.[61] What a beautiful person she was and I learned to sing all those beautiful songs and we made a record. Angela Miller led the schola.[62] I told Eleanor one time that Angela violated all the principles of education. She would intimidate us, she would scream at us. But she was a genius in music.

It was not hard to convince me to join the Grail. I saw the Grail as a movement wherein I could learn much about my faith, and

---

60 Joseph Goldbrunner, *Holiness Is Wholeness* (New York, NY: Pantheon Books, 1955).

61 During the Year's School, participants would "live work, study, play and pray with the same small group of people." Janet Kalven, *Women Breaking Boundaries: A Grail Journey, 1940-1995*, 83. Often the family unit shared a common work, such as art, agriculture, music, etc.

62 Originally, a *schola* was a musical school attached to a monastery or church. Also known as a *schola cantorum*. Today, the term refers to a group of musicians, particularly one which specializes in liturgical music. "Schola," Wiktionary, The Free Dictionary, accessed November 21, 2016, https://en.wiktionary.org/wiki/schola.

about being a woman. Yet it wasn't so much being a part of a movement of women. That developed later, through the ideas of Janet (Kalven) and Lydwine. Lydwine was such a dynamic speaker and when she talked about the responsibility of women to convert the world, I realized that, indeed, I had to convert the world.

Early on, though, I was more concerned to help our people back home. Whatever I gained from the Grail I wanted to bring back to my people. All the things I learned at the beginning about community, scripture, the liturgy—these were helping me to become a better Christian so that when I went home I could be a bigger help. For instance, the celebration of Christmas with living the life of the church during Advent and anticipating the birth coming closer on each Sunday of Advent. There was no rushing around buying gifts. In fact, Christmas Day was quiet and we opened a few presents the day after. And Lent, Holy Week, and Easter were the climax of a formation year. Just to be able to live the life of the church as it should be. And that every Sunday we sang, every Sunday was a celebration of Easter. I really cannot thank my staying at Grailville enough.

By then, I had three years of training in the Grail and during the summers I went back to Notre Dame to finish my M.A. degree. I finished in 1963. At Grailville, I became more focused on Christ. I had come with a traditional image of God as a kind father who attends to our needs but who also can be a God of spite, who punishes us. This is common among the Filipinos, just like the eruption. When the volcano on Pinatubo erupted, people immediately said, "We have sinned; it's our fault."

That has changed a great deal for me over the years, mostly as a result of my time at Grailville, and I had a real conversion at Notre Dame. When I returned to the Philippines, I wanted to say to everyone, "Look, look, this is what I learned. The story of our faith is a story of God's love for us." That was so central in my mind: that God loves us and the whole Christian doctrine is that God showed us how He loves us. It is all interconnected. Then the commandments and the sacraments are expressions of this love. I can see clearly that God loves us in our faith. Then I discovered so many treasures in our faith, like the liturgy, the scripture, which I had never known.

This was really a discovery for me, the central mystery that God loves us. I realized we have to love in return. The Christian life is a response of gratefulness and thankfulness to this love that God has showered on us. It was so much in my mind that I thought perhaps I could have been an apostle. I was so excited. Whenever I met a friend after I went home I would say, "Do you know that this is what our faith really is?"

Now I think of God as ever present in my life, as the center of my life, ever present wherever I go, Who is the source of all I am. I have full faith in Him. He is a personal God who just spotted me from all the millions, and He loves me. So I have to respond to that love.

After I went home in 1963, I taught theology at the college level and did that for twenty-five years. I was also in administrative positions and was head of the theology department. For a year I was academic dean. Then I was asked to be College Dean of Academic Affairs for the whole unit, three thousand students. The administration said they hoped I would be able to handle all of this. I knew I'd rather teach.

At the same time I was also asked to be the principal of an adult education program, high school level. And the clientele of the program were all poor people—janitors and domestic helpers and dressmakers—a thousand students, all adults. So I had to make a choice. When I look back, I think the choice I made was a good one. I chose to be the principal in that adult education program. My father said, "You're crazy." I had wanted to go for my Ph.D. in education, but that was all forgotten. I don't regret it.

Turbulent Times

As you may know, while I was in the United States, I received intensive training to be in the Nucleus, but I did not make it. After Vatican II many women left the Grail Nucleus, including my director,[63] which was very disappointing to me. In 1964, before I left Grailville, I talked to Eileen (Schaeffler) about joining the Nucleus and she replied that the Grail was in such a state at the time that the movement did not know where to go. I went on to Europe and saw the president, Magdalene (Oberhoffer), and she told me that she could not give me an answer. She told me the best thing for me was to go home. So I took the boat and I left Europe all by myself, alone.

When I got back home, I kept writing people in the Grail but I was very busy so I put the idea of the Nucleus in the back of my mind. I didn't want to think about it. I think God was telling me that I was already committed to the Grail, but back then, if you were not a Nucleus member, you were not a member of the Grail. At this time in my life, I'd rather be doing what I am doing, and besides, there are so many people here who would like to join the Grail. Explaining the Nucleus would just complicate things.

Those early times, though, were very traumatic for me—the upheaval in the Grail, the upheaval when people left. And there seemed to be such extremes at Grailville when feminism came. I heard that men were staying overnight. That was really shocking for me.

But then you realize that it's the culture and you get over it. You cannot prevent the young people, and the young women wanted

---

63 Probably Jeanne Plante, whose main work in the Grail had been "advising people while they were at Grailville," and who left the Nucleus to marry. Kalven, *Women Breaking Boundaries: A Grail Journey, 1940-1995*, 186.

to prove something. It was a reaction. Actually, the Grail seems to be more of a women's movement than it was before. When I was at Grailville, relationship with God was emphasized. But now there's more emphasis on finding who we are and also working for justice and peace. That's the one I like. It's a new reading of the Gospel with the stress on justice and peace. It's living the scriptural text, which really underlies whatever you do. Before, it was just me and my God.

Launching a Movement

In 1973, I initiated the Grail in the Philippines with some friends and my students. The first brochure we put out was made by two of my students and it was about starting a women's movement. I had been back to Grailville on a sabbatical and we had talked about women and my desire to start a movement. I was promised help to get a Grail team started but it never came.

I believed in the Grail. I felt that if I was so convinced of the Grail myself, I was sure there were other women who would think the same way. Simone Tagher, the International President, came for a visit in 1975 and that is when we really became a Grail team. She gave the stamp of approval, so we had a ceremony and commitment. Jeannette Loanzan was with me and she became my right arm. Also, there was Gloria Gallant, my student, who later came to the United States. She's married and is now part of the Boston Grail team. My sister, Teresa, was also with me. She was the supervisor of Grail projects for seven years, and she was in Nigeria for seven years before that. In 1977, Dorothy Rasenberger and Carolyn Gratton came for two months.

When we first started, we said we were a women's movement and the first thing we did was pray about it. We found a prayer room at the Marian College. We went there every Friday and others joined us. So we started a prayer team and then we took on issues such as what it was to be a woman. Then it spread and we would have our meeting at home in my flat. We were able to get money to start a children's project. Eventually we were able to get money to start leadership training. It is called "Pagbubuo," which means "to make whole" or "integration." We took that from the text of John 10, "I have come that you may have life and life in abundance."

We have a big banner where we have the training. The first week is on self-worth, self-appraisal, and the second on community skills—how to organize, how to serve. Then each person has to bring a profile of their community—where is the market, the school, the rivers, how many doctors. So they become acquainted with the resources in their communities. Then we discuss all of this. Then they make a plan of action in the second week. From understanding, knowing the needs and problems of their community, what do they plan to do when they go back?

The third week we discuss social issues like environment, family relationships, abortion, responsible parenthood, disciplining the child, and nutrition. And in the fourth week, we integrate all of this. We have a retreat for them and we take them to two places, places of affluence in contrast to poverty. We look at those big buildings in Manila and then we go to the huge garbage dumps. I refer to them as "smokey mountains" because they get taller and taller and they smoke because of the carbon. And people live on top of this garbage for their survival, scrapping whatever they can find. The government got embarrassed because we were getting to be known as "smokey mountain" country even in Europe.

So the government improved the situation, levelled it and built housing for these people. However, the lives of the people remain the same. Even with the increase in the GNP, which is supposed to make the lives of people better, their lives are the same. I don't think that the increasing GNP has ever reached them. The income of the government is much higher. The Philippine overseas workers have caused this increase. We have millions of them outside the country. And there is still much corruption.

Being a Woman in the Philippines

The needs in the Philippines are economic, so we train our women on what it means to be a woman in relation to the family. Later, when we evaluate, the women always answer, "The best learning I got here was that I discovered myself as a woman." It's not just about women helping women, but about women helping the community, helping their families.

Because of this stress on women, the bishop said that we are feminists. He liked what we were doing, but he didn't like that we are feminist. The bishops don't understand the nature of women. However, we still believe that the first role is that of homemaker, of bringing understanding and unity and peace in the family. At one time, an American politician said that he observed in his travels that the women contributed most in the Philippines; women are more interpersonal, they're more compassionate by nature. When there's a crisis, they are the ones in the forefront and they are able to solve the problems.

I know this because I work with poor women. They're the ones really providing food for the family, because men have to wait until they get their jobs, seasonal jobs like laborers or construction workers. They do it for six months. In the meantime, they don't have jobs. It's the women who really do the work, sixteen hours a day. The woman wakes to cook and feed the family, send the children to school, and then when she has about two hours she goes around selling vegetables or doing washing for some money. And then the children are home. I know that in many squatter communities, the husbands are just there talking amongst themselves while the women work.

In my country, women are really oppressed, and we see that we are in a movement and we should do something about it. There are sexual abuses—women are sent abroad as domestic helpers and they're part of white slavery. They are very much discriminated against. If you are Filipino, people think you are either promoting prostitution or part of the white slavery of going abroad as a domestic helper. That's the Filipina women's image and we get so mad about it.

We hired a woman gardener because she needed the money very badly. She was married to a man who then had no job. One day she came sobbing to our house. She had sent her husband to jail because he had attempted to rape his four daughters who were all eighteen years and younger. One of the daughters got free but she had to take the others to a doctor. She was in a trance and did not know what to do. I wept with her. She is such a good woman and works so hard. It was the end of the world for her. The husband threatened to come and kill all of them when he gets out of jail. Now every time a woman works for us, I ask her who is taking care of her children, and when she says her husband, I ask if he will take good care of them.

One of the things we discuss with women and their role in the church is their relationship with the priest and the relationship within the family. Since our women are so subservient to priests, they are victims of priest abuse and they become pregnant. And because they live on the outskirts of town, the father or the uncle or the brother can severely punish them. There is talk among people in the Filipino diocese about rethinking celibacy, questioning it because we are a very, very family-oriented society for good or for ill. We are not individualists like Westerners. Here in the family we don't just uphold one member of the family; it's the whole family's honor.

The Catholic Church in the Philippines

The church in the Philippines hasn't changed much over the years. It has always been quite conservative and traditional and very hierarchical. It's very centered on what the bishop says and that has a very strong influence on the life of the people. Things are a little different in Mindoro because of the Muslims. After Vatican II, there were some bishops who were more progressively minded but they are still in the minority. Of course, at that time, many priests left and priests and nuns were marrying, but on the other hand, I am happy because some of the liturgical practices we had at Grailville, like the Mass facing the people and the Mass, not in Latin, but in English, have been put in place. And then, there came the ruling that people could pray in their own dialect. That was really good news for me.

Our present cardinal is a good friend of the pope (John Paul II), but the people have such a blind love and loyalty to the Holy Father. When he came to the Philippines, four million people came out for one Eucharistic celebration and he was so pleased.[64] I love the pope and the bishops are trying their best to elevate the situation of the people, but I think it's not enough. There are some very vocal, progressive-minded bishops and also priests who are really trying to turn the church toward the poor. When the Oblates run a parish, they are concerned with helping the poor. They even work with poor Muslims. Their emphasis is always with the poor.

My spiritual life includes everything; it's not just my soul, but includes primarily my relationship with God and then my relationship with people and my relation with work. So it's all-encompassing. Religion can include doctrines and beliefs and tenets. But the spiritual life should underlie everything, in any religion, whereas religion without the spiritual is more abstract.

---

64 On January 15, 1995, Pope John Paul II celebrated Mass with a gathering of four to five million people in Luneta Park, Manila. It is believed to be the largest papal gathering in history. "Pope John Paul II," Wikipedia, The Free Encyclopedia, accessed July 17, 2016, https://en.wikipedia.org/wiki/Pope_John_Paul_II.

An International Responsibility

In 1988, I was elected to the International Presidency Team along with Teresa Santa Clara Gomes (from Portugal)[65] and Marita Estor (from Germany). I had been nominated before but I had refused. By 1988, I had had experience in participating in international gatherings like council meetings. In fact, I had attended all the international meetings since 1977. While I was on the International Council, I attended meetings in Kenya and Portugal and Amsterdam. And later, a regional meeting was held in Manila. Being on the IPT was hard and also a learning experience for me.

It was very helpful in understanding intercultural experiences. There were cultural stereotypes in the Grail that still exist. There are many who do not understand the cultural backgrounds of other Grail members. I can still see it. I think there should be more effort to understand each other culture-wise. "Why do we act like this? Why do we think like this?" Do we really know? We do speak of unity, of bringing peace.

The vision of the Grail is more explicit now than it was when I first met the Grail. Now we say that through the empowerment of women we can transform the world. During my early training women were more feminine. Now we look at cultural differences.

In the United States it's quite different from my country in terms of the role and needs of women. Ours are more basic, the economic and social needs. So our work then should be geared towards these. That's why our projects are for the poor. Here in the Philippines the Grail has seventeen pre-schools in all, in the squatter areas. And we have the training of women, grassroots women. We have already trained about 270 women since we started this project. It's all a process and we explain that women will reach wholeness.

---

65 See Chapter 10, 195-214.

Our problem is funding. We have a project to raise funds for our pre-school project and the training program. We make cards. The Grail does not give us any financial help.

We dream of bringing the Grail to other Asian countries. We could do this by going to other countries and living there. Jeanette would like to do it. She'd like to go to Vietnam. We could also go to Indonesia. We have a Grail member there who married an Indonesian. Two Korean women attended Pagbubuo. They came here and had interaction with the women at Smokey Mountain.[66] We could easily start one there but we would have to live in Korea for a while. To do a formation program, we would have to stay at least three months. In any new country, we would have to get to know the people first and teach them how to do the formation program. We cannot enter and just do it ourselves.

Retirement as Continuity

My retirement is all Grail work. I would get ill if I retired in the sense that retirement is a passive kind of life. My ideal retirement is getting involved up to my dying days. It's not really difficult. I get so much fulfilment from my work that it keeps me going. Part of my retirement is having the free time to do things like come to the United States. Of course, I don't have enough funds to do what I would like for the Grail. I would also like to go to Japan, to Bangkok, to Indonesia. Those are my frustrations because I don't have enough money. But the Grail work is very satisfying for me.

---

66 "Smokey Mountain" is the term used to describe a large landfill located in Manila. It was converted into public housing in the late 1990s."Smokey Mountain," Wikipedia, The Free Encyclopedia, accessed July 7, 2016, https://en.wikipedia.org/wiki/Smokey_Mountain.

For Younger Women

I would like to remind Filipino women that we are gifted people and gifted women, that we have so much to contribute for the benefit of our people. Our task is to find out what these gifts are, to help one another so that in the long run we will be able to help our people. We have to know ourselves as women. We have so much to give, and must just find out how we can develop these capacities. In a situation like ours where the majority of the people are poor, I feel that our efforts should be towards the elevation of our poor sisters. And then, we have to keep faith in the Lord, not to give up, to hope when there is darkness—when you think you cannot proceed because of many obstacles.

Maria de Lourdes Pintasilgo, Portugal, 1986

13

Maria de Lourdes Pintasilgo

> *Political power exercised by women*
> *is worthwhile only if it is*
> *power of a different kind.*

Maria de Lourdes Pintasilgo calls her appointment as the first woman Prime Minister of Portugal in 1979 a "revolutionary act." Breaking tradition was not a new phenomenon for Maria de Lourdes. Her belief that women can make a difference in all spheres of economic and political life began many years before when, at the age of seventeen, she made the decision to attend engineering school. Her choice was influenced by a conviction that remained integral to her life's work: her belief in the contribution women can make to challenging injustices in society.

By the time Maria de Lourdes graduated in 1953 at the age of twenty-three from the Instituto Superior Tecnico in Lisbon as the only woman with a degree in chemical engineering, she had begun to pose questions about the unique identity of women that would be the catalysts for all her future achievements. What role can women take in professional life? What can they bring that is different? What is their specific place in a society where being a good wife and mother is the norm?

Maria de Lourdes was born in Abrantes, in Portugal's Tagus Valley, January 18, 1930, to Jaime de Matos Pintasilgo, who was in the wool business, and Amélia do Carmo Ruivo da Silva. Maria de Lourdes and her younger brother grew up in Lisbon in a large middle-class extended family. Because the adult members of the family were republicans, they were not practising Catholics, although they had all been baptized.

Later in life, Maria de Lourdes realized the seeming anomaly of someone like herself coming from an "unbelieving" family but recognizing that she was raised with very Christian values. The home atmosphere was strict; she and her brother were raised with a sense of their duty to care for others and a respect for the dignity of all human beings, including the poor. They were also taught to assume responsibility for their own actions as well as to take responsibility for others who did not have the opportunities they did.

Thus, Maria de Lourdes's later attraction to Christianity was an appeal to the idealism inculcated by the high ethical standards of her childhood rather than to a list of rules and dogmas. She recalled another influence on her decision to adopt Christianity. A bachelor uncle who lived with the family knew hundreds of poems by heart. His love of poetry introduced Maria de Lourdes to metaphorical language and to a world of symbolism that later opened her to faith, to seeing what is beyond the eye.

Maria de Lourdes excelled in her studies as a young student, again influenced by what she terms a "tremendous sense of duty." Attending a public high school was an advantage because students like herself were exposed to young people from diverse economic and cultural backgrounds who were valued and respected for their contribution to all of the activities of the school, rather than for their origins only.

Maria de Lourdes's decision to enter engineering school was a difficult one. She was told that this was not a field for women; one female graduate of her high school had already failed in engineering. At this point in her life, Maria de Lourdes, an avid reader, had discovered the writings of Simone Weil, the French Jewish philosopher whose books on spirituality introduced Maria de Lourdes to the worker-priest movement in France.[67] Inspired by the context of Simone Weil's life, Maria de Lourdes set her horizons on engineering school as a possible way to eventually help the worker.

Maria de Lourdes's six years at university provided the atmosphere for her to develop her intellectual life as a woman who "listened differently and asked different questions." Hers was a generation that was realizing new possibilities for women and Maria de Lourdes felt free to explore her own questions about the potential of women, including her own. Again she excelled in her studies. Of the 250 students who started in her class, fourteen remained for the full six years and she was one of the four best. The other three were men.

Perhaps one of the most significant influences on Maria de Lourdes's life from these years was her involvement with Catholic Action,[68] a student group patterned to some extent after the Young

---

67 In the Worker-Priest movement, founded in France in 1941, priests worked in factories as a way of reaching out to workers. The movement was suppressed by Pope Pius XII in 1954. Windass, *The Chronicle of the Worker-Priests*.

68 Catholic Action is a term used to describe groups of lay Catholics in the nineteenth and twentieth centuries who worked to influence society with Catholic principles and practices. "Catholic Action," Wikipedia, The Free Encyclopedia, accessed July 14, 2016, https://en.wikipedia.org/wiki/Catholic_Action. See also 2016 Introduction, vii-xxviii.

Christian Workers, which had started in Belgium in the early 1920s.[69] Here Maria de Lourdes was introduced to the intellectual life of the Catholic Church that she had heard about in high school through reading the work of Pope Pius XII, himself an intellectual. She was impressed by his having counselled Catholics to be on the edge of new thinking. Maria de Lourdes joined members of the Catholic Action group for heady discussions about the purpose of student life and the place of the Bible and liturgy in their lives. This experience was instrumental in what Maria de Lourdes refers to as her "conversion" to Christianity and her later attraction to the Grail.

In her last year of university, while attending a meeting of Pax Romana, an international movement of Catholic students of which she later became the first woman president, Maria de Lourdes met Rosemary Goldie, an Australian Grail member. Five years later, in 1957, Maria de Lourdes visited the Tiltenberg, in Holland. She was already involved in a successful career, having left the Commission of Nuclear Energy after two years to be project director of research and development at a large industrial complex in Lisbon. By the time she met Rachel Donders, the International President, a few months later, Maria de Lourdes had already decided that she wanted to join the Grail.

That summer, Maria de Lourdes and Teresa Santa Clara Gomes visited Grailville and by fall, the two of them had called together a group of women students from Catholic Action to begin the Grail

---

69 The Young Christian Workers (YCW; French: *Jeunesse ouvrière chrétienne*) is an international organization founded by Rev. Joseph Cardijn in Belgium as the Young Trade Unionists; the organization adopted its present name in 1924. Its French acronym, JOC, gave rise to the then widely used terms *Jocism* and *Jocist*. It eventually spread to 48 countries. "Young Christian Workers," Wikipedia, The Free Encyclopedia, accessed November 21, 2016, https://en.wikipedia.org/wiki/Young_Christian_Workers.

in Portugal. Within a few years Maria de Lourdes was asked to serve as a member of the International Grail Vice-Presidency team for two terms, during the presidencies of Magdalene Oberhoffer and then Eileen Schaeffler. As an International Vice-President, Maria de Lourdes helped shape the guidelines resulting from the Grail *aggiornamento*.

By this time, Maria de Lourdes was already known in the Portuguese political arena. In 1959, at the invitation of one of the ministers, she set up a commission on the status of women; several other Portuguese Grail women served as members. By the end of the 1960s she had been invited by the Prime Minister to place her name on the list for Parliament. Maria de Lourdes refused because of her opposition to Portugal's one-party system and its participation in colonial wars. However, she did agree to appointments on two commissions, one having to do with social policy concerning women.

From 1974 until 1979, during and immediately after the Portuguese revolution, Maria de Lourdes served as Secretary of State for Social Welfare, Minister of Social Affairs, and Ambassador to UNESCO. In 1979 she became the first woman Prime Minister of Portugal, called by several writers at that time, "the last upheaval of the revolution." She served from August, 1979, through the first few weeks of 1980.

Subsequently Maria de Lourdes combined her Grail work with active involvement in the political life of Portugal and that of Europe. She ran as an independent candidate for the Portuguese presidency in 1986, coming in third, and sat as an independent in the European Parliament from 1987 to 1989. She served as chairperson of several European commissions and president of the World Independent Commission on Population and the Quality of Life. While on that commission Maria de Lourdes led the attempt, along with other international experts, to broaden the analysis of the population problem to include human rights and ecological issues on a global scale. She was active in working groups focused on women's employment and structural change and served as a member of the National Bioethics Council. She served on the Inter-Action Council of Former Heads of Government and the Council of Women World Leaders.

Amidst her many commitments Maria de Lourdes found time to write a number of articles and chapters for books on women's issues. She launched and participated in numerous programs concerned with the identity of women in social, economic, and cultural life, politics and development, the construction of Europe and international relations, and theology and Christian spirituality.

Maria de Lourdes's many years in the Grail and in politics strongly influenced her worldview, based on a deep awareness of the connectedness between all the injustices of our times. Her approach was always one of caring for the essential rights and needs of human beings, an approach that challenges the typical political agenda and the values that underpin it.

Perhaps Maria de Lourdes's most significant contribution to the Grail and to political life was her vision of the different kinds of power that women can exercise in society and in political life, so as to bring a "trustworthy human face" to politics. She learned from personal experience the price women have to pay when they go against the norm by speaking their own truth. As she continued to work with young women toward the end of her life, she strongly encouraged them to envision and work toward a new paradigm, that of a "life-centered" world. Although she acknowledged that we are still at the beginning of this process, she held strongly to the conviction that this can only be brought about when women participate fully in all sectors of society by using their knowledge and experience in the creation of new institutions and new social structures.

Maria de Lourdes remained active till the end of her life, urging the Portuguese government, in her final weeks, to withdraw its military from the U.S. war in Iraq. She died of cardiac arrest at her home in Lisbon on July 10, 2014, at the age of 74. European newspapers acknowledged the passing of this distinguished woman who was Portugal's sole female prime minister to date and, at the time, only the second female prime minister in European history. Grail members around the world mourned her loss.

Interview

Grail Beginnings in Portugal

When Rachel Donders explained to me what the Grail was, I knew that I had found something that would foster my interests in women's contribution to the world and my search for a spiritual life that wasn't pious but came from within and could express itself in many different ways. Also, the international dimension of the Grail was, and still is, very critical for me. Early on, I came to realize it doesn't matter where I am; what matters is what I am doing, because I am rooted in this international family. This is very important. Again it was Rachel who was the thread weaving together the network of Grail people for us in our early years in Portugal. When she came to visit she would tell us about Grail people in America, in Australia, and in other parts of the world. She had such an ability to link people together.

I was a late vocation to the Grail, having made my commitment in the Nucleus at the Tiltenberg in 1961, when I was thirty-one. Teresa Santa Clara Gomes made her commitment at the same time and we had both had what you might call "on the job training," since we did not go through any established formation program.

We had visited Grailville in 1957 after attending a Pax Romana meeting in El Salvador. By then I had been elected the first woman to be the International President of Pax Romana even though I was no longer a student but a professional woman. That was quite interesting. Before the election, a bishop from Switzerland who was responsible for the movement wired Rome to ask if a woman could head up a group of men and women. Of course, two years before this Anne Hope, another Grail member, from South Africa, had been elected vice president.

Grailville was fantastic. We arrived at the beginning of a summer program and the first evening there was a presentation of Tolstoy's "What Men Live By." At the end of a few days, Teresa Santa Clara, who was twenty-one at the time, said, "This is for me." Just like that! And indeed it was, for all of her life, without a moment's hesitation. I had to return right away to Portugal since I was on vacation from my position, but Teresa Sanata Clara stayed for a month and visited different city centers. That was in August and by October we had started the Grail in Lisbon. That's how we became a reality.

We spent the next several years building the Grail in Portugal with a great deal of help and support from Rachel. Our concentration on building community out of city centers was influenced by Teresa Santa Clara's Grail experience in the United States. And we always tried to develop a rich cultural life at each center.

An early emphasis was on liturgical life, trying to give a deeper meaning to liturgy. We studied very thoroughly the documents coming from the Vatican Council and accepted invitations everywhere to discuss them. We also had Bible study groups for women and we concentrated on injustices in Portuguese society. Before long, we began to address the role of women in society. So our focus was on current problems that ranged from those one might face as a Christian, to the political situation, to the situation of women, to a new ethics.

From our earliest days, we have been aware of equality issues. For instance, here in Europe, as in the rest of the world, there's a big gap between the salaries of men and women. And working conditions for women in this country have been very poor. In my seven years working in a factory, I learned a lot about the condition of women workers. At thirty, they looked like old women. However, our major concern has always been with women's specific contribution. We have always cared most about bringing something different to society. So again, the whole question of identity is still very important for the Grail in Portugal.

Speaking My Truth in Politics

Over the years, I have been able to bring my experience in politics to bear on the Grail. My first intensive course in politics came in 1969, before the revolution, when the Prime Minister appointed me to the Commission on Politics and General Administration.

I quickly learned how this country is run. I was the only woman among twelve men and I voted most of the time in disagreement with the majority. At that time there was strong censorship in our country, so I never could have written my own opinions for newspapers. But because what I said was coming from the chamber, it was published and then reproduced in the papers. This publicly supported what we, in the Grail, believed in. We were working on literacy, and we had started the conscientization process with people in the rural areas based on Paulo Freire's thinking. At that time we also went to Mass together with married couples and after Mass had discussions about the situation in the country, and people wanted to know what I knew.

Since our meetings were open, we sometimes had people from the secret police come. When I knew one of them was there, I would say, "Well, last week in the chamber this happened, etc." And since the Church enjoyed certain privileges, it was possible to have these little cells of resistance to the regime. After all, things had already been in the newspapers. Of course, there was suspicion of the Grail. After the revolution we were able to read the files they had about us which said we were against everything. We were against the injustices we saw in Portugal and we were against the colonial wars, such as in Angola and Mozambique. That was our motivation, not overthrowing the regime. We had no big illusions.

I could never be obliged to take a stand against my own conscience. For this reason, I never joined any particular political party; I always remained an independent. When I became a member of the European Parliament, I applied to the socialist group as an independent although I was not a member of the socialist party.

Very often I voted differently from the rest of the group. I always explained why I voted against them and some agreed with me although they felt they couldn't vote against their party. On one occasion, the Secretary General of the group told me I was sowing trouble because I was causing disunity in the group. I disagreed with him and informed him that I was speaking out of my conscience. Unfortunately, women in politics today are coming from the political system just like men, and often they cannot speak from their own consciences.

A Woman Prime Minister: The "Last Revolutionary Act"

One of the reasons I was chosen to be Prime Minister was because I was an independent. After the 1979 election, the political parties couldn't come to an agreement because there was no absolute majority. Because of this deadlock, the President asked me since I was not in any party. I was the first, and thus far the only woman Prime Minister of Portugal. This was five years after the revolution and people were still open to new ideas. It was really the last revolutionary act since our revolution. I don't think this would be possible now.

Despite the activism of the women in the revolution and their input into the new constitution that brought the principle of gender equality to the forefront, the reaction to my appointment was predictably mixed. Though I experienced great support from many who found that my style and concept of politics breathed a new life into Portuguese politics, this "revolutionary act" also brought about vehement opposition by members of the conservative parties in Parliament.

While I was Prime Minister, I tried all kinds of new things that were not then the custom in Portugal. For instance, in addition to cabinet meetings in Lisbon, I inaugurated mini-cabinet meetings in all the regions of the country so we could listen first hand to local problems. We held public sessions for people to meet and voice their concerns. And then we would formulate and announce plans for action.

This manner of meeting in different places was very important. I made it clear that the government had to work, not from the top down, but in partnership with the living, active forces of society. When a problem arose, such as—can shops be open on Sunday?—we would bring together people from various segments of society, the tradespeople, the consumers, groups who often had no say in these things.

So what I defended was that all groups in society have to be social partners with the government on the questions in which they have competence and which affect them directly. This was pedagogical, bringing together people from the Left and the Right. These ideas were used later by my successors. Just the other day at the opening ceremonies for Expo '98, I saw the president who appointed me. The speaker was talking about social partners and a civil society. The former president turned to me and said, "That's what you used to talk about and now it is a reality."

Women, Politics and Power

I do believe that women can make a difference in political life. For women, politics is connected to daily life, not outside of the events of life. It is naming things as they really are and therefore establishing different priorities. Political power exercised by women is worthwhile only if it is power of a different kind. Power, to me, is of little interest unless it corresponds to new attitudes, new ideas, to another way of managing affairs at all levels, ranging from the village to the planet.

Women express themselves differently and therefore introduce new breadth and new directions into politics. We speak with a more personal and human voice, a voice of caring and concern that can cut through the bureaucracy and create action. Of course if we really make a difference, we have to pay a price. I have experienced this, and other women involved in politics in Europe say the same thing. Certainly we work harder than men do. And the antagonisms we create often have nothing to do with the subject we are dealing with, but with our identity as women.

For instance, when I was prime minister I created a program that was heavily attacked from the right. In my presentation of this program to the Parliament I asked, "What is at stake here? Is it the program, itself, is it the time, what is it?" At the end I said, "What is at stake is having a woman for prime minister." Before I even reached that point in my speech, one of the male members of Parliament stood up and said, "It is you that's at stake." So it was really clear.

Some people even said I was an invention of the president because he had appointed me. Interesting, since I was known long before he was because of my opposition to the wars the government supported. It's the Adam and Eve syndrome that other women in politics also experience: we are taken from the rib of a man, therefore, we are invented by him.

But I have also experienced very strongly that people want politics to make a difference in their lives. Men often just cannot accommodate to these differences. Men see themselves as actors in the big drama of government that dictates their lines.

However, for women I see some dangers. Appointing and electing women can be mere tokenism. When I was part of the European Parliament, we were allowed to join three commissions rather than the usual two if the third one was not considered important. So I joined a third one, the Commission on Women's Rights.

And simple "infiltration" into politics is not enough. Women then find themselves overwhelmed by this double task of being a woman and a politician, but also by a style that is not theirs. Frequently, then, they assimilate for survival and become like men by mimicking their behavior. As a result, they become unbearable, doing the same things men do in all kinds of enterprises, including politics. And often when they "succeed," they block other women.

The other danger is that women become subdued and therefore invisible. What we are trying to do now is to find out how to walk between these two extremes. This is a new way and I think we are still in the beginning—very much in the beginning.

The strength of one or two women in politics is not enough to generate a new system. What could be significant for society is that women in politics question the established norms so that politics returns to the basics, to structuring social relations for the common good. In order for this to happen, we need to do more than apply human rights to females as human beings. This just makes them objects of a process. The challenge of our age lies in the possibility of women as subjects, leading the way in society.

Toward a Politics of Caring

I think what we need today is to go beyond an interdisciplinary approach to a transdisciplinary one where everything intertwines, where our point of view comes from a knowledge of sociology, philosophy, and economics across cultures. We thus allow new terms of reference for human knowledge to emerge and a new paradigm of social organization to take shape and gain momentum.

I call this "walking among fields of knowledge," a methodology for me which is extremely important and which is not reductionist or linear; it does not limit the issues.

The methodology I am suggesting assumes that every human being is in the center, the human person is not just dissected into small segments. We are part of a complex whole and everything relates to everything else. Therefore, not only is knowledge important, but feelings and emotions, the total context of human life.

There was a reason that the title of the book coming from my commission on population and quality of life was *Caring for the Future*.[70] The book is about much more than studying or planning or predicting the future. It's really about caring. When we care, we share with others and we learn new ways. Today there is such an escalation and fragmentation of knowledge that people don't know where they fit any more. Hence, the search for modes of belonging lead people away from community to seek refuge in a world of immediacy rather than through the bonds of basic and rooted solidarity. Participation and empowerment of people in the process of improving quality of life are the key words for a new life-supportive society. I believe we need a new set of values for knowledge to do this. At the same time, personal frontiers for knowledge ask for the realistic appraisal of the limits imposed by the higher value of life. All this is essential for me.

In addition, the method of "walking among fields of knowledge" helps us to understand the relationships between militarism, ecological destruction and poverty. I would say that the main issue for today and for the coming decade is one of poverty. Among every four human beings on this planet, one lives in total destitution. Most of these live in the southern hemisphere.

---

70 Maria de Lourdes Pintasilgo and Paul Harrison, *Caring for the Future: Making the Next Decades Provide a Life Worth Living* (New York, NY and Oxford, UK: Oxford University Press, 1996).

Something is wrong. It's not just a matter of sharing with those in need; it's more than that. It's a matter of reorganizing our national and global priorities and systems. During the Cold War we were all concerned with democracy and freedom from fear. I don't deny the value of liberty but I have always felt that, coming from a poor country like mine, liberty without housing and food is an empty word. Our world population is close to six billion, and one billion nine million of them don't even have the most rudimentary sanitation facilities in their houses. One billion three hundred million people don't have drinking water in the house where they live. Many have to walk miles to get it. For me, the revolution, or whatever needs to happen, has to involve a relentless combating of poverty.

It is now very clear that as we move towards more globalization, not only do people become disposable, but so do regions and whole countries. Take the situation of Africa. Africa now has a smaller share in international trade than they did under colonialism. This is one of the ironies of political life.

But when I think of poverty and being disposable, I think of women and children who make up the greatest number of the poor. The children, of course, suffer because the women suffer. If we don't find the mechanisms to regulate and control globalization we will have more and more poverty and women will be greatly affected.

Unfortunately, there are many women involved in decision-making positions leading to a kind of globalization that especially hurts women and children. So we need a tremendous awakening, a consciousness-raising, not as we had in the 1960s and 1970s with the women's liberation movement, but in terms of what we are doing to others. What are we doing as women? Where are the possibilities for doing for others? By what values do we live? What are we working for? What is our vision, how do we look at the world? Do we look at the world only through the eyes of professionals with one kind of power, or do we see from a spiritual perspective?

The Global Challenge for the Grail

Within the Grail, we need to study more. I am not referring necessarily to degrees and academic life, where people often just talk to themselves. People go on building theories and reproducing ideas so that praxis is often fed by very little thought. What we need is the interplay between theory and praxis that often are totally separated in the real world. So I think it is very important when we have projects in the Grail to ask why we are embarking on this, what is the rationale for this project. For instance, we need to ask, what is globalization, what does it mean? And then, what can we do about it? I see this as a necessary commitment of the Grail.

I think in order to face globalization we have to become more global ourselves. This sense of globalizing has to expand to our countries, our cultures, to other Christian denominations and to other religions where women are searching spiritually in other ways. So our first group is not necessarily the group of our country, because we work with people from other cultures.

For instance, Eileen Schaeffler and I were not close before she became International President and I was Vice President. Although we were very different we had the same vision about the Grail so there was a companionship, a solidarity between us. And the same was true with Magdalene Oberhoffer when she and I worked together. It was only after living under the same roof in Paris for two years that I realized she was a woman with a tremendous culture in music, in literature, in art. I still feel a great friendship with her and there are others in the Grail I feel the same way about.

We in the north have to look at the south in total partnership regardless of our backgrounds. At this point, the solidarity is there but sometimes it is there in a patronizing way, left over from colonialism; this undermines the international spirit. Change is structural but it also has to be psychological. We have to see the poor as ourselves. We need real networks of people within the Grail who feel the same way, who are developing new communities. This is already happening through e-mail with some of the young members.

We are a small movement and we can't change everything, but we can work with the two linking threads. The first is a very important shift in our responsibility—to denounce what in globalization leads to more poverty and to the social exclusion of people. This would not just be theoretical, but would include the actual poor in our own regions. We know that development does not necessarily bring human rights and quality of life. The president of the Grail in Brazil reminds us that Brazil is not an underdeveloped country—it is an unjust country.

Anne Hope and Sally Timmel worked on this in Africa using the best of tools from Marxist theory. We need now the same kind of analogies of society but done with the tools of globalization. Namely, the center of power is no longer in the political sphere. The center of power is with the multinationals. Power is now in the marketplace.

In my youth and early adult life, when I held political positions, one of the principal convictions was that political power had to control economic power because economics and the market are blind. The market doesn't see women, it doesn't see the poor, and it doesn't see the vulnerable or those who are not organized or are too weak to organize. Now the market only sees those who are able to make profits and not even those who share the profit.

Again, we have to understand poverty from various perspectives, not just poverty in itself. With poverty come issues such as the disappearance of systems of life, our exploitation of the environment and nature that is criminal because it destroys life support systems. This analysis of our societies is a very important element. Then we need to take a stand against the specific aspects of globalization that bring about and maintain poverty in our own countries.

A Personal Challenge

Change, though, is both structural and personal. So there is another thread that links to our concerns in the Grail, one that is very important for us in terms of globalization. Not only do we have to confront economic power but we need to take care of ourselves by supporting and being in solidarity with all Grail members as we strive to embrace a certain lifestyle, one that is a spiritual expression of the dignity of all things and beings in God's creation.

Even if we want to live according to certain values, the pressure of the milieu is very strong, with the power of the economic market. And conversion doesn't happen once and for all. Conversion comes from understanding at any time in our lives what prevents us from seeing the face of God. We know that's not the same at twenty, forty, or sixty years of age. We live in a world in transition and we are experiencing a tremendous change of paradigms. This makes the need for lifelong renewal very important.

For my own spiritual life and renewal, I have to remind myself that my work is only a little drop; it's not going to change the world, and sometimes I won't see any results. I spend time in nature and I also read a lot. In the evening, I read the text for the next day's liturgy.

Occasionally I go to Taizé, a Protestant monastic community in France that attracts people from all over Europe. Talking to the young people there is so stimulating. I feel a tremendous bridge to the future with the younger generation. Taizé has a very joyful and prayerful atmosphere centered on the essentials. I am reminded that prayer for me is not a dialogue but is part of an orientation and direction—to be quiet and silent before God. For me, also, while traveling in other countries, the meeting of people from other cultures and sharing in conversation has often touched me at the core of my spiritual being.

All of these experiences continue to deepen my conviction that across the spectrum of those who have nothing and those who have a lot, the solidarity of women is something we have to build in a very clear way. Our very survival depends on this, so that somehow we have to create another type of world and other types of rules, mechanisms, values that emphasize our global reality and the creation of a more humane world for all.

PART - IV

A Vision of a Justice-Filled New World (1957-2001)

Elizabeth Namaganda, location and date unknown

14

Elizabeth Estencia Namaganda

I longed for you my God—
to be one with you, to experience your touch.
You were present and yet far away.
Your silence puzzled me
till the moment the space
between heaven and earth opened
and I walked on Holy Ground.[71]

"Pioneer" is a word not to be used lightly, but Elizabeth Namaganda was truly a Grail pioneer, and especially in her own country, Uganda. Born on December 6, 1938, in Ggulama, Masaka, Elizabeth was a member of the first class to enroll, in 1954, at the Grail's Christ the King Secondary School in Kalisizo, Rakai.[72] She was also the

---

[71] From "In Appreciation ... ," memorial flyer from the Grail in Uganda upon the death of Elizabeth Namaganda, published after her death on December 12, 2012.

[72] For its first year, the school was located in Kasabala, but moved to Kalisizo in 1955. Mary Gindhart and Demmy Kyangye, *Histories of the Grail in Indivdual Countries* (Loveland, OH: Grailville, 1984), 73.

only member of that class to graduate, and, for many years, the only woman in her village to have completed secondary school.

That Elizabeth achieved all these pioneering successes does not mean that they came easily, however. The British curriculum used at Christ the King was strikingly unrelated to Elizabeth's culture and experience; she had no choice but to persevere, acquiring British cultural practices as well if she wished to succeed. It was worth it, she believed, because it enabled her to help change attitudes toward women's education in Uganda.

After leaving Christ the King in 1957, Elizabeth worked in Kampala as assistant to Scottish Grail member, Joan Dilworth, participating in Grail work with women in villages, helping with women's clubs, and teaching. Then, in 1958, she travelled via Europe to southwest Ohio, to Grailville, the center of the Grail in the United States, to begin three years of training. While she was at Grailville, according to Australian Grail member and journalist, Elizabeth Reid, Elizabeth Namaganda was "a radiant young woman," with "poise and dignity and charm."[73]

Elizabeth found her time at Grailville exciting, describing it as a place where she got "real formation." She received training in "family and community service" and was deeply influenced by the celebration of the liturgy there, as innumerable other women before and after her have been. During her years in the U.S., Elizabeth also lived for a time at the Grail house in Burlington, NJ; Lydwine van Kersbergen, co-founder of the U.S. Grail, was in residence there at the time, and directly influenced Elizabeth's spiritual development. Elizabeth also received more intensive formation at Super Flumina, the small Grail retreat center about ten miles from Grailville.

Upon returning to Uganda in 1960, Elizabeth continued her own education even as she threw herself into the education and social

---

[73] Elizabeth Reid, I *Belong Where I'm Needed*, 175.

welfare of other women, a Grail work to which she would dedicate the rest of her life. In 1961 Elizabeth and Kevine Nabwani travelled to the Netherlands where they each made their dedication in the Nucleus of the Grail; they were the first Ugandan women to do so.

In 1968 Joan Dilworth and Imelda Namkula Tibasoboke set up the Uganda Catholic Social Training Center[74] in Rubaga. Elizabeth became the director of that center in 1970,[75] and continued working there as director for the rest of her life, that is, for forty-two years. The Ugandan Catholic Bishops Conference established the Center with funding from Misereor, the German Catholic Bishops Organization for Development. The center provided education for voluntary adult leaders from all sections of the Ugandan population, primarily girls and women, and was used for Grail courses as well. Beginning in 1980, for example, the center offered a five-month residential program for girls who had recently left school. The courses prepared the girls for a life after school, including equipping them with skills with which to earn a living. Elizabeth brought to the Uganda Catholic Social Training Center "remarkable strength, leadership, determination, commitment."[76]

During the years after her return to Uganda, Elizabeth also made an amazing number of other contributions to the Grail, to the Catholic Church, and to Ugandan society. For example, she served on the Roman Catholic Council of the Laity at the Vatican for ten years, representing Central and East African countries. She was one of the trustees of the Uganda Grail from 1970 to 2012, and a member of the Grail National Finance Team from 1972 to 2012.

---

74 The center is now called The Uganda Catholic Management and Training Institute.

75 Some records say 1971.

76 From "In Appreciation…," Elizabeth Namaganda's memorial flyer from the Ugandan Grail.

She was also a member of the National Leadership Team of the Grail in Uganda for more than twelve years, and for eight years a member of the International Grail Nucleus Team. Elizabeth was also the Chairperson of the Catholic Women's Association for Central and East Africa Committee, a local committee member of the Uganda Catholic Women's Bureau, Deputy Secretary to the Uganda Joint Christian Council, and a member of the board of the Ecumenical Church Loan Fund.

In light of all this, one cannot help suspecting that Elizabeth Namaganda was a genuinely humble woman. In the interview that follows this introduction, she spends amazingly little time emphasizing her accomplishments, speaking instead at length about the Grail in Uganda. It remains to us, her Grail sisters, to share the details of her lifetime of achievement.

After suffering from cancer for some months, Elizabeth died on June 12, 2012, in Rubaga Hospital, the hospital in Uganda that the Grail had administered from 1953 to 1973. She was surrounded by many of her Grail sisters, who had taken turns sitting by her bedside throughout her hospitalization. Elizabeth's Requiem Mass was celebrated in St. Mary's Rubaga Cathedral on June 15. She was buried at the Grail's farm, Nakirebe, the first Grail member whose body blessed the communal burial space there. Each year on the anniversary of Elizabeth's death, the Grail holds a special Eucharistic celebration in her honor.

Interview

The Great Experiment: Education For Women

In my family, I was considered the "black" sheep, or the "white" sheep, since I was the only one to leave home. And also, at that time, not many women had a chance to go beyond primary school. What really made my childhood special was that around my village I was the only girl who went for and finished secondary schooling.

Oh, yes, people asked my father a lot of questions and my mother wondered if the whites weren't taking me in since I went to the school run by the Grail. Although my mother never really said much, she was not for what I was doing.

Frances van der Schott[77] had started the school; Alice McCarthy and Josephine Drabek came a little later. I was a bright student; I finished primary school in four rather than the usual six years. But secondary school was quite hard. I had to learn new languages; I had to learn many other difficult subjects that I was not accustomed to. And since I was a pioneer in these stages of education for women and with the Grail, things were not that easy. I felt at times that I was being experimented on because they (the Grail) were just beginning this whole new thing. They were still shaping up, so to speak.

We started with about twenty-seven young women. But others kept dropping out to get married. Others who didn't marry, and those were very few, went into convents. They were attracted to the convent. And at the end I was left alone, the only one to finish secondary school in my group.

The Underside of the Experiment

Our system of education in Uganda had come from England, so it was the British system. And it was very much the same in the Grail school. Even the examinations came from England. These examinations did not relate at all to my culture. They didn't relate to anything I grew up with and therefore all these things were strange to me.

But I had to cope; I had to learn it. The kind of geography and history we learned had nothing to do with us. It was British geography with British scenarios and we had to deal with it. We were taught about the Ice Age and those kinds of things that didn't

---

77 See Chapter 3, 41–60.

mean a thing to us, but we simply had to memorize them, cram them and answer the questions.

None of it ever meant anything to one's life. It did not add anything to what we knew and saw and grew up with. I have given this whole thing a lot of thought. It was difficult but it was the only thing we had, so I managed to pass the exams.

On the other hand, this did give me a lot of background for other experiences later in life. I had not really even dreamt about the kinds of things my education would lead to.

It certainly gained me access to other avenues. For instance, I was sent on an international exchange program. Before I went, though, I had to go to a certain place to be prepared: to learn how a white man eats, how to hold a fork and knife, how to hold a spoon, how to make a bed, how to do everything in a British home in a white British culture. If you can do it like the British do it, then you are accepted in the civilized society. At the time I took this for granted. I thought that this was all part of life. But now, this kind of regime could not be forced on us.

The positive side of this is that, as a pioneer, I was able to break through objections to education for women. Very quickly the fever caught on and many parents became interested in sending young women to the Grail's social training center at Rubaga, near Kampala. People in my country, and in my village, where at one time they thought I was very strange, now have different values toward education than they had when I started out. At the beginning, I set the example.

Blending Continuing Education Into Life

After secondary school, I became involved in Grail activities, in the Grail movement. So even though my education continued, it was fragmented. I was going from one thing to another.

For instance, I left this country and went to Europe; from Europe I went to America. When I returned, I went back into formal education, and even that was interspersed with Grail activities. So my education didn't follow a straight line. At a certain point, while I was in America, I decided to take up social work and I had to deal with the fragments; I was pursuing studies and participating in Grail activities.

A very important part of my education took place at Grailville. I was sixteen when I went there.[78] I could have used this time for other kinds of formal education, learning about other things. At that age, of course, I was full of life and full of inspiration to explore. Yes, I was in the age of exploring, so it did not matter that I was away from my home for so long.

The Grail as I knew it at that time attracted me because it was made up of women from different professions and women who could work in society as laypeople. I went to Grailville because it was exciting. In fact, I had an exciting teenage life. I could move overseas at the age of sixteen[79]; at the time, this was quite unusual and, of course, it made me feel good. And everybody admired me.

On the other hand, when I thought things over seriously, I didn't know if I was doing the right thing; I didn't know if this was going to be my life. I was full of these kinds of questions until later in life but at the time I felt very confident, very, very happy.

---

78 If, as other records indicate, Elizabeth was born in 1938, then it seems she was nineteen or even twenty when she arrived at Grailville. Perhaps her seemingly incorrect recollection here tells us more about how old Elizabeth felt when she landed on another continent than how old she actually was.

79 See previous footnote.

I was at Grailville for three years and I learned a lot during that time. I learned about many different cultures, about religious education. Grailville is where I got a real formation, a spiritual formation.

During this period of time, I went to Burlington,[80] where Lydwine van Kersbergen was living at the time. I can tell you that that was a very special period of time where I was just soaked in a very real spiritual and religious training. As a young person, I was being trained to put God first in my life and nothing else. Forget about all the other cares, sit down and think of spiritual things. This is what matters.

So I had to go deep into my faith. And I remember Lydwine giving me a card on which was written, "Faith can move mountains." I thought at the time that she gave me this card because my faith was not deep enough. I had to reflect on that for quite some time because she kept insisting and asking me all kinds of questions. At times, I felt Lydwine was testing me. But what she was about was making sure that I had it really in my blood. She was quite special. When she got into something, she, herself, forgot about everything else. The food could burn on the stove when Lydwine was talking about God. You could think of nothing else. At times we got angry, we blamed her for leaving us, for intoxicating us with all these spiritual instructions, but later on we came to appreciate her very much. She gave us a firm foundation. It was something we could not have gotten anywhere else and it is something we value as very special.

---

80 The Grail had a house in Burlington, New Jersey, where Lydwine van Kersbergen and other Grail leaders went for more intensive prayer and formation. Often, those preparing for leadership roles were invited to participate.

I also spent time at Super Flumina.[81] That was quite an experience, something else that I value very much. At that time it was tough; it was really hard on us; but now I appreciate it because if it hadn't been for those kinds of experiences, I think that religion would have meant very little to me. A lot has since changed. We don't have all that rigidity of spiritual exercises. But I think that those of us who lived it, appreciate it. It built me up, I must admit. As a result, religion is something I have committed my whole life to; it is the foundation on which the spiritual part of me is built.

All in all, my experience at Grailville was very enriching. So much of that was ahead of Vatican II; we did things that were not yet permitted and that we had not even thought of, like receiving Communion in the hand. And the wonderful celebrations, Holy Thursday, for instance. And we prayed the Psalms. I missed all of this when I came home. Now when we have these practices, it is part of my history, but it is new here. I feel I owe a lot to God and all those people who have enriched me. And I wish I could perhaps enrich others in the same way.

Bringing the Learning Home

When I returned home to Uganda, I was received like the prodigal son. There was a big celebration in the village and almost everyone came—look at my child who was lost, now she is found.

My mother insisted that I come home because she knew if I remained longer I would never come back. She couldn't understand or appreciate that I was not looking for a man to marry. She still thought I was too influenced by the white world. Later on she realized she was fighting a defeating battle; she gave up.

---

81 Super Flumina was a small Grail retreat center in Foster, Ohio, about ten miles from Grailville, the national center of the U.S. Grail in southwestern Ohio. It was situated on a few acres of land and was used for intensive spiritual formation.

As for me, I was trying to look at a future where I would perhaps be in a professional occupation. This was somehow mixed with my Grail aspirations—a profession and the Grail. So I projected myself toward that end. Back then, I felt I had gained a lot; I was spiritually happy and comfortable even though some of my family still did not know what I was about. But I said, "As long as I am happy, I don't care, as long as I am not doing anything wrong, and as long as I haven't rejected God in my life."

Although my father also did not understand what I was doing, he supported me. He said to me as I travelled all over, "Now, whatever you do, you must always pray. Say your prayers every day, every day—prayer means that you are still with God." In fact, when we were young, we were not allowed to stay overnight at the home of relatives who were Moslems or Protestant since it was difficult in these places for us to say our prayers.

I had wanted to come back to my country and immerse myself with my fellow women, and girls especially, from my home area where I had had a chance for an education that they did not have. I started with my sisters. One of them is now in Kampala with her family. She completed her secondary education and went into professional training and is now working. And this is what I wanted for her.

Even though today it seems normal for woman to complete school and even go on to university, there are very few who do; there is still a lot of pushing that one has to do. Some of the ones who drop out after secondary education really end up with a lot of problems and a lot of difficulties. We need to do something about this since it affects a very large number of people. Boys experience the same, but they can learn other skills. They can go into technical education, which is just opening to girls. Although we push very hard, very few girls go this way. There are very few openings for skills that are actually more attractive to women.

But now, with the computer age, things are opening up more and girls are going into banking and other occupations. Some of them are taking engineering; a lot of them are studying medicine. Women have to persevere, and once they have access to a university, the opportunities are many.

The employment situation, though, is another story, another struggle. We need to create opportunities for employment. This is a challenge. But the good thing is that the government and the church see many advantages in encouraging women with their education.

The church, however, has not really honored the participation of women in the activities of the church as fully and as freely as we would like. For instance, in terms of pastoral life, there is a lot more that women could do. But now, they are not allowed. I am not really propagating for the ordination of women, but I think the church can recognize women's contribution, a push can be given, encouragement and inspiration.

If women were even allowed to study theology, we could do a lot. I have been working in church structures all the years of my working life and I do feel there is a lot to be desired. But we can't hope that this is going to change in the very near future; it will take a long time. Women also have to ask for this, to put themselves forward.

In Uganda, many women only see real participation in being a nun or in being ordained. But they have a role as laywomen. They could be involved in catechetical instructions. There are things women are doing like working in the bishop's office or in the presbytery as typists and cooks. This is fine, I have no objection to all this, but I feel that the women can do a lot more in the way of educating the young, in pastoring the community.

When I look back, it was the women, like my mother, who were the educators of the children, of the adolescents, of the young women, and they were preparing them for marriage. Although Vatican II opened many doors, I feel that women could be of great service to the church and be more effective if they were given training, the skills in the way of passing on spiritual formation. These are my dreams and they come from my own experiences and reflections, things I hope for the future.

Responding to Women's Greatest Needs

But to go back. The beginning of the Grail here and the beginning of my real participation in the development of the Grail in Uganda started when the first two of us, Kevine Nabwani and I, committed ourselves in the Grail. This was in 1961. We were the first two Ugandan members. Later Imelda Gaurwa joined us; she had come from Tanzania for her formation since she was alone in her own country at that time.

We worked a lot together in the beginning and we took turns in taking the leadership roles. We saw that women lacked education, especially in looking after their homes and feeding their children—just that kind of practical education. And this is what we started with, together with Joan Dilworth and the White Sisters who had been doing this kind of work for a long time.

We taught women nutrition, child care, simple methods of preparing food. Along with this we taught the women to read and to write. This was really the greatest need at that time.

Now that the women have been to school and learned a lot more, their needs are different. They are much more articulate, and they want to engage themselves in their own economic development, which in the past was the role for men only. They also want to provide the possibility of education for their children, which in the past was not recognized as an important part of life.

Early on, we also went around to different schools taking the gospel, the Grail gospel, thus giving information about our different apostolate. We worked with Joan Dilworth who later on did much through her social work profession. But before we got involved in our professional activities, we did go around to bring the message of the apostolate and organizing young women into groups in various schools. Sometimes, this would take place at Christ the King School that was still run by the Grail.

As our group grew, we moved on and changed our style. We invited women to different Grail programs. In many of these programs, I had a leadership role or I was responsible for trying to organize finances, something I am still doing, and which, of course, we cannot do much without.

There were many Dutch women here who contributed to the Grail. There is a litany of names. They have all contributed through their practical work, through their professional work. They were working in hospitals, others were teaching, others were doing social work, but we always met together. On some occasions we just came to reflect and plan for the Grail and to work for the development of the Grail as such. It has been quite a full program for each one of us in our lives, but it has also been a joy because many of us feel fulfilled in these tasks just by the fact that the Grail has been built up.

The Lord has called some of those women. And I am sure now that even those the Lord has called are happy to have left the Grail established here. You see, the responsibility was shared with others, but I was still called upon to help here or give advice there. That has been my life here.

We will continue the Grail as Ugandaized. The Ugandan women in the Grail are very committed and they have definitely built up the movement. And this gives us, those of us who are now getting on in years, the feeling that yes, it will grow, it will continue, it won't die and that is really a good feeling.

I must say that this has been due to the efforts of Ugandan women, this building up of the Grail. It is in their hands; they are mature, they are no longer children, and they can stand on their own feet. And they are now also building up our centers. We don't have many but we feel that the few that there are are slowly growing for sure. And we have also spread to Kenya and Tanzania.

Imelda (Gaurwa) has contributed a lot to our beginnings in Uganda and to the Grail in Tanzania.[82] And we are all working together to establish the Grail in Kenya. We are working with women who are quite committed and are working hard to get the Grail to take root there, and for that we are happy. We have great hopes that it will continue and eventually we would like to be joined by others from West Africa and Mozambique. And now that South Africa is open, we are making connections there, and these connections will definitely bear returns.

Yes, there are differences on a cultural level between all of us. Our values sometimes are not the same. But it is almost impossible to make comparisons between one culture and the other. One difference between Africa and countries elsewhere, of course, is that in African countries women are expected to marry. Religious life is very acceptable, but the value of the Christian woman who is not married or not a religious, but has dedicated her life to celibacy, is still questioned. The society, and the church as a whole, still question.

I think that slowly people are beginning to realize that such a life of celibacy is possible and they can see that it has been done, and is still being done. In the Bible you find that in the times of Christ there were such women.

---

82 See Chapter 15, 297-324.

But on another level, they were invisible and I think it is the same with us. In the past, there were even women in our culture who were not committed to the church or to Christ but they were set aside not to marry. When we had kings as leaders, these women played a special role in the houses of these kings. They were there but always in the background. Their role was behind the curtains, preparing meals for all the gatherings. They were seen by society as the women who were working with the king or were there to be played with, enough women for the king, set apart for the king, alone, to be available. Now we can compare our own culture to that one, and say that now it is possible for a laywoman to be living in society, to lead a life in community, a life of celibacy dedicated to Christ. It is possible, but before it was unheard of.

A different side of the coin is the experience of married women in the Grail in our country. Society sees us, the celibate ones, in a different way; we live in community, we have a spiritual life, we also dedicate ourselves completely to the community, the life of community and to the service of the church.

But even the married members also commit themselves permanently in the Grail to serve. At times they are away from their families. These women need public recognition by the Grail because they go out of their way as married women, committed to the service of the church, to serve within the Grail community in addition to their family responsibilities. I do hope that through them also society will understand the Grail better, rather than through us, the "spinsters" whom others regard, no matter how we explain it, as religious without a veil.

I think such understanding will come with time and we do feel that we are becoming more understood than we were in the past. In the past we were there, something like a club. But now others are seeing us as a community, a community that has other categories of membership. So this gives us hope for the future.

I think people have come to know more about the Grail in Uganda and appreciate the services we have extended to the needs of society. I feel that wherever the Grail has been, the women have been opened up and understood. There is an appreciation of women and there are models of women we have that can be looked to and admired and aspired to. My hope is that there will be more of a sense of community, especially for young women with education who have been affected by either the war or results of war. We want to give our younger generation the knowledge to sustain themselves and their families.

And now, protecting the environment is a big area. We all have to be creative to promote the care of the earth. It will not only contribute to the Grail, but to the whole of society. If our women can learn the skills of knowing how to care for the earth, I think we will have contributed a lot to other sectors—education, economics, the survival of our mission. We will achieve what we are attempting to achieve.

The Future of the Grail and of the Church

I believe the Grail will survive, not with large numbers but with a few who will be committed to carry on even when some of us are gone. It is also true on an international level with the Grail. Our hope, of course, is that we still build on what we already have, and that the changes of the times don't really change us to the extent that we bury the Grail.

I get a bit anxious when I look at the numbers among the membership. If young ones don't come forward, will the Grail survive? I think we need to look at the issue very seriously and find ways and means of taking care of it so that the Grail can survive before all these old ones go. Something ought to be done, although we need to be careful that we don't take young people simply for the sake of taking in young members so the Grail will survive. It still won't survive.

We need a real committed new generation. How can that be secured? I think we need to study it. Also, science has brought about a lot of changes in attitude, a change in our faith, and somehow that has to be looked at, studied, in order to relate these changes to the life of the Christian, the believer. Some of the young ones who are coming come with an understanding that they want to commit themselves. I think Father van Ginneken is also responsible for this inspiration. And some of the women who started with him are responsible for this inspiration. We could have just said, "Well, this was an idea brought by some white women from Europe and America and it doesn't really work for us. Let them go away and we will find something that will suit our culture."

We have had the opportunity to really look at our culture and the relationship of our spiritual life and how we can bring them together. Vatican II accepted the fact that culture is an important element in one's life. Therefore, wherever the change is, it should look at culture, should address the issues of culture, and should make the church part of the culture of the people. That has encouraged us to look at our culture as to how we are related to the Grail objectives in our community and how we can interpret those objectives.

And that is what we have to study, to work out, so we don't alienate ourselves. This is coming. We are also looking at language so that we don't always express our Grail identity in a foreign language. Speaking only English has given the impression that the Grail is élite.

So, we have to translate the Grail into our culture, and language is very important in doing that. It is hard; it's a struggle because we even take home a white culture from international meetings. The idea of unity amidst diversity is just beginning to be addressed on an international level. There are signs of development in this area, not only here but also elsewhere; Grail members around the world are reflecting on these issues. So we aren't really that far apart, because we recognize this as a need in our lives. I hope that the Grail will continue in some way or other to carry on the spirit of service and the spirit of growth in the church as Christians.

One of our fears has to do with secularism. The world is becoming more secularized. This is a new concept we see developing in the Western world as related to God and the church, where the church may have to change structures in order to accommodate everyone.

This has hit us differently. I think we are still somehow behind. Christianity is much older in Europe. There are things permissible there that are not permissible with us. I wonder about why this is always so.

Our young people go to Europe and sometimes come back with the attitude that it doesn't matter whether they go to church, you don't need the church, and you don't need God. These are some of the developments we fear might destroy the values we have lived with for a long time and still hold on to. People who come to live with us often say: "I don't even pray." That shocks us and we say, "How can we survive?" This sometimes puts off our young generation here, too—when they see young people from other countries training for the Grail who say they don't need God, they don't need to pray.

This worries me and I think that we as Grail have failed to somehow work together with the proposals that have been made to bring young people who are aspiring to the Grail here in our country. Things are different, the attitudes change, but I do hope and pray that we will not divert into a secular kind of life. This is my message to younger women in the Grail. We need that spiritual deepening and enrichment, the going back all the time to the life of Christ, to ensure that it remains. I hope we will never lose touch with the word of Christ, the word of God, and the imitation of God in our lives.

Actually, when I was a young person going to school and even in my early Grail days, I did participate a lot in other youth movements such as the white Young Christian Students. We moved a lot in groups, mainly trying to live out our own faith, trying to practice charity with each other and the community around us.

Later on, when I joined in the lay apostolate movement, I served for fourteen years on the Consulate for the Laity in Rome as an African representative.[83] It was during that time that I gained a lot of experience that has contributed to my spiritual life, to the life of my faith, and has also enriched and encouraged me to continue and to stand firm in the Grail and my Grail vocation. In turn, it was through the Grail that I met a number of church people who enriched and inspired me. And this made me realize the importance of women working within the structures of the church in order to participate in the life of the church.

---

83 Once again, there is some difference between what Elizabeth remembers here about how long she served as a representative to the Vatican Consulate on the Laity, and responses from the Ugandan Grail to questions posed to them in 2015 regarding Elizabeth's life.

Imelda Alfred Gaurwa, location and date unknown

15

Imelda Alfred Gaurwa

*The Grail succeeded here in Tanzania
because wherever the Grail went we left a kind of sisterhood.
Wherever we have gone
we have built a community of people.*

From the time she was born, in 1938, Imelda Gaurwa was surrounded by models of strong leadership. Her father was a chief of the Haya tribe in Tanzania and she remembers him presiding, when she was a young child, over meetings of local people. They had gathered in the community hall to address their problems, things that were happening in the village. Sometimes they came on a daily basis to talk. They talked, they made decisions together, and everyone was encouraged to put the results into practice.

Years later Imelda would assume the leadership role in establishing the Grail movement in her country, the first African Grail member to do so. Previously, Grail women from Europe or the U.S. took on the task. And in 1993 she was elected to the Grail's International Presidency Team, another first for an African Grail member. It is highly likely that Imelda's role as the oldest in a family of six children and her enrollment at the age of seven in a mission boarding school influenced her sense of independence and nurtured the capabilities later reflected in the responsibilities she assumed as a Grail leader.

Because of her father's position and his ownership of a large banana plantation, Imelda grew up in the city of Bukoba in what she describes as a "privileged" home.[84] There were maids and a number of other servants in the household and therefore Imelda did not learn how to do any practical manual work until she went to boarding school. Her most outstanding memory of her early life is the care and concern shown by her father and mother, although, as she notes, her mother was somewhat passive and went along with whatever her father wanted.

For instance, he made sure his children were always dressed appropriately; he was very specific and very precise while her mother was not fussy and just abided by the wishes of her husband. Imelda's mother could, in fact, read and write but, as was the custom concerning male and female roles in the household, she could not participate in discussions with her husband when they were with other people.

Imelda's mother was Catholic, and her father later converted to Catholicism. Early on, he was not interested in any Christian practices, but he never opposed Imelda's mother's efforts to have her children baptized and raised Catholic. In fact, her father encouraged her mother to take Imelda, when she was a two-months-premature newborn, to a mission hospital where the baby received the kind of care not available in the village and was baptized there. And though her mother sent Imelda to a village preschool where she was taught prayers and prepared for first Communion, it was her father who arranged for Imelda to

---

84 Bukoba is a city and a region in northwest Tanzania on the western shore of Lake Victoria. "Bukoba," Wikipedia, The Free Encyclopedia, accessed July 16, 2016, https://en.wikipedia.org/wiki/Bukoba.

attend a Catholic boarding school run by the Missionary Sisters of Africa.

Attending a Catholic school was another privilege accorded Imelda in her early years; her brothers and sisters went to a government school. Imelda attended boarding school until she was seventeen. She went home for holidays and, as a result of long separations from her family, did not grow close to her siblings until later in life. The greatest influence on her religious and spiritual life did not come from her own family, then, but from living in the boarding school community and receiving a Catholic education from the nuns. In fact, when she went home for visits, she was the one who got the family together for prayer.

Although Imelda's father was not a Christian, according to Imelda he was a man of faith who understood the meaning of Christianity. She remembers him as a very thoughtful person, reflecting on his own knowledge, what he knew and did not know, and on his relationships with others. She eventually taught him religion and what it meant to be a Christian by reading passages to him that she chose from the prayer books and the missal, since the family did not have a Bible. She was trying to teach him, but often it was the other way around; he was always the one to interpret the meaning of the reading from a Christian point of view. Not until later did Imelda realize that his ability to convey the message to her was due to his own insight rather than the fact that he was older than she was.

Imelda describes herself as having been an average student, in the boarding school that she attended. She does see herself as a lifelong learner, however, someone who is constantly learning and being educated. She recalls one woman teacher at the boarding school whom she greatly admired for the ways she taught. Imelda remembers that she impressed a lot of young girls, including herself.

During Imelda's teenage years, Tanzania achieved independence. Imelda knew that there were wrongs in her society. Her education continued until the age of twenty-two, when she finished secondary school. Then, after meeting the Grail in 1959, she finished a course in adult education and took a leadership training course.

Because of the influence of the Catholic sisters in her boarding school, Imelda had at one point decided to become a sister, as well as a teacher. Her father objected but she did go to a teacher-training school. She had been teaching one year when she heard about the Grail from a priest who told her about Coleta van der Ploeg, a Dutch Grail member who had come to set up a program for prostitutes and who knew about Christian women working in Uganda. Imelda was nineteen, she was searching for something, and she thought that the Grail might allow her to serve in the community while still maintaining a close relationship with her family. She took the initiative to find Coleta and invited her to meet her parents. When they met, Imelda had to do the translating —Coleta did not speak Swahili and Imelda's parents did not speak English. Her parents, nonetheless, encouraged her to become involved with the Grail since it seemed quite different from a convent.

Imelda spent the next two years in a Grail formation program in Mubende, Uganda, where she was introduced to new liturgical celebrations and the role women could take in Catholic Action. She made her lifetime dedication in the Nucleus of the Grail at the Tiltenberg in August, 1963. Her parents were opposed to her making a commitment for life but Imelda was searching for a permanent community. Eventually, they approved, thinking her dedication was temporary. That same year she went to Moshi, back in Tanzania, where, with Ton Brouwer, she helped to start the bookshop.

When the request came to start a Grail training program in Tanzania, Imelda was the obvious person to do so. She was the only African Grail member in Tanzania who had been through a formation program. Another Tanzanian, Honorata Mvungi, joined her. They opened the center in Kisekibaha in 1970 with six young women. The program was, from the beginning, developed by Africans, for Africans. When the center began, it was considered a two-year experiment. It progressed very slowly and with much hard work and support, it continues today.

Imelda stayed at Kisekibaha for twelve years. Then, beginning in 1982, at the invitation of Bishop Lebulu, she took charge of the Catholic Women Development Program of the Same Diocese. Imelda also played a significant role in the International Grail, becoming, in 1993, the first African to be elected to the International Presidency Team (IPT).

After leaving the IPT in 1998, Imelda became head of school at the Grail's Emy Gordon Vocational Training Center at Rau, a suburb of Moshi, in Tanzania. She still lives with the Grail team at Rau, and serves as Technical Advisor at Emy Gordon. Retirement is not a part of Tanzanian culture, but in recent years, Imelda has suffered from some health problems, including diabetes and high blood pressure. She continues to walk between one and one and a half kilometers a day, and is able to participate in the liturgy.

In the following interview, done in 1995, one of the strongest convictions Imelda expresses is that she found a spirituality in the Grail that she never found in any other community in the church. She refers to this as a "Grail culture," a unique way of living, of celebrating, which for her is the root and the essence of the Grail vision. Her role in the International Grail has convinced her that, although the vision of the Grail is expressed in accordance with the needs of each country in which the Grail exists, it is the core vision of the Grail that binds members together in community. Her life has been devoted to a continuous search for how the Tanzanian Grail can sustain its own cultural identity and, at the same time, be faithful to making this Grail vision a reality.

Interview

Family Life and Education

I was born in 1938 in a family where my mother was a Christian but my father was not. My mother told me that I was born prematurely at seven or eight months old, and since we didn't have proper hospitals then, my parents were specifically advised to take me to the mission, because that's where there was good care for premature kids. I don't know how long we stayed. But later I was baptized, when I was still very small. So I grew up under the supervision of my mother, as she was the only Christian.

My father was the chief of the village at that time, so we had many privileges. When I was around the age of five or six, I went to the village pre-school and also got my first Holy Communion. The person who was behind me in all this was my mother. My father was never interested in practicing Christianity, but he didn't oppose it, either. And after receiving my first Holy Communion my father wanted me to go to a boarding school that was under the supervision of a community of the sisters. So from the age of seven I grew up in a boarding school.

I had two brothers and four sisters, but I was the first child in the family. For education, we had government schools and mission schools, but I am among the few who had the privilege of going to a mission school; the rest of my brothers and sisters went to the government school. So my spirituality came from the school, in fact, not from the family. And that separation from my brothers and sisters from an early age—I came home for holidays of course—meant that we didn't grow close until later.

My mother was supportive of me but she was not very active. So what I cared about most during my life came from the school. When I was home, I was the one who was preaching to my parents, telling them what they should be doing—and that my father should be baptized. I, in fact, was the one who convinced my father to become a Christian.

What I remember about my family is the care and concern. My father even would tell you to change the dress you were wearing if it was not fitting. He was very precise. My mother was not very fussy, but she was obedient about the way my father wanted us to appear.

We grew up in a family where we had people working for us, maids and other servants doing things for us. Myself, I was not a hard-working person like other African women who were expected to dig and so forth. I had never done that practical work of digging at my home. We did fetch water and wash clothes, but not all the manual work. But later—I am very grateful to the Lord for this—I learned how to dig at school. And, also, I think, although my father was not Christian as I was growing up, he was a man of faith. Very often he would sit down and reflect on what we know or we don't know; he'd reflect upon his work and also about his relationship to the people around him.

And I remember when I started teaching my father religion. I would just take a passage and read to him and I thought I was the one teaching him but it was the other way around. He was the one telling me what the passage meant from the Christian point of view. So I felt that my father had a very good insight but, of course, I did not realize what that meant. I thought because he was a grown up person, he understood more than I did, so that's why he could translate for me the message of what I was reading. But now I realize that although he was not a Christian at the time, he had faith. This is why he could understand certain aspects of what was in the Missal, the prayer books. So I would use those for praying and teaching him prayer, but then he would tell me what they meant. This happened very often. I think he had a sense of who God was and the mystery of God was alive for him.

My father was a chief in the Haya tribe. As a chief, you call people together in the *baraza*, a kind of community hall. This came from the old times, when the British set up a kind of community hall where people would meet, where people would come together to discuss and solve the problems with their leaders. And if they didn't go to the *baraza* they would come to our place. I remember we had so many people around almost every day. They would come and discuss whatever was going on in the village. Then my father would tell the people to put into practice whatever the discussion had been about.

Unlike some families, my family didn't gather together for rituals or prayers. On the contrary. After I went to school I was the one pulling my family together for prayer.

I really have an image of God from what I was taught as a child at the missionary school. And also before that, from the pre-school where we were taught reading and writing and religion. So that's when I started getting the image of God. I understood from the catechism that God could see everything you were doing. And I understood that God would punish us, as our parents did. Like my father—if you'd do something wrong he would punish you immediately by beating you, so I think I understood God in relation to the way I understood my parents. I believed that God is a punishing God. I had that mentality.

But my image of God today is really different. I see God now as good, as very good. He understands me. I see God as a loving father who has cared for my entire life up to now. I see God as somebody who is very good to me. I see God as a father because my relationship to God comes through Christ, Jesus Christ. This is the Jesus who is present, who is expressing his Father to us in the Gospel and this has gone into my mind so many times. So I try not to relate the way I understood God at that earlier time, as today that understanding is very different. He is a loving God, yes, loving and caring. And a very nice friend. Because in the readings that we read in the Gospel of St. Luke, God is very loving and very patient. God does not pay back. There are many things that are not right going on and God isn't quiet. You know, he is working for us as well as listening—he waits for us to change, and to see if this is not the right way, then you better take it the right way. God is a patient God.

The mission school was run by an order of nuns, the Missionary Sisters of Africa, called the White Sisters. But they had a lot of laywomen who were teaching at the school. Perhaps there were forty of us in the class. I was not the fastest student, but I was not the last, so perhaps that encouraged me to carry on studying.

I was in the boarding school until I was eighteen. Then I went to what we called secondary school, which was up to age twenty-two. Then later I joined the teacher-training school and after that training I taught for one year. Then I met the Grail, and went into the Grail. After that I took a course in adult education for one year and several other courses. I took a course in leadership; I took courses in Red Cross first aid.

In my life I really wanted to become a teacher. And there was a time when I wanted to become a religious in a sisters' convent. But this was not supported; it was not my father's choice so I stopped it. So when I met the Grail and discovered that it was serving us in communities—that you can serve God and at the same time you can keep your relationship with your family—I felt this was good. I didn't know whether it would be possible but I said, perhaps I will try it.

So my expectations changed quite a bit from wanting to be a nun to joining the Grail. But for me I really wanted to become a teacher. But I also wanted to find my way in what I thought was a Godly direction.

So many things have changed over the years. But for me, what has not changed is faith. You know, faith doesn't change—it develops.

You grow in faith, you get a better understanding of how to live as a Christian. Vatican II made what we once regarded as dreams not dreams anymore. Things change, but the changes give us a direction and a new way of looking at faith. I think this is where the Grail movement is, too.

Vatican II brought a lot of joy into my life. I recall that festive time when we were told we could go to the midnight Mass on Christmas because Jesus was born in the night. For me, it was something very new. And then they said there could be an Easter celebration in the night—all those things were new for me. I never thought that things would change in the Catholic Church; it used to be very rigid.

The old way of worship has moved on now, it's more expressive—I think there is a lot of freedom. It is like finding a flower, which for a long time never sees light, but when light comes—boom, it opens up. The same for me, I think. Vatican II was a way of opening up. Coming and giving us directions, and then we had a new understanding.

The Grail

I first heard about the Grail from a priest. He knew I was searching for something but I didn't know what, because my family members did not support me in my desire to join the sisters. He didn't know much about the Grail but he told said there was a woman in town who could tell me about it, Coleta van der Ploeg.

When I met Coleta and told her about my search, she said she would come to my home. She told my parents about the Grail. My parents did not speak English and Coleta did not know Swahili; at that time she was learning Swahili but she did not know enough yet, so I was the one who did the translating. And at the end my parents said, "Okay, you can try if you want to." They did not want to disappoint me.

So then I went right away to Uganda for formation because there was no formation here in Tanzania. Coleta took me to the Grail in Rubaga. There I met Elizabeth Weigand, Magdalene Oberhoffer, and many other Grail women. Elizabeth Namaganda was not there at the time; she was in America. When I went to Uganda it was December, the end of the year. So I stayed for the Christmas celebration at Rubaga and I was exposed to how the Grail women celebrate, which interested me very highly. For the first time I saw the Advent wreath. I did not understand what it was.

Then Christmas came and they had a very big celebration. All the Grail members were there. I said, "Oh, this is what Christianity means." I was really impressed, as if I was in heaven. I will never forget this, my first time of being in the Grail; it was Christmas time.

Then, in the new year, we had a program at Mubende. There was Jane Namugenyi[85] and Theo Namule. Then Kevina Mabwami joined us. And Theopista Lukwago. There were about six in in the formation program, for one year.

During the program, we heard a lot about the lay apostolate. It was very much emphasized. We learned how working with women's groups was also part of Catholic Action. And parents would bring students to different courses—Holy Week, Easter, Christmas—at which their daughters would discuss how to use their time in school and what a young woman should know and practice in her life as a Christian. So I came to understand that the purpose of the Grail was to assist young women to discover their talents so they could use those talents properly to build up the Kingdom of God in their society. The emphasis was on them using their talents very well.

---

85 Jane Namugenyi's family name is sometimes spelled Namagany.

When Father van Ginneken talked about women contributing to the conversion of the world, I think he meant that the world was big. I think he wanted the Good News to be spread all over by reaching out to as many people as possible so that the Christian faith would reach all corners in the world. And I think the women wanted to participate because women are the ones who always keep the faith—more than men, I think.

And for me, what Father van Ginneken meant when he spoke about converting the world was not just working to have people become Christians, but converting the world to become a better world. This means to overcome poverty, to overcome miseries from which most of the people are suffering—and at the same time to enable them to feel the joy of becoming a Christian. You put all your tasks aside and make a joyful sound and then you pray and praise God and also meet friends. You know, as people come together for worship, they meet friends and then they get new ideas. You don't get new ideas when you are just in your own nuclear family. But you get new ideas when you get out. This idea of converting the world is very much connected to spiritual as well as physical development.

When I met the Grail I was not very much aware of the situation of women here in Tanzania. I was not aware that women were oppressed. I learned this through the Grail. When I went to Uganda for the formation program I was not aware, as I am now, that women are oppressed.

If I can think of my own mother, she had education only up to primary two. She could read and write but she was not allowed to participate in discussions with my father when people were around—she could speak to him only when we were among ourselves, at home. She was allowed only to serve bananas—we had a very big banana plantation and a lot of coffee. But it was not my mother who controlled the family. It was my father. When I was going to school, my mother would go to my father to say, "Imelda is going to school, she needs this and this." She really had no final say in what was going on in the family. I think that most of the women were like this.

It helped that my mother was very smart. There were many women at that time who did not know how to read and write and it was awkward, except that it was accepted, of course. And although I had gone to school I had not begun looking critically at the situation of women and questioning it as we do today.

You know, of course, the Grail from the beginning has been a woman's movement. And when we speak about the Grail being a woman's movement, it means that we educate Grail women to help other women who are not liberated, and also to assist other church groups who are working toward women's liberation. So, for me, a movement is a magical word which involves women of different life choices. The Grail brings all those women of different life choices together in order to sit down and share their vision so that we can work as a movement toward the creation of a better society.

In the Grail today we are not making headway on that because the women we meet need massive help. The Grail is not that massive. We are a woman's movement but in reality we are just a very small group. And you see that such a movement could have different meanings. It could mean having a mass of women working towards the coming of God, or it could mean a group that is ready to change and move in a different direction. Just as things are changing in the society, things are changing in the church, so the Grail, as a movement, is also bound to change. Being a movement brings us into a different way of living, a different way of looking at things. Changes happening elsewhere could also happen in the Grail.

Early Years in the Grail

Since I have been in the Grail, I have been working with women—not with youth, but with women. And from the beginning I have enjoyed it very much.

In the beginning I didn't know that I could teach adult women. But when I began to, I found that the women were enjoying our teaching. So, you know, this gave me confidence. This is what made me continue, that the women were taking the learning seriously and enjoying it. We would teach them subjects like childcare and hygiene and other things, and they enjoyed it all. I never knew where the time went.

In my early years the strengths of the Grail were very much connected to community life. The early Grail members were women who were committed. But there were different tasks that they wanted to do. I remember still a woman I worked with in the program for young people, for one year, in Uganda.

She was a bit quiet, but I came to realize that she was fully committed to whatever we had to do—talk about the program we had to lead, do the activities, teach, work in the garden—a whole range of different things. And she was a hard worker. From watching her, I realized that in the Grail we have to live in the community, we have to be committed to our work and take on this responsibility, and of course, we also knew that prayer was a given.

On the other hand, one weakness of the Grail in my early years of involvement was that the Grail women never spoke about themselves. This made it difficult to explain the Grail. Even when we were living together the older members still didn't talk about what the Grail is. I felt this was kind of a weakness.

The Vision Develops

I think the growing awareness of women's oppression changed the emphasis of the work of the Grail. You see, the leaders of the Grail in the early days used to give the final word on everything, while today the emphasis has shifted and everybody is discussing and expressing their feelings. There is more sharing, and one person is not making decisions for everybody. I think this is very much connected to how women are more involved in decision making today, not just in the Grail, but also in the wider community.

There has been a progressive development in the vision of common faith and hope from the time I joined the Grail until today. When I joined the Grail they were talking about converting the world; those terms were used often in my Grail formation program. But in the document issued by the International Grail in 1979 we began to speak about our "vision," so I came to understand that the language is changing.[86] But the original vision, I think, is there because it is radical—converting the world is something we have not yet achieved. And even if the whole world were Christian still the conversion must happen every day in our lives. Now today we have the mission statement—which is based on the vision statement. So, for me, I think it is very often one building on top of the other.

There was also that big turning point at the IGA in 1979 when we decided to have an International Presidency Team instead of one International President. And I never thought that I would be on the I.P.T. but when the time came, in 1993, I thought perhaps I had some contribution that I could offer to the community. So I accepted.

When I came to the Grail I didn't know that it included different life choices. I turned to the Grail because I was looking for a community. When I was in formation they never spoke about the Nucleus. Perhaps I was searching for a community to be part of and where I could do service to the church. At that time it was enough.

---

86 "Grail International Vision Statement 1979," The Grail, An International Women's Movement, accessed April 14, 2016, http://www.thegrail.org/index.php?option=com_joomdoc&view=documents&path=Grail+Statements/Vision_Statement_1979.pdf&Itemid=86.

But when I did decide to join the Nucleus—I made my dedication at the Tiltenberg in 1963—my parents opposed it. They said you don't know what kind of commitment you are getting into. But it was done; I made that commitment.

One change in being in the Nucleus between those days and today is the commitment to community life. Today we are not bound to live in the community as we once were. You can live in a smaller community, or you can live by yourself if you can find a way of supporting yourself individually.

After my dedication I requested that we start a formation program in Tanzania. I was the only Tanzanian woman who had gone through the formation program in Uganda. So we were given a period of two years to see if Tanzanian women would accept the ideas of the Grail. Honorata was the first. She had been not very happy as a Catholic sister but then she met Ton Brouwer and Lenie Schaareman, two Dutch Grail members who were working in Kisekibaha. She went to live with them while teaching religion during the day and they introduced her to the Grail. Since there was no formation program yet in Tanzania, she went to Uganda for a certain period and then when the Grail started here she came back and we were a team of two. For me, I felt that it was very important to make these young women first acknowledge the reality of the Grail, that it was a lay movement.

The process went slowly but it had some support. Two priests here didn't know the Grail, but they valued the ideas of the Grail because we gave them the Grail documents that we had read and they supported us. I think this was because we concentrated very much on the Grail issues—what does it mean when we speak about the Grail as a lay movement, what does it mean when we speak about women working towards the conversion of the world. And we used the Vatican II document about the laity: we had the material translated into Swahil, so it was very good for us.

At that time also in Tanzania there was a lot of emphasis on *Ujamaa*, which means socialist, working together.[87] It was a political view that was very important in relation to the building up of the Grail here. Because, you know, normally the community of the Grail was the only community that was lay and was still working for the outside community, and yet it was in the church. And for us the ideas of *Ujamaa* was very much linked to the Grail. You know, living the community life and working together for the development of yourself and for the entire community. And, therefore, when we started we adapted what we thought was very related to our situation here by having community subjects taught and also by having practical activities going on. This was twenty-five years ago, in 1970, at Kisekibaha, when we started.

At first, it was very difficult, people did not understand us. But I think what helps is community living together. Sometimes when women come here we try to clarify for them, you know, the questions which people have towards the Grail, and this strengthens the community. And we clarify *Ujamaa*, especially the part that means power. But for us it was not only for the sake of our community, but also to prepare these young women so that they could later facilitate the possibilities of community living in the different places where they would be. So, luckily, the bishop at that time—he was Dutch but even so he did not know the Grail well enough—he came to know the Grail by associating with us. We would give him material to read, but also I think he trusted us—even when the Grail started here he supported us financially for two years. Then after two years we evaluated and decided to

---

87 *Ujamaa*, a Swahili word, means "'extended family,' 'brotherhood,' or 'socialism'; as a political concept it asserts that a person becomes a person *through the people* or community. Tanzanian President Julius Nyerere introduced it in 1967 as part of his model for African development. "Ujamaa," Wikipedia, The Free Encyclopedia, accessed July 8, 2016, https://en.wikipedia.org/wiki/Ujamaa.

continue for another two years, and he supported us for those years too. So in fact we never depended on the International Grail financially—we were very lucky.

Meanwhile, the International President, Simone Tagher, came here several times and she gave us moral support, telling us that it was good to carry on. When we started working educationally, many of our young women had just finished primary school, but I understood that we needed to look beyond that. My understanding was that if the women we were training were going to learn what they needed to do the work of the Grail, they would need upgrading courses, which were going to help them to take the responsibility.

In the first educational group we had six. The next year only two. But then people started coming every year. We realized that we wouldn't get women to be interested in the Grail if we didn't train them. Training was the way to make people interested and also convince them that it is possible to live the lay life, to be committed to the vision of the Grail as well as doing the work of Christ. After some time we got young women who were really convinced and who have given themselves fully to working for the conversion of the world, as we used to call it. Yes.

During that time the bishops were trying to translate the ideology of *Ujamaa*, to show how it is related to the church. One bishop had written several articles showing that *Ujamaa* is not opposed to the Christian faith. That was when the bishops were trying to educate lay people, trying to encourage them to understand their lay function, including empowering women to be active in the church.

And the Grail was looked upon as people who could motivate women in that area, and from the very beginning the Grail worked very closely with diocesan staff to involve women. So the Catholic Church was a very big supporter of *Ujamaa*—they were trying to translate it and to show how Christians could put into reality the ideas of *Ujamaa* in a Christian way. So the Grail was also reaping the benefit of using the ideologies of *Ujamaa*.

The greatest need of women here at that time was education. We took the girls at whatever level they were and encouraged them toward higher studies. Even in the little villages we would encourage the girls and speak to the parents. We were assisting them in making the application to attend school, and so forth, to bring the possibilities of women's education to all. And I am still hoping that the ideas of converting the world and reaching out will get many more women to work on that mission

Today, of course, we use the language of the Grail which now is "transforming the world." This is the phrase we use now when we are speaking to the women. And, also, we are emphasizing the reality that women have a special position in society. And the Grail is trying to help make women realize their potentials, their possibilities—how can we succeed in transforming the world? I think these things are very important even today.

I am very grateful for what I have, for the training I received. For me, I see that aspect which is following the dream that you are given, to realize its possibilities; it is very important. This is what I was given. I was given a chance at the time to grow. I did not grow at once but gradually, that gradual development and growth with which I was entrusted by the Grail communities. This is what also made me do whatever I did. That gradual development, giving me the possibilities of growing, this for me is the biggest contribution of the Grail, which made me what I am.

Further Life Developments

In 1964 and '65 I was working in the Moshi bookshop. After my training in Uganda (1960 and 1961) I had to go to Tabora, then I made my dedication at the Tilt in 1963 and from there I came to Moshi, and in 1964 we started the Moshi bookshop. I was not a bookseller type of person. But I enjoyed that work because of the communication with the wider community. Because most of the people—primary school teachers, secondary school teachers, priests and many other people—came to the bookshop. But then I shifted from there to the secondary school for two years. Then I went for another year of studies, and came back to Kisekibaha to do the work here, for twenty-five years.

Looking back I can see that my first twelve years of working at the Grail formation center here was, for me, a very important time, because I was a Grail woman who was maturing into her life vocation while I was here. Then it was training the young women, you know, the reason why we—the Grail—were there. After a few months we started the women's group. They used to come here so that they could learn how to write to the other women and how to teach them. And from that time on, the emphasis was towards the Grail movement committed to working with women. Today most of the women we work with are rural, but they have come to respect the presence of the Grail and they understand us; they know what we are doing and they don't call us "sisters." There are other people outside of here who are calling us sisters. But the community of Kisekibaha and nearby here know very well that the Grail are not to be called "sisters" because they understand what the Grail is up to.

Since 1982 I have been working in the diocesan development program for women. Doing this is my contribution as a Grail member working towards development. We teach women wherever they are to realize their capacities in leadership—whether in the family, or in youth leadership positions, or in the church, or in the wider society—so that they can participate fully as citizens of the country. At this moment in our work we also want to train our women to realize what they have been suffering, so that they can have a different stand on what are their rights, for example, understanding the marriage laws so that they are not abused by their husbands and by society. There are many things that a woman needs to know at this moment and so this is our responsibility to them now, to make our working women realize there are possibilities in social development so that they can contribute.

Grail Culture and Spirituality

I think for me Grail culture is women culture. Grail culture is to live as a Christian woman and exercise the Christian way of life in everyday life. So, for me, I think we have tried to live as Christians in witness to our own society, and we still remain lay and live as committed Christians. Grail culture, also, for me, is the greatest spirituality. Grail spirituality, what I found in the Grail, which I had never found anywhere else, is a community where people were meeting in the evening to discuss their readings for the next day. I call this the Grail culture. Now we are at Eastertime. Grail women have a beautiful way of celebrating the Easter season. The Grail way of celebrating is different, and these festivities have contributed quite a lot to the rest of the church and to Christian communities around here.

You know the Grail is often not understood. Many people say they don't understand the Grail but those who are close to us come to understand it. For example, the bishop, Josephat Louis Lebulu, understood the Grail from the very beginning; he supported us fully.[88] Even before he was the bishop he supported us. He understood what we were aiming at and he always came here to

---

88 In response to a questionnaire updating this 1995 interview, Imelda Gaurwa wrote that the first bishop to support the Grail in Tanzania was Holy Ghost Father Henry Winkelmolen, a Dutch missionary, who financed the Grail program in Moshi for four years. Tanzanian Bishop J. Lebulu was Bishop Winkelmolen's successor, and, as Imelda noted, also a great supporter of the Grail.

stay for some time and to learn more about the Grail. He saw the Grail as a continuation of the entire church, yes.

I think God has done a lot of work—this was really Providence who has done a lot of the work here. Consider how we started and people didn't know us, but we got some donors and the bishop did not know us but he gave us priests to stay here. I think that God has left us a tremendous gift. We always say that we have to thank Him every day—we have to be grateful.

Of course, always there were times of difficulties. For me, the greatest ones were connected with funding, the programs running out of money—how to carry out all the programs. I remember in the early days, we told the bishop and our International President that we couldn't stand on our own because we didn't know how to raise funds. You don't have any other source except the communities you came from. Then we depended very much on the Moshi bookshop, of course. Ton and the others would always give their income here to make the program possible. We were not in a crisis but at times it was problematic. Yet even in a critical situation you go on.

There were certainly times when I wish we could have expanded the community, putting all our resources in one place. You know, you live in a small cluster here and another one there and another one there. This is because there were never the resources needed to move to a larger community space. This happened several times. We didn't have a view that we needed a larger place.

I think that the Grail succeeded here in Tanzania—and in other African countries—because wherever the Grail went we left a kind of sisterhood. Wherever we have gone we have built a community of people. We got the feeling that Grail women are very committed. I think we always contributed a spirit of hard work.

For all of us, I think the task is to interpret the international vision of the Grail according to our own way of living. The vision or the mission speaks about, you know, living according to the Gospel for the most part. This can be expressed in one sentence but living up to the word of the Gospel takes an entire lifetime. The Gospel speaks of things but when you take a passage and if you have time to discuss a given topic, you see how much that message can have an influence on you; you adapt to that message according to the way you live your life. And we say we are trying to live by the life of Jesus but for me the challenge in Jesus' life is that what he requests is extreme. And extreme is difficult.

For instance, when you reflect on the cross, the one who dies for others is Jesus. But I don't know if I can die for my friends. That's why I say that the message of the vision for each person is different: it's up to the people to translate it and to see how they can live up to it. What women can do here is different from what people can do in America. Here it is very different. For me, I see that we cannot create our own vision but we are trying to share, to learn together the vision that the Grail has internationally and to see what we can do as the local Grail in Tanzania.

What I learned most from my experiences with the International Grail was from that different kind of openness, that rich openness which is in the Grail. We would go to different countries and meet women who were highly qualified, women of different levels of education; this was very good. I think the Grail is one of very few communities where people who are different in their life vocations and with different levels of education can enrich each other and be happy together.

I have been in the Grail more than thirty years. And I have seen the Grail coming up here, but now I am also seeing the Grail coming up in different parts of the world. In the beginning the Grail was missionary-oriented, and the women came already prepared with university or secondary school educations; they were professionals. They came ready because the Grail had a specific role to play. But it's different now. The mission statement will be implemented in different countries, but in order to allow more women to participate, we have to renew our vision. What we are doing is renewing our vision, but some people are going to ask, "What is our vision today? And how are we going to promote this?" When you have a vision you need people to discuss it with.

Getting Older

Sometimes I feel I am the only one who is thinking about the category of old people now, but clearly we have to do it together. Thirty years of my life have been dedicated to the Grail and then what? I have been thinking that I should be training myself in skills using my hands so that when I cannot do much else I can do a lot of hand work. That is, I think, a way of meeting the challenge, but I don't know exactly how.

My spiritual way of life is not very good. It is not very good. For me the place that provides a good spiritual development is here where people live together and have different tasks. But after your tasks you have time to sit down and pray. In that case, for me, I find spiritual development and time for prayer comes very naturally.

When you are living in a community, discussion leads to spiritual growth, and when people are not too tired they come here to share deep things. But when I am tired, I don't hear anything. Then there are times when if I am not going to pray with the community, I will sit and pray by myself in the house. Personal prayer helps me deeply

Aging, for me, is that you can't do certain things that you used to do. It begins with the inability to see or hear or move, or finding it harder to stand up when you have sat down, physical disabilities and handicaps which happen. And memory—remembering—you start forgetting. But I think even as you age and have a physical disability it can also be a time rich in spiritual development. I have seen many old people who are very close to God, and when I asked how this happened, I understood that it did not happen in one day. It is a process of trying and trying, even from the time when that person was young, trying and trying to pray, until in old age when you perhaps are not able to do anything, but you can do one thing and that is to pray. So, I think, also aging means coming closer to better times of praying than in the early times of your life.

As I get older, I think about what I will do if I cannot go out any more and teach the women, and I cannot depend on people to take me to the groups. I must do something, and in that case I have to develop another responsibility so as to still contribute to the people around me. One thing I think about is that if you can sit down and read and have a good memory, then you can help a lot of people with that knowledge of reading and passing on what you have read.

As I reflect on my life, my life in the Grail here and now, I don't know how old I'm going to be when I die because getting old does not mean that you are going to die soon. So, for me, I know that death can come at any time, but the one thing I pray for is to have the chance of expressing my gratitude to my community before I die. This is my wish.

But you can't think too much about death. Think of the people who have died in their sleep, so there's no point in worrying about it. I'm putting my trust in the Lord. Whatever happens, I am not afraid.

My great hope is for spiritual development. If you develop spiritually, you and your companions around you, it is a journey, step by step, having time for reflection and trying to build a relationship with people near you to build up your spirituality.

Of course, even as we get older, some of us talk about finding a way of creating an understanding with the younger people. It is very important. But when older women are living with young people and are helping them, they are helping themselves also. Yes, for me, these people are complementing one another, especially here in African culture where older people are still expected to contribute. My advice to younger people coming up in the Grail is that they should listen to the Spirit because the Spirit, the Spirit of Jesus, is very close to us.

I also value very much the decisions that are made by small communities. When people come together to reflect on different issues and make decisions, the decisions are the true decisions that God wants. I am finding this to be true because I have seen how important it is that leadership listen to the spirit of community sharing. And, of course, it is important to value the community's vision. It is this vision that has drawn many women to the Grail, as well as the hard work of our Grail women.

Honorata Mvungi, location and date unknown

16

Honorata Lubero Francis Mvungi

> *The International Grail has widened my way of understanding, by my meeting different people, face to face, discussing different opinions of different people from different cultures— to see the way others see things.*

Honorata Mvungi's life manifests a profound openness to following her own inner voice and embracing the most demanding of challenges. She evolved, from a timid and shy young person who experienced deep disappointments and frustrations, into a competent leader who helped establish the Grail in Tanzania. And as the first girl born into a family of four girls and five boys, she was early in life given heavy responsibility for the economic survival of her family. By the time she reached grade four in primary school, she had reluctantly left school to help her mother work in the fields and attend to childcare and household duties. Her brothers were encouraged to continue their schooling, but all of them quit during middle school because they preferred to have jobs outside the home.

Honorata's father did not provide for his family and was away a great deal of the time, leaving the burden of supporting and raising the children to Honorata's mother. And even though Honorata had a good relationship with her father, who often turned to her for advice, Honorata grew up being aware of the poor relationship that existed between her mother and father and witnessing the severe hardships her mother endured as the sole provider for her children and their primary educator. Without any income, family subsistence depended mainly on working in the fields, work that was done primarily by the girls and women. Honorata also grew up with the desire to remain single and to receive an education.

As was the custom, Honorata received the name of her father's mother, Lubero, and her clan name, Mvungi, from her father. Her mother's father had, at one time, been captured as a slave and forced to work in the fields. Later, missionaries who were trying to recover slaves bought him and they baptized him. They also trained him as a catechist.

When his family finally heard that he was still alive, they brought him back to his village where he married and became the first catechist there. In his travels, he met a young man he influenced to become a catechist because this young man wanted "to preach the word of God." This same man later became Honorata's father. Although the relationship between her mother and father was not good, Honorata is able to say, "They were people who cared about God." Both of them taught their children how to pray and when her father was home, he was very strict about the family coming together for prayer. She recalls what was very important—seeing them pray together. She credits them both with influencing who she is now.

A turning point came in Honorata's life when she persuaded her father to allow her to enter the convent. When convent life became almost unbearable, Honorata wanted to come home but her mother refused to allow this. So she stayed and was sent on to finish middle school. However, despite very good reports, she did not pass the exam for secondary school. Most of these places went to boys. And despite her desire to become a teacher, she was not selected for teacher training college.

Though initially disappointing, this turned out to be an auspicious occurrence; at the encouragement of the local bishop, she joined the Catechist Training Center, which eventually moved to Kisekibaha. She was still training for the sisterhood and teaching in a catechetical program when, through this same bishop, she met Ton Brouwer and Lenie Schaareman, the two Dutch Grail members who were working at the bookstore. She went to live with them while teaching religion during the day, and in the evenings, Ton and Lenie gave her an introduction to the Grail. It was 1968 and she was twenty-six years old. She eventually left the convent and became part of the Grail movement.

Since the Grail did not yet have a training center in Tanzania, Honorata went to Rubaga, Uganda, for four months of Grail training. When she returned, she joined Imelda Gaurwa, who had just finished her adult-education studies in Dar es Salaam, on the eastern end of Tanzania. Together they started the first Grail training center in Tanzania, at Kisekibaha.

It was a difficult task. Honorata describes herself as a very shy person who did not know what to teach the six young women who came for training. She had originally thought that her role would be one of taking care of the environment through such practical tasks as gardening and maintenance. Also, the venture was a whole new concept in the church and the parents of young women were quite sceptical. And material resources were very limited.

But since Honorata sang in the church choir, she was well known in the area and this helped in gaining acceptance and attracting new students. Very important was the clergy's changing attitude toward the position of laity in the church, and women in particular, which provided a much-needed support to the work of the Grail. And as the work of the Grail grew in strength and visibility, the support from the clergy increased.

At about the time the Grail was beginning the center at Kisekibaha, the new national government of Tanzania inaugurated a liberation movement known as *Ujamaa*. Using socialist concepts, this movement fostered more cooperative means of earning a living among citizens. Although there was no financial support from the government, the new Grail center, with its emphasis on community living, was able to apply this approach in its training; this added to their credibility.

In the midst of her first years at Kisekibaha, Honorata went back to school. Being an older student among younger people was hard, but she finished her secondary education in three years. In 1974, after careful deliberation about the future direction of her life, she became the first Grail member to made her dedication in the Grail Nucleus in Tanzania itself. From the beginning, she saw this commitment as a way to give her the freedom to respond to the needs of her own community in Tanzania and to the larger community of the International Grail. Even today, as she reflects on her years with the Grail, she feels that her greatest contribution to the movement has been her availability for its work.

Honorata knew first hand about the oppression of women and this awareness informed her approach to teaching young women at Kisekibaha. Although the word "feminism" was not in her vocabulary, and many Grail documents were unavailable due to language barriers, Honorata, from her experience and observations, was acutely aware of what the needs of women in her society were. "How can these young women gain self-esteem and a sense of their own identity?" was the question around which the Grail developed its programs.

Eventually weekend programs were offered to local women around similar issues. Men, out of fear, often objected to the content of the education their wives were receiving and some refused to allow them to attend courses. And childcare was an obstacle. Nonetheless, the Grail in Tanzania has been able to provide education for the emancipation of many women, not only through its training program for Grail members, but also through centers and teams in various parts of the country. Despite the difficulties Tanzanian women have had in finding their own voices, gains have been made in the liberation of women in Tanzania and the Grail has been a significant catalyst in this development.

Soon after the turn of the century, Honorata, along with Tanzanian Grail member Maria Goretti William Semvua, began giving talks about the practice of female genital mutilation (FGM), reaching out especially to the Masai people.[89] The Masai are an indigenous, semi-nomadic group in northern Tanzania. FGM has long been considered normal practice for Masai girls, a rite of passage into adulthood. If a girl has undergone FGM, she is ready for marriage.

In 2003, Honorata and Maria Goretti met a Masai couple, Moses and Lea Mbuyik. Lea explained to them that for her daughters to escape FGM, they would need to leave their home and get an education. She asked the Grail women to take her daughters, Asifwe and Margaret, raise them, and help them go to school. In a leap of faith, Honorata and Maria Goretti agreed to do just that.

---

89 Female genital mutilation (FGM), also known as female genital cutting and female circumcision, is the ritual removal of some or all of the external female genitalia. UNICEF estimated that in 2016, two hundred million women had undergone the procedure in twenty-seven countries in Africa, as well as in Indonesia, Iraqi Kurdistan, and Yemen. "Female genital mutilation," Wikipedia: The Free Encyclopedia, accessed July 7, 2016, https://en.wikipedia.org/wiki/Female_genital_mutilation.

By 2010, Moses and Lea's daughter Asifiwe was in form 5 at school and her sister Margaret was being raised by Honorata's sister, Victoria Francis Mvungi, in the mountains nearby. Others have joined them and thirty-five Masai girls are now living at Chekechea, just outside the gate to the Kisekibaha Grail center. Felisiana Mathey, a young Grail member, lives with them and they call her "Mama." Another young woman assists her. As a result of Honorata's leadership, the Grail has gradually brought these girls to live at Chekechea at the request and with the blessings of their birth mothers.

In the beginning, these women believed that the only way for their daughters to escape FGM, early marriage and the difficult life of a Masai woman, was to get an education and live outside Masai culture. In recent years, the work has become more complex, with the primary goal continuing to be keeping the girls safe from FGM and early marriage and enabling them to get an education. But now, another goal is for these young women, as adults, to be able to make their own choices about how to relate to their own Masai culture. Some Masai women who have gotten an education seem to be moving back to their communities, trying to walk the fine line between introducing aspects of modernization that make life possible (clean water and sanitation, health care, and so forth) without losing the richness of their traditions. This can be a difficult task.

This work with Masai girls is, of course, a continuation of Honorata's lifetime commitment to women and girls, and to the Grail in Tanzania and around the world. She is particularly concerned about the future of women in the Catholic Church. In referring to the present role of women in the church, Honorata speaks about Vatican III, something she believes the Grail already embodies. She understands the Grail movement to have a much wider vision than the church, which seems, according to her, to be still having trouble dealing with the changes introduced by Vatican II.

Honorata also believes her participation in the International Grail has shaped her openness to people from other countries and cultures. She recalls how intimidated she and other African women were when they first attended international meetings, and how they have since gained confidence in their own ideas and in their rootedness in cultural values that can be different from those of Grail members elsewhere.

At the same time, her contact with the International Grail has made Honorata more aware of implementing the Grail in a Tanzanian culture without losing the Grail's original vision. She sees a great need in the Grail today to find unity in the midst of diversity, "to work together, to listen to one another, so that we can encourage and support each another in our common, and sometimes diverse, struggles." This kind of solidarity, according to Honorata, is what will build the Grail internationally and enable it to flourish.

Interview

Saying "Yes'" to the Challenges

At first, when something new comes to me, it's a shock and my initial reaction has always been "no." I may say no, but after a while I go back and say, "Let me think about it," and I pray about it also. From childhood to now, prayer has been very important to me. And then sometimes I find someone I trust and I talk to this person and I hear what she or he says. Then I compare this advice with my own opinion and in the end, it's my decision. Some changes are very easy for me and others are very hard. So this is what happens when something new comes: first it shocks me, but when I get into it, I relax. Change always frightens me, but when I go deeper, the fear goes.

For instance, my coming to the Grail. At first, I was going into the sisterhood, but then that changed. There was just something in me. And people said to me, "You had better make a decision, what are you going to be in your life? What is your plan for your life? You don't seem like someone who wants to marry or join the sisterhood." The truth is, I wasn't planning anything, but there was something in me that told me to wait even though I did not know what I was waiting for.

Then it happened. While I was a catechist, I was helping a priest with his celebration of twenty-five years with the missions. The celebration was at Kisekibaha and Ton Brouwer was there. I did not even meet or talk to her then, but just looking at her impressed me. I knew she was not a sister and she was the only white person there. I asked and the priest told me that she was a member of the Grail and she worked at the Moshi bookshop. He only knew that the Grail was committed to the church and that they were good people. He suggested that I go to Moshi to meet her and find out more about the Grail.

But then I did not even know where Moshi was. I had a brother who was working there, so my younger sister took me one Sunday and we asked around and found Ton and Lenie in their apartment around the corner in the bookshop. When Lenie answered the door, I thought I had made a mistake, but she told me Ton was there and she invited me in. They did not speak Swahili, so with my little English I told Ton that I had seen her at Kisekibaha and that she had impressed me very much. I told her I wanted to know who she was and what she was doing. Then she and Lenie started telling me about the Grail and I just said, "I would like to come and be with you."

It was decided that I could live with them and continue to teach catechetics. What I didn't know at the time was that the bishop of the diocese wanted me to join the Grail. He knew I was not suited for the sisterhood and he had already been talking to Ton and Lenie about me.

Ton and Lenie came to my home and arranged the move to their place. I was so happy. I told my parents, "I am joining the Grail." My mother asked what the Grail was about and I told her that I would know when I got there. When I came to the Grail, I was told I had three choices. I was told about marriage, I was told about the single life, and I was told about the Nucleus of the Grail. And even though I knew I did not want to become a nun or be single in society, which is not a choice in our African tradition, I hesitated for a long time about the Nucleus. I had had only a few months of formation and I was in school; I was just not ready.

I went to a two-month formation program in Italy where Simone Tagher, who was then the International President, asked me if I would be ready the following year. There was to be an international Grail meeting called, "Growing Together in the Grail" in Tanzania the following year, a first for my country. And I said, "No."

But I went away and prayed over the decision and decided that my formation could continue even after I made my dedication. So, I said, "Yes." That was in 1974. I made my dedication alone at the "Growing Together in the Grail" meeting. It was the first time anyone had made her dedication in Tanzania. I think my ability to respond to the call came from the influence of my parents, their strictness about our praying together, and of course the goodness of God. It was a mystery because of the way it came about.

The Great Leap of Faith

When we started there were only two of us. The bishop had closed the catechetical center at Kisekibaha and he wanted Imelda and me to start a Grail center there. So two weeks after Imelda returned from her studies in Dar es Salaam and when I had finished my formation in Uganda, we went around to the diocese to meet the girls in the parish to talk about the Grail. And on the tenth of May 1970, we arrived at Kisekibaha.

It was a Sunday and Ton drove us to there. When we arrived, Ton prayed with us and then she said, "I wish you all the best. Good-bye." That was all. Ton and Lenie really stayed away. They had said to us, "You can start this center. You do it yourselves. If you have any questions that we can help with, come to us, but it is not for us to be there." They wanted us, as Africans, to do this in our own way. They would come on weekends and ask how we were doing, but they never proposed that we do anything differently. They completely let us go our own way. So in that way it happened that indigenous women started the Grail in Tanzania; the Grail in Tanzania has always been in the hands of Tanzanians. This has been our greatest strength.

Ton had wondered before we went to Kisekibaha if we shouldn't prepare the rooms and the rest of the environment for the six young girls who were going to come. We said, "No, let the girls come and prepare their own environment." And that's what we did; we spent the whole of Sunday cleaning up and we even had to go to the local priest to ask for food for our dinner. We continued working and when the first person arrived the next day, we told her to put her things down and come to work. As others came we said the same.

When we had prepared the environment, we were ready to start the program. Imelda called me in and said that now I had to teach such things as how the girls could teach others to read and write, about prayer, English, the Bible, literature, education, what was happening politically in society. I was so shocked. I did not have that much Grail training and I remember thinking when I came back from formation in Uganda that I needed more.

I thought that I would be a student at Kisekibaha; I didn't count myself as staff. I thought, "I can't do this." Imelda said that there were books to learn from. And she said that through doing I would learn. She also suggested that I could attend classes she taught on the Grail. That is how I eventually learned more about the Grail.

But I thought I would need time to prepare and then who would do the outside work. But Imelda decided that we would have classes in the morning and all of us would do the outside work in the afternoon. I saw that there was no one else; we could not afford to hire anyone to teach. So I said, "I will try."

We divided up the teaching and I took prayer and the Bible. I even composed a prayer we used for many years. Imelda had an adult-education background, so she taught literacy, which was then heavily emphasized by the government. She also taught about the Grail and did teaching about home management, so that the girls in formation could teach these things later. We also taught biology and methods of teaching religion or catechetics. One of the greatest influences the Grail has had on me was this experience, since I was shy back then and had not taught in this way. I even refused to go to the International General Assembly at Grailville in 1971 with Imelda because I did not have the confidence. But teaching is real formation, through doing. So I am glad I did this because that's the way I educated myself. Now I have changed. I am able to speak publicly, to stand in front of people and talk.

We Reap What We Sow

Our biggest struggle was making the Grail known to the people and I had a lot of doubts. We even heard that people were talking and saying that this thing would not work. We were the only ones convinced that it could. However, we were encouraging and supporting one another. And then I decided that it was not really us doing something but we are God's instruments, so it will work.

After convincing myself like that, I began to just relax and hope that it would work. And later the bishop came and he saw that it was working. We started with six students and Imelda and myself. As women, we knew what the issues were and we spent time talking with the women, and learning, too, from them. After we had been preparing the way for several months, we divided into small Christian communities to work with young children, the youth, women, and in the parish. We found out what the girls who were training with us could do and we helped them to choose which group they wanted to go with. I went to work with the women. And we had some help from other Grail members: Fini van de Rijdt, a Dutch member, as well as Jane Manugeni, Regina Bashasha, Elizabeth Namaganda, Eliza Nvungi. All of them had been in Uganda.

Vatican II made a big difference in Tanzania. Previously, the church had belonged to the priests and nuns, but now we were told that we were also part of it, and that is when the lay apostolate movement started here. People were very happy; they accepted this and they really involved themselves.

I was the first woman here to read during Mass, and people said, "Oh, what? A woman at the altar?" And women were happy that they could participate because previously they were not being used. It was not always easy for them to go in public and do something, but gradually they did and especially in the area where the Grail was. They saw us doing things and they said—if these women can do this, we can also. So it was a time of new experience.

When the bishop saw what we were accomplishing, he started coming and giving us some reflections about conscientization.[90] So in the end people said, "Now we know what the Grail is," and that was my hope—that it would work and, as you know, it is working.

---

90 Conscientization is a popular education and social concept that was developed by Brazilian pedagogue and educational theorist, Paulo Freire, and grounded in post-Marxist critical theory. It focuses on achieving an in-depth understanding of the world, allowing for the perception and exposure of social and political contradictions. Conscientization also includes taking action against the oppressive elements in one's life that are illuminated by that understanding. "Critical consciousness," Wikipedia, The Free Encyclopedia, accessed July 7, 2016, https://en.wikipedia.org/wiki/Critical_consciousness.

The Grail is now appreciated in our country because we really do a lot in the church. The women in our village, because we have worked hand in hand with them, appreciate us, they accept us. When they see things happening they say, "It is because the Grail is here."

Even the nuns, who were sceptical at first, have accepted us. They know we have a place in the church, especially in the diocese of Moshi. In the past, things were quite conservative, but now the nuns say, "We need you, so let's work together," and now we are working together.

A Time to Grow

Our greatest need was to help women trust themselves, to be more confident, to know what their talents were. Often they knew how to do things, but they were afraid. So our education has been to train them to do their best and play their part in church and society. Now you can see these women running programs and workshops and meetings and seminars.

One of the difficulties for us in relationship to the Grail has been the language barrier. For a long time, all the Grail documents were in English and we could not understand many things that were in them. Due to the problem of language, I couldn't grasp much. So we translated them into Swahili and gave everyone a copy. We started together, we read it together going line by line and discussing what people understood.

From this we were able to make our own vision according to what we understood and then we could talk about how to implement in our lives what we had read. Many times, that is how we conduct women's groups. We use the idea of the Grail vision for discussion and what it means to us and how we can apply it in our own situations. In this way, it helps us. I know that African women, due to colonization, in the past usually felt inferior in front of white women. They had strong feelings about this and it took a long time for women from my country to speak out at International Grail meetings. It has come gradually and now we are used to this, but before, it was not easy.

The meaning of my dedication in the Grail Nucleus has certainly deepened since 1974. My vision has become more international. You see, when we started the Grail, we wanted to see it get its roots in Tanzania. However, the challenge has always been to see the Grail rooted here without us losing the vision of the whole International Grail. It is very important that I have been more available to the community because I can move about and take on many responsibilities, which married women cannot. It has been a real struggle for women in my country who throughout their lives have family responsibilities.

This is truer in Tanzania than in some other African countries. It depends on the culture and the way it functions. In our country, the church and government work hand in hand. So the Grail has a place in the government and in the church. Now in Kenya, all the Grail members are married, but here women find it hard to use their talents for both the family and the Grail. That is one reason the movement in this country is mostly Nucleus members.[91] However, when you are in a family, you bring that Grail spirit into your family. This is what we have been trying to explain to women, to help them understand they can manage both.

When we started out, we said that we wanted to make this place a better place to live, not just by catechism or work, but by a combination of all things in life. And the emphasis was always on women, to help the woman have a good standard of living,

---

91 While this was the case when Honorata gave her interview, the Grail in Tanzania in 2011 had a hundred members, of which fifty-two were in the Nucleus.

that was our goal. At the time, the church and the government were encouraging the participation of everyone. In fact, it was the government who realized that if we leave aside the women, the progress of the whole society will be very affected—after all, the number of women is bigger than the number of men.

So the government began to say that we have to find ways of helping women to also participate in the progress of the society. It was very hard for women to hear that, because for most of their lives they had lived by the African tradition, that women had no place in society. Women have been just like an instrument to be used by men. There was no dialogue whatsoever. Whatever they were told, they would say "yes"; there was no "no."

The Grail early on began to speak about the influence women could have in church and society. Before our priest, Joseph duBulu, became our first African bishop, he studied sociology in Belgium. When he returned, he wrote a booklet on the Christian faith and the environment. Imelda helped him write a section on the role of women. Always in the formation programs and in our own formation, we talked a lot about women's awareness. Right from the beginning the Grail was involved in anything concerning women, especially in this diocese. The women have learned from us and we have learned from the women. There is certainly a little more light than when we started.

As time has gone on, the whole society is working toward the development of women, not just the Grail; it is something for the society. We now have the Unit of Women in Tanzania and we have the Catholic Women's Movement, which focus on women's development. Many women previously did not have professions, because, as I have said, due to the culture, women were supposed to do work in the house, not in the offices. Not until the government realized that women had to be involved did women start coming up.

And now in Tanzania I think it's very good. Employers do not choose between men and women; it depends on your capacity. If you are able, you have the job; you have it whether you are a man or a woman. It's only a matter of capacity, ability. For instance, we have a lot of women ministers and many women holding high positions in the government. So we all have the same goal, because it's all work with women.

Women now are realizing their position in society as well as in the church. They are trying to find their own identity and it's not easy. The talk now is about self-reliance, self-determination, in very basic grass-roots ways. Each woman is trying to find her own way to becoming a full human being. I know that a long time ago the women could never question their husbands, but these days, they do, which means that men are trying to see and realize their wives as human beings. My role is trying to support them with what they have, what they are developing in themselves, so that they have a greater sense of their own dignity.

And right now the emphasis is on how to bring up their children in a better way. We are realizing that children are the future of the nation and the future of the church also. Children need to be brought up in a certain way so that they will also be responsible for themselves and to society and the church. This is our main emphasis at the moment, especially among the women.

We also wanted to try to find ways of involving men, so that men and women can work together as a family at home. When the responsibilities are left up only to the women, it is not easy to bring up the children, especially now-a-days. It is not a job for one person. We have organized this work through small Christian communities at the local and diocesan level. So whatever we are doing locally goes also to the diocesan level and then to the national level.

We are also looking at economics, because people need money in order to travel to meetings at the diocesan and national levels. Where we are it is very difficult to have projects to raise money. We have tried to start some things but they haven't worked. When we make things to sell, we lack the market and the transportation. And it became too much of a burden for the women who had many other commitments in their families. Our latest project is planting and raising beans to harvest and sell. Last year we had too much rain and we are hoping this year it will work.

My role is mainly giving ideas and giving moral support. When it comes to the actions, we don't participate much because we lack enough Grail people. One of our greatest difficulties is in communication. We have teams in Tabora, in Moshi, in Same, in Dido, in Kisekibaha and in other places, but communication is a big problem. Sometimes it takes a month to get a letter from one place to another. If we hand deliver a letter, it can take up to two days since we have to walk and take the bus and it's too tiring. This kind of thing complicates our work.

But the situation of the Grail in Tanzania today is that we have many women coming along, many of them who are able to take some responsibility, and they are also reliable women and we can trust them to do the job. We have Grail people managing everything I have talked about and they also have connections with other women. The Grail is always trying to support itself and stand on its own legs—on the ground. It's still not easy because the process of formation is long. We get young women from primary school and we have to educate them. They have three years at Kisekibaha and then they go back to school to study so they will have something to give in the way of service to their people. And when they are ready, they are really ready, but it takes a long time.

So this is what is happening to us. The harvest is ripe but the laborers are few. We have so many invitations to come here, come there, but we can't because we don't have enough people.

People are still in the process of getting ready to meet the needs. There are so many needs. But yes, it is promising.

One of the signs of life for us is that we have different groups of women who are of different ages. We have older women and younger women, the young generation. This is providing for the continuation of the Grail. Sometimes this brings conflict because of different opinions—the younger generation sees it this way and the older generation sees it that way. Each generation has its own way of thinking and they do tell each other.

But as Grail, we have to find the way of working together, of finding unity among diversity while seeing diversity as positive. Cooperation is very important, and it is important that we all struggle together. At the same time, the Grail in Tanzania is still Catholic. We haven't come to the point of mixing other denominations. I know that we say the Grail is a movement rooted in the Christian faith, but we have not gone beyond our own tradition yet. In other countries, the Grail is more ecumenical. This is one example of how the vision of the Grail is adapted to the needs of each country. Ecumenism has not yet been applied to our own country.

And a Time to Reflect

I am happy about what we have done in Tanzania. And the best contribution the International Grail has made to us has been to make the existence of the Tanzanian Grail possible. When I look at the work the Grail has done here, I realize that if the Grail were not here, all that has been done, especially for women, would not have been done. I thank God for the one who invited the Grail, the one who was on the leadership team at that time, accepting the idea and accepting us, of course. Our international connections have helped us with our lay apostolate, especially the women's groups. We use the vision and we have built it in our own way as Grail, as well as women. We see the international vision as part of our lives, it has strengthened us, it helps us in our search. We use this vision in our formation, our own Grail formation. We use it in our own women groups and discussions and reflections. The vision supports us in our daily lives.

We have been through very hard times, very taxing times, and we have been tested. But when I look back and realize how many women have passed through our centers and programs, how many of them are with us now, and when I look at the responsibilities they take on, the influence they have, I realize I have not labored in vain. I have made myself available for the work of the Grail and I have done it with my whole heart, my whole mind, my whole body, and I have seen the Grail develop. Whatever the Grail has asked me to do, I have accepted, and I have tried many things, simple and difficult ones, but I think through it all, somehow I have managed the difficult ones. This has been the goal of my life.

Prayer, reading the Bible, reflections, retreats—these have all sustained my own spiritual life. And I usually like the homilies, when the priest who preaches is able to tie together what he is saying with the real life of the people.

I remember when I first learned as a child to pray. Prayer was vocal, from a book or based on what the catechism taught. Later I found that praying is not only saying some words but I can sit quietly without any words or any thought and just be there in silence. I just look at nature and listen to the birds, to the wind, to other creatures, thinking about God. So what gives my life meaning now is my faith, yes, because I think the faith I have is what makes me be who I am.

Conclusion

The Daughters Weave On

As we approach the centenary of the founding of the Society of the Women of Nazareth in 1921, and the Grail Movement that emerged from it, we express our thanks to the sixteen women whose lives comprise the subject of this volume, for the vision and commitment that they, and their Grail sisters around the world, have contributed to the building of this movement. To honor these sixteen women of vision, we conclude with the International Vision Statement, formulated and affirmed at the International Grail General Assembly in Kleinmond, South Africa, in 2011.

International Grail Vision Statement 2011

We are an international movement and community of women of different cultures, social backgrounds and generations. We trust in the Spirit of God, Mystery and Source of Life.

We are called to create a sustainable world, transforming our planet into a place of peace and justice.

We acknowledge that we are part of the whole of creation, striving to live simply and to nurture a culture of care for all the earth.

- We are determined to look for signs of hope in a complex world.

- We are strengthened by the compassionate energy and creative action of women.

- Born in the Catholic tradition, the movement is grounded in the Christian faith and challenged by the radical call of the teachings of Jesus. Today we are women of various religious traditions and on life-giving spiritual journeys. And we share the same Grail vision. We recognize that in each of our Grail countries, our expressions of faith, religion and spirituality reflect our own realities and cultures. We respect and acknowledge these differences.

Recognizing the global realities we confront, we are committed to growing together and learning from one another's wisdom, experience and spiritual search. [92]

---

92 "2011 International General Assembly Report," The Grail, An International Women's Movement, accessed November 2, 2016, http://www.thegrail.org/index.php?option=com_joomdoc&view=documents&path=Reports/2011+IGA+Report.pdf&Itemid=86.

Bibliography

Brown, Alden V. *The Grail Movement and American Catholicism 1940-1975.* Notre Dame, IN: The University of Notre Dame Press, 1989.

Brown, Stewart J. and Nockles, Peter B. eds. *The Oxford Movement: Europe and the Wider World 1830–1930.* Cambridge, UK: Cambridge University Press, 2012.

Campbell, Debra. "The Struggle to Serve: From the Lay Apostolate to the Ministry Explosion." In *Transforming Parish Ministry: The Changing Roles of Catholic Clergy, Laity, and Women Religious,* edited by Jay Dolan, R. Scott Appleby, Patricia Byrne and Debra Campbell, 212-213. New York, NY: Crossroad Publishing, 1990.

Derks, Marjet. "Female Soldiers and the Battle for God: Gender Ambiguities and a Dutch Catholic Conversion Movement." In *Gender and Christianity in Modern Europe: Beyond the Feminization Thesis,"* edited by Patrick Pasture, Jan Art and Thomas Buerman, 173-190. Leuven, Belgium: KADO Studies on Religion, Culture and Society, Leuven University Press, 2012.

Dolan, Jay. P. *The American Catholic Experience: A History from Colonial Times to the Present.* Garden City, NY: Doubleday and Co., Inc., 1985.

Donders, Rachel. *History of the International Grail 1921-1979: A Short Description.* Loveland, OH: Grailville, 1983.

———. *Lydwine van Kersbergen 1905 –1998: Een vrouw van de twintigste eeuw: Lydwine aan het word.* The Grail in the Netherlands, 2000.

Editors, The. Encyclopedia Britannica, The. "Catholic Action." Accessed October 25, 2016. https://www.britannica.com/topic/Catholic-Action.

Gindhart, Mary and Demmy Kyangye. *Histories of the Grail in Individual Countries.* Loveland, OH: Grailville, 1984.

Goldbrunner, Joseph. *Holiness is Wholeness.* New York, NY: Pantheon Books, 1955.

Grail in the U.S.A., The. "Where We Are: The Bronx Grail Center." Accessed August 24, 2016. http://www.grail-us.org/where-we-are/the-bronx-grail-center/.

———. "What We Do: About the Sofia Fund of Tanzania." Accessed August 24, 2016. http://www.grail-us.org/aboutthesofiafund/.

———. "What We Are: The Grail Link to the United Nations." Accessed August 24, 2016. http://www.grail-us.org/what-we-are/grail-link-to-the-united-nations/.

Grail, The, An International Women's Movement. "What We Do: The Grail Link to the United Nations." Accessed August 24, 2016. http://www.thegrail.org/index.php?option=com_content&view=article&id=67&Item id=81.

———. "Where We Are: Australia," Accessed October 25, 2016. http://www.thegrail.org/index.php?option=com_content&view=article&id=69&Item id=95.

———. "Where We Are: Brazil." Accessed October 25, 2016. http://www.thegrail.org/index.php?option=com_content&view=article&id=101&Item id=96.

———. "Where We Are: The Philippines." Accessed October 25, 2016. http://www.thegrail.org/index.php?option=com_content&view=article&id=78&Item id=104.

———. "Where We Are: South Africa." Accessed October 25, 2016. http://www.thegrail.org/index.php?option=com_content&view=article&id=81&Item id=107.

———. "Where We Are: Sweden." Accessed August 13, 2016. http://www.thegrail.org/index.php?option=com_content&view=article&id=82&Item id=108.

———. "Where We Are: Tanzania." Accessed August 23, 2016. http://www.thegrail.org/index.php?option=com_content&view=article&id=83&Item id=109.

Harmon, Katharine E. *There Were Also Many Women There: Lay Women in the Liturgical Movement in the United States 1926-59.* Collegeville, MN: The Liturgical Press, 2012.

Kalven, Janet. "Living the Liturgy: Keystone of the Grail Vision." *U.S. Catholic Historian*. 11:4 (1993): 29-35.

———. *Women Breaking Boundaries: A Grail Journey, 1940-1995.* Albany, NY: State University of New York Press, 1999.

Kim, Susan. "*La Croix.*" *French Media Studies.* Accessed October 20, 2016. http://frenchmediastudies.blogspot.com/2010/10/la-croix-susan-kim.html.

Leo XIII, Pope. *Humanum Genus* (On Freemasonry). The Vatican. Accessed August 11, 2016. http://w2.vatican.va/content/leo-xiii/en/encyclicals/documents/hf_l-xiii_enc_18840420_humanum-genus.html.

———. *Rerum Novarum* (On Capital and Labor). The Vatican. Accessed October 18, 2016. http://w2.vatican.

va/content/leo-xiii/en/encyclicals/documents/hf_l-xiii_enc_15051891_rerum-novarum.html.

Lidman, Melanie. "Q & A with Sr. Imelda Gaurwa, the First Tanzanian Grail Sister." *The National Catholic Reporter Global Sisters Report*, January 21, 2016. Accessed August 12, 2016. http://globalsistersreport.org/blog/q/q-sr-imelda-gaurwa-first-tanzanian-grail-sister-36661.

Maestrini, Nicholas. "Four Years with Lay Missionaries." *America* 86 (October 6, 1951): 12.

"Nuns in Mufti." *Time* (July 21, 1941). Accessed August 25, 2016. http://content.time.com/time/magazine/article/0,9171,765827,00.html.

"Obituary: Maria de Lourdes Pintasilgo." *The Independent*, July 13, 2004. Accessed September 1, 2016. http://www.independent.co.uk/news/obituaries/maria-de-lourdes-pintasilgo-550094.html.

O'Brien, Mary and Patricia Miller. "A Woman of Vision: An Interview with the Founder of the Grail Movement in the United States." *U.S. Catholic Historian*. 15.4 (1997): 95-105.

O'Malley, John W. *What Happened at Vatican II*. Cambridge, MA: Harvard University Press, 2008.

O'Toole, James M. *The Faithful: A History of Catholics in America*. Cambridge, MA: The Belknap Press of Harvard University Press, 2008.

Pintasilgo, Maria de Lourdes and Paul Harrison. *Caring for the Future: Making the Next Decades Provide a Life Worth Living*. New York, NY and Oxford, UK: Oxford University Press, 1996.

Pius XI, Pope. *Ubi Arcano Dei Consilio* (On the Apostolate of the Laity). The Vatican. Accessed August 19, 2016. http://w2.vatican.va/content/pius- xi/en/encyclicals/documents/hf_p-xi_enc_23121922_ubi-arcano-dei- consilio.html.

"Pope Leo XIII." *Notable Names Database* (NNDB). Accessed August 20, 2016. http://www.nndb.com/people/387/000088123/.

Reid, Elizabeth. *I Belong Where I'm Needed*. Westminster, MD: The Newman Press, 1961.

Sparr, Arnold. *To Promote, Defend and Redeem: The Catholic Literary Revival and the Cultural Transformation of American Catholicism, 1920-1960.* Westport, CT: Greenwood Press, 1990.

Van Kersbergen, Lydwine. *Woman: Some Aspects of Her Role in the Modern World.* Loveland, OH: Grailville, 1956.

Vatican, The. "The Congregation for Institutes of Consecrated Life and Societies of Apostolic Life. " Accessed October 21, 2016. http://www.vatican.va/roman_curia/congregations/ccscrlife/documents/rc_con_ccscrlife_profile_en.html.

Windass, Stanley, ed. *The Chronicle of the Worker-Priests.* New York, NY: Humanities Press, Inc., 1966.

Zwick, Mark and Louise Zwick. "Virgil Michel, Benedictine Co-Worker of Dorothy Day and Peter Maurin: Justice Embodied in Christ-life and Liturgy." Casa Juan Diego, February 1, 2000. Accessed August 22, 2016. http://cjd.org/2000/02/01/virgil-michel-benedictine-co-worker-of-dorothy-day-and-peter-maurin-justice-embodied-in-christ-life-and-liturgy/.

Index

"A Parable of the Grail" (Gallant), xxxiv–xxxvii
Aba Grail (Burundi), 75
Abbey of Solesmes, xvii
    acceptance, 57, 122, 123, 200
Adam and Eve syndrome, 266
Adebola, Queen, 142
Aengenent, J.D.J., Bishop of Haarlem, ix, 7, 34, 62
Africa, 14, 24
. *See also* Burundi; Congo (Belgian Congo); Congo (Zaire); Kenya;
    Nigeria; South Africa; Tanzania; Uganda
African Grail, Tanzania, xiii, 164–66, 297–98, 300–301
"AgeWise" (newsletter), 45, 90, 103
aggiornamento, 140, 183–84, 207, 259
aging, 17–18, 79–81, 148–49
    letting go, 58–59, 80, 189–90, 228, 232
    retirement, xxxii, 90, 103, 111, 132, 146–49, 175, 189–90, 252,
        253–54, 301
AIDS, 180
Akiko (Japanese Grail member), 35
Allard, Elisabeth, xi–xii, 68, 90
Alter, Karl, Archbishop of Cincinnati, *149*
Amsterdam Grail houses, 28
Amsterdam Stadium performances, ix, xx, 8, 41, 62
Anthony, Saint, 239–40
Antigonish Movement, 136–37
Ark (retreat house at Tiltenberg), 32
Asia-Pacific Forum, 238

Australia (Ladies of the Grail), x, xxiii, 41, 44, 47–53
autonomy, xv, 8–9, 16
Ave Maria, 90

Baganda tribe, South Africa, 55, 56
Bagley, Catherine, 49
baptism, 100
Bashasha, Regina, 336
Bauduin, Dom Lambert, 216
Beguines, 45
Beguinhoff, Netherlands, 45, 58
Beijing Conference on Women, 238
Belgium, 215–16
Benedictines, xvii, 11, 93
Bible circles, 203–4, 262
bishops, 116, 249–50
. *See also* individual bishops
bookshop, Moshi, Tanzania, 162–64, 167, 300, 315–16, 318, 332
Bosch van Drakestein, Yvonne, 51, 70, 91
Bourne, Cardinal, Archbishop of Westminster, x
Bowman, Judith, 50
Brazil, xxvi, 95, 107, 109–10, 114–21, 130, 183
    conscientization, 119–20, 143
    cooperatives, 120–21
    Holland-Brazil connection, 122–23
    social justice, 107, 118–19, 127
    as unjust country, 271
Brien, Dolores, 130, 175, 177, 183
Brouwer, Antonia (Ton), xiii, 78, 151–69, *170,* 300
    Africa as unshakeable goal, 156–57
    Africanization of Grail, 164–66
    beginnings of work in Africa, 157–60
    in Burundi, 154, 158
    difficult times, 160–61
    early years, 151–52

in Nucleus, 153, 165
return to Netherlands, 167–68
in Tanzania, 153–55, 161–66, 327, 332–34
Brown, Alden, ix, xxiv
Brust, Ingrid, 93
Buckley, Mary Imelda, 127, 134–35
Burundi, xiii
Brouwer in, 154, 158
Canters in, 63, 73–76, 79
hospital work, 160–61

Cabana, Archbishop, 177
Cabrini Nursing Home, Manhattan, 132–33
calling, 39
Camanada, Elizabeth (Bep), xii, 107–25, *126*
in Brazil, 109–10, 114–21
early years, 107–8
as Grail president, Holland, 117–18
later decades, 121–25
War, Grail, and ecumenism, 111–14
Canada, Madonna House, Toronto, xviii, 51
Canters, Hilda, xiii, xxii, 61–81, *82*, 157, 160
in Burundi, 73–76
early years, 61, 66–67
early years with Women of Nazareth, 67–72
on getting older, 79–81
new directions after War, 72–77
return to Netherlands, 77–78, 77–79
in Zaire, 76–77
capitalism, 44, 203, 271
Cardijn, Father (later Cardinal) Joseph, xviii, 215, 217, 258–69
caring, politics of, 267–70
Caring for the Future (Pintasilgo and Harrison), 268
Caritas International, 155, 169
Carmelites, 23, 175–76

Catechist Training Center, Kisekibaha, 327
Catholic Action, vii, xiv–xv, xx, 307
    Australia, 50
    Belgium, 216–17
    Brazil, 116
    Netherlands, 6
    Portugal, 195–97, 257–58
    . *See also* lay apostolate
Catholic Center, Hong Kong, 100, 101
Catholic Center, South Africa, 54
Catholic Central Bureau of China, 100
Catholic Intellectual Revival, xvi, xviii, xix, 11
Catholic Interracial Council (Philadelphia), 87
Catholic Truth Society, 88
Catholic University, Belo Horizonte, Brazil, 115
Catholic Women's Association for Central and East Africa
    Committee, 280
Catholic Women's League (Australia), 48
Catholic Women's Movement, Tanzania, 339
Catholic Worker, xviii, xix, 90, 97, 128, 137
celibacy, 157, 174, 185, 249, 290, 291
Chacara Manhangawa, São Paulo, Brazil, 117
change, 38, 41, 45–46, 57–58, 70–71, 206
China, 87–88, 101
. *See also* Hong Kong
choirs, 137
    in Africa, 327
    in Australia, 49, 52
    New York City Labor Chorus, 132, 148–49
Christ the King Secondary School (Uganda), 277–78, 289
Christian maturity, 184–85
Christian Unity (Rome), 182
Coffey, James, Monsignor, 96
Cold War, 269
College of St. Theresa (Minnesota), 85, 93

Commission for Foreign Affairs (Portugal), 199
Commission for the Participation of Women in Society (Portugal), 199
Commission on Politics and General Administration (Portugal), 263
Commission on Women's Rights (European Parliament), 267
committed families, 97
The Commonweal, xvi, xvii, 90
communion
. *See* Eucharist
communion within the people of God, 184
communism, 44, 49, 75, 101
community, 9, 58, 135, 166, 189
    Brazil, 122
    Gomes and, 200, 201
    in northern Netherlands, 23
    Tanzania, 311, 318
community development, 171, 178, 188
community of memories, xxxi–xxxii
concentration camps, 29, 175–76
    Catholics in, 172
    threats to Grail members, 30, 71
Congo (Belgian Congo), xiii, 63, 72–73, 159–61
    hospital work, 72–73, 154, 158–59
    independence, 154, 159
Congo (Zaire), 64–65
    conscientization, 188n46, 336
    Brazil, 119–20, 143
    Portugal, 202–3
contemplation, 26
conversion of the world, vii, 7, 26, 32, 44, 79, 184, 222, 243
    Hong Kong, 99–102
    as transformation, 230
Cooney, Nancy Hennessey, xxix
cooperatives, 63–64, 76, 120–21, 136

Cornwall-on-Hudson, Grail retreat house, New York, 133
cosmic awareness, 36–39
Costuna, Jeana, 238
Council of Churches, 155–56
Council of Women World Leaders, 260
Crookall, Adelaide, 52
Crusaders of St. John (Knights of St. John), vii, x, xxii, 67
Cultural Center, Lisbon, 204
cultural diversity, 185, 206, 229, 251, 256, 270, 290, 293–94, 331
cultural events, 11
"Cultural Exchanges: Currents of a Common Future," 205–6
cultural identity, 151

Daniélou, Jean, 174, 179
Day, Dorothy, xviii, xix, xxi, 128
de Hueck Doherty, Catherine, xviii, xxi, 3, 51, 97
de Klerk, Sis, 63, 64, 75, 161
de Martini, Corinna, 182–83
death, concepts of
    Brouwer on, 160
    Canters on, 80
    Gaurwa on, 321
    Gomes on, 211, 212
    Maréchal on, 219, 227–28, 230–32
    Oberhoffer, 190
    Schaeffler on, 133–34
    van der Schott on, 59
DELTA method (Development Education and Leadership Teams for Action), 188
democratic processes, 64, 78, 175
Derks, Marjet, xix–xx
Dilworth, Joan, 178, 278, 279, 288, 289
Doddridge Farm, 96–97
Doesburg, Hanny, 73, 75, 157
Dominicans, 23, 119

Donders, Rachel, xii, xxiii–xxiv, 21–39, *40,* 102, 135, 139, 160, 176, 261
    Brazil visit, 116
    on cosmic awareness, 36, 37–39
    early years, 21–23
    Grail culture, 200
    Grail quest concept, 25–28
    as International President of Grail, 15, 21, 24, 31–35, 156, 258
    in Japan, 35–36, 217–18
    optimism, 28, 39
    on religious discrimination, 21
    at Tiltenberg, 25, 27–32
    World War II and after, 28–31
Dougan, Alice, 178
Drabek, Josephine, xxii, 55, 179, 281
duBulu, Joseph, Bishop, 339
Duinhage, The Hague, Netherlands, 11
Dutch East Indies, xix
Dwyer, Bishop, 47, 49, 50

East Africa, xxvi, 166
economic power, 271–72, 341
Ecumenical Church Loan Fund, 280
ecumenical/interfaith work, xxv, 112, 114, 155–56
Eighth of May movement, 168
Emy Gordon Vocational Training Center, Tanzania, 301
England, (Ladies of the Grail), x–xii, xxiii, 32, 51, 85, 91–92
Enlightenment, xvi
Escaler, Federico, Bishop, 238
Espinosa, Rosaurora, 237
Estor, Marita, 236, 251
eucalyptus plantations, 121
Eucharist, xvii, xxv, 42
Eucharistic Congress (Dublin, 1932), ix–x, 8, 47

European Community for Professional Training, 205
European Liturgical Movement, xx
European Parliament, 264, 267
European Union, 204

factory girls, work with, viii–xix, 7, 62, 69, 71
family movement, 154, 157, 178
Feldhauser, Louise, 68
female genital mutilation (FGM), 329–30
"Feminine Youth Movement for Catholic Action, the Grail," x
feminism, 39, 146, 166, 168, 245–46, 248
fidelity, 46
"fiery core," viii, xxii, 44, 186
First Holy Communion, xvii, 42
Fleischner, Eva, xxix, xxx–xxxi
forgiveness, 100
Francis of Assisi, 173
Freire, Paulo, 118, 119, 121, 188n46, 202, 263, 336n90
Friendship House (New York), 97
fundraising, 318

Gabriel House, Cincinnati, Ohio, 241
Gallant, Gloria, 246
Gallant, Ruth, xxxivn59
Garland, Joy, 132
Gateway, Detroit Grail Center, 128, 132, 136–38
Gaurwa, Imelda Alfred, xiii, xxii–xxiii, 35, 78, 141, 288, 290, 297–322, 323, 339
  on aging, 320–22
  early years and education, 297–99, 302–6
  early years in the Grail, 309–10
  on Grail culture and spirituality, 317–20
  hospital work, 161–62
  Moshi bookshop, 162–64, 167, 300, 315–16, 318, 332
  Mvungi and, 333–35

Index   361

    in Nucleus, 300, 311–14
    starts Grail training center, 154–55, 164
    on vision, 310–15, 318–19
gender training, 189
German Grail, 182
Germany
Misereor lay mission group, 172, 175, 178, 187–89, 279
. *See also* Nazis
Ghana, 35
"Glittering Words" (Schaeffler), 133–34
globalization, 269, 270–72
God, concepts of, 58–59, 66, 80–81, 212, 294, 318
    artistic images of, 216
    as the God of history, 124
    as love, 243–44, 304–5
    presence of, 37–38
    traditional image, 243
    Zen applied to, 225
Goldbrunner, Joseph, 241–42
Goldie, Rosemary, 258
Gomes, Teresa Santa Clara, xiv, 141, 195–213, *214,* 236, 251
    after Portuguese revolution, 203–6
    Bible circles, 203–4
    early years, 196–97, 200
    Grailville visits, 196, 198
    health, 199–200
    International Grail and government experiences, 207–8
    as member of Parliament, 199, 207
    "Paradise," 200
    Pintasilgo and, 195–98, 201, 258–59, 261
    turning points, 210–13
goodness, 212–13
Gospel of the Good Samaritan, 100
Gospel of the Last Judgment, 100
Grail

362 Index

aggiornamento, 140, 183–84, 207, 259
choice of name, 9
conflict, xxii–xxv
"fiery core," viii, xxii, 44, 186
future of, 292–95
global challenge for, 270–72
"Guidelines of the Grail," 184–85
international structure, 182–84
Liberation Task Force, 146
mission statement, 209, 311, 319–20
NGO status, 146
Vatican II assistance, 182–83
Vice Presidents, xiv, 33, 129–30, 139, 259
as women's movement, 7, 16, 33, 39, 69, 71, 93, 190, 309
. *See also* Grail Youth Movement; International Grail Movement; International Presidency Team (IPT); International Presidents of the Grail; Nucleus; presidents of the Grail, country-level; individual countries
Grail, myth of, 25–26, 70
Grail Center, Edinburgh, Scotland, 217
Grail culture, 200, 301, 317–20
Grail house, Burlington, New Jersey, 278, 284
Grail International Council, 121, 130
Grail Missionary Training Center, Ubergen, 176
The Grail Movement and American Catholicism 1940-1975, xxiv
Grail National Finance Team, 279
Grail Youth Movement, 27, 43n19, 62, 69–70, 109, 112, 185–86
    Amsterdam Stadium performances, ix, xx, 8, 41
    Donders as president, 24
    expansion, ix–xi
    origins, 69–70
Grailville, Ohio, xiii, xxiii, 98–99, 285n81
    Camanada visits, 116
    Donders visits, 33
    Gomes at, 196, 198, 261–62

music, 236, 242
Namaganda at, 278, 283–84
Nebrida at, 241–43
Pintasilgo at, 196, 261–62
Schaeffler at, 127, 128, 135–36
Super Flumina retreat center, 51, 241, 278, 285
training for overseas work, 13–14
van der Schott at, 50
"Year's School," 9–12
Gratton, Carolyn, 246
"Growing Together in the Grail" (Tanzania), 333
Guéranger, Dom Prosper, xvii
"Guidelines of the Grail," 184–85

Halkes, Catharina, 168n43
Harmon, Katharine, xx
harmony, 36
Harrison, Paul, 268n70
Hawthorn, Sheila, 238
Healy, Allison, 141
Hellriegel, Monsignor, 98
hierarchical leadership, xxiv, 98–99, 139–40, 178, 183
    in Zen Buddhism, 226, 227
Holiness Is Wholeness (Goldbrunner), 241–42
Holland-Brazil connection, 122–23
Hong Kong, xii, 85, 87–89, 99–102
Hope, Anne, 142, 188, 262, 271
hospital work, 30, 34, 63, 64
    Burundi, 160–61
    Congo, 72–73, 154, 158–59
    Uganda, 55, 171–72, 177, 178, 180
Houselander, Caryll, 61n22
Human Trafficking Network, 169
Hutus, 63, 74–75

364 Index

immigrants, Netherlands, 107, 124
"In Appreciation ... " (memorial flyer for Namaganda), 277
Indonesia 188n46
India, 188
individualism, 155, 221–22, 249
Indonesia, xi–xii, 6–7, 32, 62
infant nutrition, 64–65
"inside out" happenings, 134
Institute for the Blind, Gravaan, Netherlands, 72
Institute of Overseas Service (Brooklyn), 13
Instituto Superior Tecnico (Lisbon), 255
integrated life, 9–11
interaction, 186
Inter-Action Council of Former Heads of Government, 260
Inter-American Foundation, 120
interconnectedness, 38
International Board of the Grail, 198, 207n51
International General Assemblies
    1961, 181
    1971, 207, 335
    1979, 207, 311
    1993 (Grailville), 143, 199, 209–10
    2011 (South Africa), xxv, 345
International Grail Movement, 325, 328, 331
    autonomy of, xv, 8–9, 16
    emergence of, viii–ix
    as enemy of the state, 29
    expansion of, ix–xi, 9, 24
    Gaurwa and, 301, 311, 314, 319
    Human Trafficking Network, 169
    post-war growth of, xi–xiv
    toward centenary of, xxv–xxvii
    Vision Statement, 2011, xxv, 345–46
    wider context, xiv–xvi
    . See also Grail

International Grail Nucleus Team, 280
International Leadership Team, 78, 237
International Movement for Fraternal Union Among Races and Peoples (U.F.E.R.), 15, 131, 146
International Presidency Team (IPT), xiv, xxix–xxx, 146, 199, 207–8, 236, 251, 297, 301, 311
International Presidents of the Grail, xii
    Donders, 15, 21, 24, 33–34, 156, 258
    Oberhoffer, 117, 161, 181–87, 259
    Schaeffler, 130, 140–41, 270
    Tagher, xii, 236, 246, 314, 333
    van Gilse, 14, 31, 47, 99
    . *See also* presidents of the Grail
international teams, 180
"International Union of Women's Leagues," x
Irish mysticism, 223–24
Israel, 24, 37
Italian Christian Democracy Movement, xviiin28
Italy, xviii

Jadez, Victoria, 103
Japan, 24, 35–36, 215
    collective mentality, 221
    Maréchal in, 217–18, 220–24
Java, 62
Jesus, 104, 124, 304, 306, 319
Jews, 29, 30, 95, 112
Jocists
    . *See* Young Christian Workers
John Paul II, 168n43, 250
John XXIII, 183
Johnston, William, 223–24, 226
Jordan, 145

Kalven, Janet, 96, 243

Kane, Mary, 97
Kartini, Raden Adjeng, 6
Kenya, 165, 290, 338
Kersters, Josette, 183
Kew, Rosaline, 100
Kilasara, Joseph, Bishop of Moshi, 161
Kisekibaha, Tanzania, training center, 164–65, 301, 312–13, 316, 327
Kiwanuka, Josef, Bishop, 177
koan, 224
Korea, 252
kulturkampfs, anti-Catholic, xvii

Ladies of the Grail (Australia), x, xxiii, 41, 44, 47–53
Ladies of the Grail (England), x–xii, xxiii, 32, 51, 85, 91–92
LaGrange Citizen, 87
Lamb, Joann, 136
L'Arche, 129, 138
Lassalle, Enomiya, 226
lay apostolate, vii, xiv–xv, 6, 92, 97–98, 196, 307
    dimensions of, xvi–xxii
    Swahil documents, 312
    . *See also* Catholic Action
leadership, 96–99, 139–42
    hierarchical, in Church, xxiv, 98–99, 139–40, 178, 183
    International Leadership Team, 78, 237
    National Leadership Teams (NLT), 180, 237
    in Zen Buddhism, 226, 227
    . *See also* International Presidents of the Grail; presidents of the Grail
Leahy, Catherine, 18, 96
Lebulu, Josephat Louis, Bishop, 317–18
Legion of Mary, 102
Leo XIII, vii, xiv–xv, xvii–xviii
Let Us Celebrate (newsletter), 25

letting go, 58–59, 80, 189–90, 228, 232
Liberation Task Force, 146
liberation theology, 16, 118, 143
life support systems, 271–72
Ligutti, Luigi, 10–11, 97
Lisbon, Cardinal of, 198
literacy classes, 119, 121, 202–3, 263
Liturgical Movement, xvii
liturgical seasons, 101
Loanzan, Jeannette, 237, 246
love, 46, 80–81, 87, 100, 104, 304, 319, 322, 346
    as essence of religion, 16
    God as, 243–44, 304–5
Lucker, Alberta, 141, 174, 176, 183
Lukwago, Theopista, 307
"Lumen Gentium," 183
Lumumba, Patrice, 159
Lutheran Grail members, xxv
Lydwina, Saint, 8

Mabwami, Kevina, 307
Madonna House, Toronto, Canada, xviii, 51
Maes, Father, 76
Maestrini, Nicholas, 87–88, 99–100
Malone, Maria, 50
Manugeni, Jane, 336
Maréchal, Emma, 215, 217
Maréchal, Gerard, 215
Maréchal, Marie Elizabeth (Mimi), 35, 79, 167, 215–32, *233*
    bringing Zen to Holland, 226–27
    early years, 215–17
    health, 219, 227–29
    mission to Japan, 219–23
    Zen Buddhism and, 215, 216, 219, 223–28
Maria Laach Abbey, xvii

Mariengaerd senior care center, 17
marketplace, 271
marriage preparation courses, 49, 50
Marxist theory, 271
Mary Farm, Pennsylvania, 128
Masai people, xxvi, 329–30
Masaka, Bishop of, 55
Mass, 43, 98
    dialogue, 101, 216
    underground, 143
Mathey, Felisiana, 330
Matthews, Anne, 37
Mbuyik, Lea, 329
McCarthy, Alice, 55
McGarry, Anna, 97
McNicholas, John T., 9
McSorley, Francis, 240
    meditation, 123, 224
Melbourne, Australia, 50
Mercier, Anne, 136
methodology, 267–70
Mexico, 15
Middle East, 131, 145
Milcent, Benedicte, 130
Miller, Angela, 242
Misereor lay mission group, 172, 175, 178, 187–89, 279
Missa recitata, xvii
missals, 216
mission statement, 209, 311, 319–20
Missionaries of Africa (White Fathers), 76n27, 162–63, 175, 179
Missionary Sisters of Africa (White Sisters), 178, 288, 305
Missionary Sisters of the Sacred Heart of Jesus, 132
missions, 31–32
Monica House, Brooklyn, 128, 132, 138
Morishita, Akiko, 217, 223

Mundelein, George Cardinal, Archbishop of Chicago, x
Muslims, 250
Muwonge, Elizabeth, xii–xiii, 55
Mvungi, Honorata Lubero Francis, xiii, 155, 163, 301, 312, 325–43, *344*
    community work, 335–37
    early life, 325–27
    growth of Grail, 337–42
    leap of faith, 333–35
    in Nucleus, 328, 333, 338
    reflections, 342–43
    saying "yes" to challenges, 331–33
Mvungi, Victoria Francis, 330
Mystical Body of Christ, theology of, xv–xvi, 98
mysticism, 216

Nabwani, Kevine, 278, 288
Nakirebe, Grail farm, Uganda, 280
Namaganda, Elizabeth Estencia, xiii, 56, 179, 277–95, 296, 307, 336
    continuing education and life, 282–85
    early years, 280–81
    education of women, 280–82
    on future of Grail and church, 292–95
    return to Uganda, 285–88
    on women's greatest needs, 288–92
Namuesh, Albina, 238
Namugenyi, Jane, 307
Namule, Theo, 307
National Bioethics Council (Portugal), 260
National Catholic Girl Guides, 63
National Catholic Reporter, xxii
National Catholic Rural Life Conference, xxi, 10, 97
National Liturgical Week, xxi
nature movements, 10–11, 51–52

Nazis, x, 28–29, 62–63, 71–72, 92–94, 109, 111–12, 151–52
    concentration camps, 29, 30, 71, 172, 175–76
    . *See also* Germany; World War II
Nebrida, Rebecca, xiii–xiv, 235–53, 254
    beginning of work with Grail, 239–44
    on Catholic Church in Philippines, 249–50
    early years, 235–36, 239–40
    international responsibility, 251–52
    lauches Grail in Philippines, 236–37, 246–47
    retirement as continuity, 252
    upheaval in Grail and, 245–46
    on women in Philippines, 248–49
    for younger women, 253
Nebrida, Teresa, 246
Netherlands, vii–ix, xxvi, 4, *Se also* Tiltenberg training center (Netherlands)
    Amsterdam Olympic Stadium performances, ix, xx, 8
    migrant workers ("guest workers"), 15
    Nazi invasion, x, 62–63, 71–72, 92–94, 109, 111–12, 151–52
    Nucleus, 28, 42, 43n19, 62, 167
    Protestants, 21, 23
Network Women 2000, 204–5
New York City Labor Chorus, 132, 148–49
New Zealand, 50
Newman, John Henry Cardinal, xvi, 12, 18, 58, 61n22, 71
Ngobese, Jane, 143
Nigeria, 35, 130, 141–42
non-governmental sector, 145–46
Nosko, Carol, 90
Nucleus, viii, xiii, xxiii–xxiv
    Australia, 42, 51
    Brouwer in, 153, 165
    Camanada in, 109
    departures from, 140, 185, 236, 245
    Gaurwa in, 300, 311–12

Mvungi in, 328, 333, 338
name change, 33
during Nazi era, 185–86
Netherlands, 28, 42, 43n19, 62, 167
Oberhoffer in, 171, 177
Pintasilgo in, 261
Schaeffler in, 129
Tanzania, 165
Tully in, 85, 98–99
Vatican II and, 182–85
nuns, 74, 92, 98, 337
Nvungi, Eliza, 336
Nyerere, Julius, 313n87

Oberhoffer, Magdalene, xiii, xxi–xxii, 130, 162–63, 171–89, 190, 270, 307
African experience, 177–79
African experience, reflections on, 180–81
early years, 172–73
as International President, 117, 161, 181–87, 259
Misereor lay mission group, 172, 175, 187–89, 278
new focus, 189–90
in Nucleus, 171, 177
time of decision, 176–77
Oblates, 250
O'Hara, John, Archbishop of Philadelphia, 91
Overboss, Joan, x, xxi, 12, 87, 94, 137–38
at Doddridge Farm, 96
The Gateway, 128, 136
in Nucleus, 98–99
"socialist heart," 128
van der Schott and, 42
Oxford Movement, xvi, xx

"Pagbubuo" training, 247, 252

Index

Palestinian refugees, 131, 145–46
Papal Volunteers, 103, 117
Papua New Guinea, 238
"Paradise" (Gomes), 200
Pax Romana, xiv, 196, 258
Pintasilgo as International President, 261–62
pensionato, 115–16
Pentecost play, Amsterdam, 1932, 8, 42, 62, 71
Philippines, xiii–xiv, xxvii, 235–53
    Catholic Church in, 249–50
    East Samar, 238–39
    Graill launched in, 246–47
    "Pagbubuo" training, 247, 252
    Pinatubo volcano, 243
    poverty, 247, 250
    squatter communities, 248, 251
    women in, 248–49
Pintasilgo, Maria de Lourdes, xiv, 130, 141, 255–73, 274
    early years, 255–56, 261
    engineering degree, 255, 257
    in European Parliament, 264, 267
    global challenge for Grail, 270–72
    Gomes and, 195–98, 201, 258–59, 261
    "life-centered" world, 260
    in Nucleus, 261
    personal challenge, 272–73
    in politics, 263–64
    politics of caring, 267–70
    as Prime Minister of Portugal, 255, 259, 261, 264–65
    as Vice President of Grail, 270
    "walking among fields of knowledge," 268
    on women, politics, and power, 265–67
pious unions, 8
Pius X, xvii
Pius XI, xv–xvi

Pius XII, 129n37, 257n67, 258
Plante, Jeanne, 242
political power of women, 265–67
Politics and Spirituality Group, New York, 132, 148
Pontifical Mission for Palestine, 131, 145–46
Pontifical Society for the Foreign Missions, 88
popes
    John Paul II, 168n43, 250
    John XXIII, 183
    Leo XIII, vii, xiv–xv, xvii–xviii
    Pius X, xvii
    Pius XI, xv–xvi
    Pius XII, 129n37, 257n67, 258
"Popular Catechetics," 117
Portugal, 24, 95, 259–61
    Catholic Action, 195–97
    colonial wars, 259, 264
    Grail after Portuguese revolution, 203–6
    political changes, 263–64
    politics, 263–64
    poverty, 263
    revolution of 1974, 198–99, 259, 264
poverty, 268–72
    Brazil, 128
    Philippines, 247, 250
    Portugal, 263
praxis, 270
prayer, 26, 36–37, 38, 93, 103, 123–24, 189, 294
    aging and, 320–21
presidents of the Grail, country-level
    Elizabeth (Bep) Camanada, Holland, 117–18
    Schaeffler, United States, 130, 259
    van der Schott, Australia, 50
    van Kersbergen, United States, 4, 139
    . See also International Presidents of the Grail

priest abuse, 249
priesthood for women, 16
prophetic tradition, 213
Protestants, 21, 23
Pugh, Evelyn, 141–42, 144

Quadragesimo Anno (Pius XI), xv
Quitorio, Pepe, Monsignor, 238–39

racial justice work, 97, 134, 137–38, 145
Rahner, Karl, 183
Rasenberger, Dorothy, 132, 246
refugees, 156
    Dutch women, 31
    Palestinian, 131, 145–46
Register, 87
Reid, Elizabeth, 49, 278
Rerum Novarum (Leo XIII), vii, xvii–xviii
retreats for non-Catholics, viii–ix
Rhomberg, Hubert, 129
Robertson, Mary, 238
Roman Catholic Council of the Laity (Vatican), 279
Ronan, Marian, 89n32
rosary, 22, 49
Rose, Betty, 103
Rotterdam, 44
"The Royal Road of the Cross" (play), ix, 8, 41, 49, 62
rural life movement, 10–11, 97
Russian revolution of 1917, 21–22
Rwandan genocide, 63

Sacred Heart Sisters, 57
sacrifices, 27, 79
San Francisco, 103, 139
San Jose, 103, 139

Santa Clara County Social Welfare Department, 103
Schaareman, Lenie, 312, 327, 332–34
Schaeffler, Eileen, 127–49, 150, 245
    in Africa, 142–43
    in Brazil, 143
    Fulbright scholarship, 129, 130, 138
    "Glittering Words," 133–34
    as Grail president, United States, 130, 259
    at Grailville, 127, 128, 135–36
    grassroots struggles, 134–38
    as International President, 130, 140–41, 270
    leadership roles, 139–43
    in Nucleus, 129
    in the New York City Labor Chorus, 132, 148-49
    retirement, 146, 147–49
    return home, 144–47
    in South Africa, 130, 131
    at Women's Bureau of the Department of Labor, 131, 144–45
Scheveningen, courses, 28
Schoenherr, Walter (Joe), 129
Schomer, Audrey, 144
schools
    Congo (Zaire), 64
    Kalisizo, Uganda, 45, 56–57
    Masaka, South Africa, 55–56
    Philippines, 244, 251–52
    Portugal, 204
    Uganda, xiii, 34, 45, 55–56, 179
    "Year's School," 9–12
Schreiber, Bishop (Berlin), x
Secretariat of the International Grail, 130n38, 169
secularization, 222, 294
Seijbel, Ifis, xii
Semvua, Maria Goretti William, 329–30

September 11, 2001 attacks, 90
sexual abuse, 248–49
Seybel, Ifis, 76
Shamansky, Margaret, 103
Sheed, Frank, 85
Sheed and Ward publishers, xvi, xix, 85
Sheehy, Beatrice (Kathleen), 49
Silvestre-Galang, Luz, 237
Singapore, 24
Sisters of Charity (Adelholzen), 176
Smith, Dorothy, 56
Social Formation Center, Bukava, Zaire, 76–77
social justice, xvii–xix, xxi, 5, 9, 50, 203
    Brazil, 107, 118–19, 127
socialism, 203, 313
    . *See also* Ujamaa (working together)
socialist youth groups, ix
Society of the Women of Bethany, vii
Society of the Women of Nazareth, vii–viii, xix, 4n3
structure, viii
Sophia University, Japan, 220
Sorrento, Audrey, xiii–xiv, 18, 241
South Africa, xii, xxvii, 130, 142–43
    apartheid, 54
    International General Assembly, 2011, xxv, 345
    Schaeffler in, 130, 131
    van der Schott in, 52–55
    van Gilse in, 45, 54
    van Kersbergen in, 14, 45, 53
Souza, Ethel, 103, 139
Spirit, 127, 135
Springwood (Australia), 49, 51–52
St. Andrew's Missal, 216
St. Leo's parish, Detroit, 129
St. Mary's Rubaga Cathedral (Uganda), 280

St. Meinrad's Abbey, xxi
St. Vincent de Paul Society, 43
Stevenson House, Palo Alto, California, 90
Stuber, Jessica, xxii, 179
Super Flumina retreat center (Foster, Ohio), 51, 241, 278, 285
Swahili language, 158, 163, 306, 337
Sweden, xxv, 206
Switzerland, 130
symbols, 16, 25, 201

Tagher, Simone, xii, 144, 236, 246, 314, 333
Taizé, 272–73
talents, development of, 4, 6, 9, 12–13, 58, 71, 79, 151, 177, 202, 253, 260, 307, 337–38
Tanzania, xiii, 65, 78, 130, 141, 288
    African Grail, xiii, 164–66, 297–98, 300–301
    Catholic Women's Movement, 339
    diocesan development program, 316
    employment, 340
    Gaurwa and, 297–322
    Haya tribe, 297, 304
    independence, 299–300
    Kisekibaha program, 164–65, 301, 312–13, 316, 327–28, 330, 332–34, 341
    Moshi bookshop, 162–64, 167, 300, 315–16, 318, 332
    Mvungi and, 325–43
    Nucleus, 165
    oppression of women, 210, 308–9, 316–17, 328–29, 337–38
    Ton Brouwer in, 154–56, 161–66
    Ujamaa (working together), 313–15, 328
    Unit of Women, 339
Tay Creggan, Melbourne, Australia, 50
Teresa of Avila, 18, 173
Thérèse of Lisieux, 173
Tibasoboke, Imelda Namkula, 279

Tiltenberg training center (Netherlands), x, 62
    Ark retreat house, 32
    Brouwer at, 155
    closing of, 111
    conflicts, 167
    Donders at, 25, 27–32
    Gaurwa at, 312, 315
    Maréchal at, 217
    Nazi takeover, 29–31
    Oberhoffer at, 175, 176–77
    Tully at, 85–86, 89, 102
    van der Schott at, 44, 46–47
Time magazine, xxii
Timmel, Sally, 188, 271
trafficking of women, 169
training centers
    Kisekibaha, Tanzania, 164–65, 301, 310, 312–13, 316, 327–28, 330, 332–34, 341
    Rubaga, Uganda, 279, 282, 307, 327
    . *See also* Grailville, Ohio; Tiltenberg training center (Netherlands)
transdisciplinary approach, 267–69
Tully, Mary Louise, xii, 85–104, 105
    "AgeWise" (newsletter), 45, 90, 103
    decision to join Grail, 90–92
    at Doddridge Farm, 96–97
    early years, 86–87
    English Grail and, 85, 91–92
    experiences during World War II, 92–96
    in Hong Kong, 87–89, 99–102
    leadership training, 96–99
    at *pensionato*, 115–16
    post-Hong Kong years, 102–4
    return to United States during war, 94–96
    support of parents, 96–97

Index 379

Tutsis, 63, 74–75

Uganda, xii–xiii, xxi–xxii, 130, 141, 165
    British system, 281–82
    Christ the King Secondary School, 289
    Elizabeth Namaganda, 277–95
    hospital work, 55, 171–72, 177, 178, 180
    independence, 56, 180
    Mubende Grail formation program, 300
    Oberhoffer in, 171–72, 177–80
    Rubaga training center, 279, 282, 307, 327
    schools, xiii, 34, 45, 55–56, 179, 277, 280–82
    women's education and employment, 286–88
Uganda Catholic Social Training Center, 279
Uganda Joint Christian Council, 280
Ugandan Catholic Bishops Conference, 279
Ugandan Grail, 171, 289–92
    National Finance Team, 279
    National Leadership Team, 280
Ujamaa (working together), 313–15, 328
UN Commission on the Status of Women, xxvi
uniqueness of each person, 12–13
United Farm Workers, 103
United Nations, 131–32, 144–46
    International Movement for Fraternal Union Among Races and Peoples (U.F.E.R.), 13, 15
United States, x, xi, 86–87, 186
    presidents of the Grail, 4, 130, 139, 259
    rural life movement, 10–11
    success of Grail in, xxiii–xxv
unity, 21, 32, 184–85, 251, 293, 331, 342
University of Leiden, 109
University of Notre Dame, xiii, 90, 236, 240–41
University of Wisconsin, 63–64, 76, 78
US Grail International Team (USIT), 147–48

Valtorta, Henry, Bishop of Hong Kong, 87, 99, 101
van Cleef, Helen, 50, 57
van de Rijdt, Fini, 336
van der Ploeg, Coleta, 300, 306–7
van der Schott, Frances, x–xiii, xxiii, 41–59, 281
    acceptance, 57–58
    Australia, experiment with change, 51–52
    in Australia, 47–50
    early years, 41–43
    letting go, 58–59
    president of Grail, 50
    in South Africa, 52–55
van Gilse, Margaret, xii, 14, 27, 31, 45, 47, 99, 175
    Donders and, 31–32
    Elizabeth (Bep) Camanada and, 113
    as Mother Margaret, 68, 69, 92n33, 181n44
    in South Africa, 45, 54
van Ginneken, Jacques, xi–xii, 61n22, 153, 206, 293, 308
    in Australia, 51
    concerns about, 67
    Donders and, 24
    on dying, 18
    on flexibility, 182
    on prayer, 189
    retreats for non-Catholics, viii–ix, 62, 63
    on technological change, 68–69
    van der Schott meets, 44
    van Kersbergen, influence on, 5–6, 8
    vision for women, vii–viii, xix–xx, 93, 206, 229
van Kersbergen, Leentje, 17
van Kersbergen, Lydwine, x–xii, xx, 3–18, 19, 43, 94, 127, 139, 150, 241, 243
    delegation, gift of, 12–13
    at Doddridge Farm, 96

early years, 4–5
integrated life, search for, 10–11
at New Jersey Grail house, 278, 284
in Nucleus, 98–99
president of Grail, United States, 4, 139
in South Africa, 14, 45, 53, 175
"Year's School," 9–12
van Neerven, Joke, xiii, 161–62, 238
van Voorst tot Voorst, Beatrice (Trees), 152, 163, 167, 169
Vanier, John, 129, 138
Vatican
    Consulate for the Laity in Rome, 295
    Roman Catholic Council of the Laity, 279
    Vatican II, xxiv, xxvi, xxx, 35, 103, 118, 130, 167
    culture, acceptance of, 293
    influence on Nucleus, 182–85
    laity document, 312
    Philippines and, 236, 245, 250
    Portugal and, 262
    Tanzania and, 306, 330, 336
    Uganda and, 285, 288
Vatican III, 330
Vice Presidents of the Grail, xiv, 33, 129–30, 139, 259
Vision Statement, International, xxv, 345–46
Vogelenzang, Netherlands, 62
von Trapp, Maria, 3

Wagawaga, Australia, Bishop of, x
Wald, Barbara, 96, 129–30, 139, 144
Walker, Eleanor, 242
"walking among fields of knowledge," 268
Weigand, Elizabeth, 307
Weil, Simone, 257
Werner, Christa, 238
West Africa, 166

Whelan, Bishop, 53
White, Carol, 79, 167, 219
White Fathers (Missionaries of Africa), 76n27, 162–63, 175, 179
White Sisters (Missionary Sisters of Africa), 178, 288, 305
Willebrands, Monsignor, 182
Wilson, Teresa, 18
Winkelmolen, Henry, 317n88
"Women and Decision-Making" (Portugal), 205
"Women and Structural Change" (Portugal), 205
Women of Nazareth, x–xi, 43–44, 181n44, 345
. *See also* Nucleus
"Women Shaping the Future: Building Justice and Solidarity, Facing Cultural Change and Contributing to the Survival of the Planet," 209–10
Women's Bureau of the Department of Labor, 131, 144–45
women's movement
  caring, politics of, 267–70
  Grail as, 7, 16, 33, 39, 69, 71, 93, 190, 309
  Philippines, 246–47
  political power of women, 265–67
  Portugal, 262–63
worker-priest movement, 129, 257
World Independent Commission on Population and the Quality of Life, 259–60
world religions, 78, 224
World War II, xi, 28–29, 172
. *See also* Nazis

Year's School, 9–12
Yeung Kwok Woon, 101–2
Young Christian Students, 295
Young Christian Workers, 97, 98, 215, 217, 257–58
youth movements, 7–8, 31
. *See also* Grail Youth Movement

Zaire, 64–65, 76–77
Zen Buddhism, 59, 215, 216, 219–29
    in Holland, 226–29
Zentrum (German Catholic party), 172
Zimbabwe, 188n46

About the Authors

MARY O'BRIEN earned her Ph.D. and Specialist Certificate in Aging from the University of Michigan, Ann Arbor (USA). She is a retired professor of Gerontological Studies from Mt. St. Vincent University, Halifax, Nova Scotia (Canada) and lives in Ann Arbor, Michigan. In autumn 2017 she will have been a member of the Grail for sixty years.

MARIAN RONAN is Research Professor of Catholic Studies at New York Theological Seminary in New York City. She is author or co-author of six other books, including *Tracing the Sign of the Cross: Sexuality, Mourning, and the Future of American Catholicism* (Columbia 2009) and has been a member of the Grail Movement since 1965.

www.ingramcontent.com/pod-product-compliance
Lightning Source LLC
Chambersburg PA
CBHW031844220426
43663CB00006B/486